Learning Space Design in Higher Education

Lennie Scott-Webber
John Branch
Paul Bartholomew
Claus Nygaard

THE LEARNING IN HIGHER EDUCATION SERIES

LIBRI
PUBLISHING

First published in 2014 by Libri Publishing

Copyright © Libri Publishing

Authors retain copyright of individual chapters.

The right of Lennie Scott-Webber, John Branch, Paul Bartholomew and Claus Nygaard to be identified as the editors of this work has been asserted in accordance with the Copyright, Designs and Patents Act, 1988.

ISBN 978-1-909818-38-5

A CIP catalogue record for this book is available from The British Library

Cover design by Helen Taylor

Design by Carnegie Publishing

Printed by TJ International Limited

Libri Publishing
Brunel House
Volunteer Way
Faringdon
Oxfordshire
SN7 7YR

Tel: +44 (0)845 873 3837

www.libripublishing.co.uk

Contents

Foreword

In my role as General Manager of Steelcase Education I meet with hundreds of students, faculty, college presidents, provosts, deans, superintendents, and academic administrators. I am constantly triangulating on their comments, looking for patterns, common themes and unmet needs across all types of institutions. In short, I am looking for the problems that keep educators up at night, the biggest problems worth solving; and I see a consistency in the challenges facing education wherever I go. I also see widespread confusion, sometimes a lack of confidence, and often desperation around how to solve for today's challenges. But I am happy to report that I also see encouraging pockets of innovation.

In my conversations, educators express their challenges in questions like:

"How might we attract and retain the best students and faculty?"

"How might we improve student success, and prepare students for 21st century jobs that don't exist?"

"How might we address our ever increasing costs and deliver an education that is deemed worth that cost?"

"How can we stay relevant on our campus in the face of lower cost online alternatives?"

In spite of significant cultural, social, and geographical differences, the questions are amazingly similar. The pressures on education to improve are global, and span elementary, secondary, and post-secondary education. It may not be surprising given that the world is becoming so 'flat'. The speed and ubiquity of communication, the depth, breadth, and ready access to information, and the socialisation of that information, are creating new expectations in students that are challenging the ways we teach, the ways we learn, and the ways we will help them prepare for success as global citizens. I am most surprised that the dialogue is so similar, from Europe to North America, the Middle East to Latin America, and Asia. When I ask educators what they think is needed to solve the problems in education they typically point to areas like *technology, pedagogy, and talent*. What is mentioned far less, but I believe critical, is the power of a new learning and teaching *environment* to help enable change and improve the ecosystem of education.

Technology is a major transformative force in education, and some forward thinkers hold it up as the best way to address many of the ills in the system. They say it promises to move us from an obsolete, one-size-fits-all, 'monolithic' approach, where all students are marched through the system in unison regardless of capability, to a more learner-centered, personalised and tailored learning experience that addresses the wide variation in student learning abilities, learning styles, and knowledge levels. Technology *IS* helping. Internet access, online courseware, mobile devices, learning management systems, learning analytics, and MOOCs (Massive Open Online Courseware), can help improve how teachers teach and assess, and how students learn. Venture and corporate investment in new education technology solutions have accelerated over the past 10 years and some of these new technologies, like MOOCs and online courses, are challenging the very business model of education institutions, promising to lower costs. Many of these new technologies will change learning and teaching forever. Surprising? It shouldn't be, given that technology is changing the ways we work, changing our lives at home, changing politics, and changing cultures. Why wouldn't it change education as well? It can, and it will.

But technology alone is not the salvation. It is not the complete solution for helping an ever more diverse student body succeed. How many times have you heard an education leader say that the key to student success is to have more great teachers in the classroom? More *talent*.

We all probably remember that teacher in 7th grade math, or the history professor in college who made coming to class a pleasure. There is truth to this notion that great teachers can have a big impact on our desire to learn and impact our learning in very meaningful, tangible ways. Through passion, commitment, and sheer force of will, many teachers have overcome limitations imposed by shrinking budgets, limited technology, and poor facilities, to make learning more interesting, engaging, effective, and fun. We must continue to find, enable, and reward great teachers if we are to improve learning. But we must also identify new ways to help them succeed so that they remain passionate and inspired.

One of the tools that great teachers employ is effective and engaging *pedagogy*. If we look back 50–100 years the dominant pedagogy was the lecture. Before the invention of personal computers, the Internet, and easy access to ubiquitous digital information, lectures were a common, and you could argue, adequate strategy for 'transferring knowledge'. But with advances in digital technology, coupled with a new generation of students steeped in rich digital media, expectations of the classroom experience have changed. When content is available anywhere, anytime, learning is no longer dependent primarily on an instructor 'transferring' their deep content expertise to masses of uninformed students. Lectures are no longer sufficient. Research on how people learn has shown that 'active' pedagogies, those that allow students to 'construct their own knowledge' (Dewey 1929; Kolb & Fry 1975), are more engaging and effective than passive lectures alone. Active teachers create multi-modal learning experiences in their classrooms, and online, including activities such as problem and project-based learning, peer-to-peer learning, small group discussion, and team presentation. These approaches are more interactive and dynamic than passive lectures, and our (Steelcase Education Solutions) research has shown them to be more engaging (Scott-Webber et. al., 2013). A strong trend is to combine these active pedagogies with new learning and teaching technologies to create a hybrid or 'blended' learning model where both face-to-face and online strategies are employed in one course. But with these new models come new classroom behaviours, and with the new behaviours come new requirements and opportunities for the learning environment.

So, as with new technologies and great teachers, new pedagogies can help improve learning and help students succeed. Not surprising, but again, not sufficient. There is another tool we can use to gain leverage in this global quest to grow a world of passionate, effective, leaders, collaborators, and team members; in short, educated citizens of the 21st century. This tool is often neglected, overlooked, or misunderstood, and is just possibly a surprising tool. It is the tool of space, both physical and virtual – the learning *environment*. The environment in which we learn, teach, build community, collaborate, and problem solve, is an under-leveraged tool that compliments the power of new technologies. And when intentionally designed, learning spaces can enable a great teacher to be more effective, more efficient, and more inspired. But there is a problem. The problem is that most learning spaces, particularly formal *actual* classrooms, look the same as they did 100 years ago. Neat rows of tables and chairs, or tablet-arm chairs, all facing forward, ready for students to 'sit and get', and teachers to 'stand and deliver'. How can this be? How is it that in a world of 24/7 content availability, where students can use *Google*, or *Blackboard*, or *Wikipedia*, or *Instagram* to access more content than any one teacher could know, the dominant design of education spaces is for lecture (at least in actual classrooms)- inadequate at best, or worse, obsolete? Could it be that our learning spaces have been the same for so long that most educators just don't think of space as a tool they can use to change learning and teaching much? Could it be that we just take the dominant for granted? Might it be that most educators and education leaders don't have an image in their minds of how the space could be different? Maybe they don't think (enough) about how space affects behaviour and how new behaviours are needed in learning environments if we are to maximise the learning that takes place there – for today's students, today's pedagogies, and today's technologies. Well maybe this situation actually shouldn't be all that surprising.

After all, education decision makers are typically not trained in the fields that are responsible for designing space, namely architecture and interior design. Without an awareness of the connection between physical space design, and human behaviour in these physical places, educators may be unaware of the importance of designing spaces to foster activities and behaviour that lead to better engagement, and better learning. So maybe the lack of innovation in learning spaces, as a new normal, shouldn't be all that surprising. But here in lies a golden opportunity. If we can connect space, or more broadly, the learning environment, as a tool to support new behaviours to improve learning, and also address the myriad pressures that education leaders are under to attract and retain the best faculty and students, compete in a new world of cheaper/better alternatives, and justify ever rising costs, then maybe, just maybe, we can get the attention of the leaders who are tasked to solve these problems. And then we may just be able to help them make a more holistic and enduring change happen.

Pedagogy, technology, and space can and should work in concert to create a synergistic ecosystem that can maximize the effectiveness of great teachers. Adding the learning environment, both physical and virtual 'spaces', as an equal partner, a new tool in our mission to improve student success, just may lead to surprising results.

Thank you for the opportunity to share some thoughts relative to the important work shared in this anthology.

Sean Corcorran
General Manager
Steelcase Education Solutions

Chapter One

Practising Learning Space Design

Lennie Scott-Webber, John Branch,
Paul Bartholomew and Claus Nygaard

Space: the final frontier

These words are known to fans and many non-fans alike as the first
sentence of the opening sequence in the original Star Trek television series.
Narrated by the main character Captain James Tiberius Kirk (played
by Canadian actor William Shatner) they declare, rather unequivocally,
that the world beyond earth is the only remaining unexplored territory
for humans. And it is this other-worldliness which provides the series'
basic plot device, and which is captured – immortalised perhaps – in the
sentences which complete the opening sequence:

> "These are the voyages of the starship Enterprise. Its five-year
> mission: to explore strange new worlds, to seek out new life and new
> civilizations, to boldly go where no man has gone before."

To some extent, we as editors of this anthology feel a lot like Captain
Kirk, because learning spaces are a kind of final frontier of educational
research. Indeed, a quick glance at the literature finds a notable absence
of work on learning spaces in education. To be fair, architecture and
the built environment have figured prominently in calls for universal
design in education over the last decade or so. John wrote about this in a

previous anthology. And proxemics has also frequently been cited as an important concept for teachers to understand when it comes to classroom management. But compared to pedagogy, curriculum design, educational psychology, learning theory, special education, and other 'mainstays' of educational research, learning spaces remains relatively under-researched.

There is also a kind of starship *Enterprise* mission about learning spaces today – to explore… to seek out… to boldly go… Modern technology, globalisation, and other forces of change have completely reshaped the landscape of countless institutions and activities. Consider the once noble hand-written letter. The classroom, however, has changed little from the early one-room schoolhouses of yesteryear. As one of Lennie's colleagues said so aptly, *"We have 21st century students, 20th century teaching practices, and 19th century learning spaces."*

Finally, this anthology could be considered as a kind 'captain's log', chronicling the exploratory voyages of its authors. It is a collection of chapters which document various dimensions of the universe, which we call learning spaces. We make no claims that it is exhaustive. Instead, we treat it as simply the beginning of a long journey… a journey which we undertook with the same brio as the infamous Captain James Tiberius Kirk.

LiHE

The anthology is the product of *Learning in Higher Education* (LiHE), an academic association which, as intimated by its name, focuses entirely on learning at the post-secondary level. The focus of the association reflects the shift from a transmission-based philosophy to a student-centred, learning-based approach. And its scope is limited to colleges, universities, and others institutions of higher education.

The main activity of the association is a symposium. About 10 years ago, Claus noted that professors attend conferences at which they present their scientific research in a 10-20 minute session, receive a few comments, and then very often 'head to the bar for a drink'. He proposed an alternative, therefore, which *au contraire* returns to that ancient Greek format – the symposium – at which co-creation is key.

So, about 6 months prior to a symposium, a call for chapter proposals which has a relatively tightly focused theme is announced on the association's website and on various electronic mailing lists. The June 2013 symposium, for example, had the theme *Case-Based Learning in Higher Education*; previous themes have revolved around games and simulations, classroom innovations, and creativity (in higher education).

Authors submit chapter proposals accordingly, which are then double-blind reviewed. If a proposal is accepted, its author is given 4 months to complete it. The whole chapter is then double-blind reviewed, and if it is accepted, the author is invited to attend the symposium. There, all authors revise their own chapters, work together to revise each other's chapters, and collaborate to assemble an anthology which, about a month later, goes off to the publisher.

A serendipitous fieldtrip

In the summer of 2012, John was asked to sit on a special Dean's committee at the Ross School of Business, whose mandate was to explore the future of business education. Inevitably, the question of instructional technology arose, which then led to discussions about distance education, 'flipped classrooms', and new curricular designs. Consequently, the chair of the committee arranged for a visit to Steelcase Inc., the global leader in the office furniture industry.

For years, Steelcase has been conducting research into the changing nature of work and the workplace, and more recently with the growth of its Educational Solutions division, has likewise been questioning basic assumptions of how (and where) people learn. To that end, in 1999 the company created Steelcase University, repurposing one of its old furniture assembly factories. "*A 60,000-square-foot-facility, Steelcase University features formal and informal learning spaces, nine high-tech classrooms, various breakout and touchdown spaces, a Discovery Learning Center, a Distance Learning Center, practice installation labs, a café and a dedicated area for staff.*" (www.steelcase.com)

Throughout the tour of Steelcase University, it became plainly obvious to John that learning spaces was a subject of great interest— and great challenge— to not only the Ross School of Business but to all institutions of higher education. Pedagogy (or its Latin equivalent education), he mused, has traditionally focused on the operations of teaching and learning. But the context of teaching and learning – the places in which learning occurs – is equally important. Indeed, it seemed to him that these 'learning spaces' can limit the types of activities which can be used by the teacher. They can also influence the social interactions between teachers and students, and between students themselves. And they can impact the affective and cognitive, the behavioural, and even the physiological responses of students. Learning spaces, he concluded, can either help or hinder learning.

By the end of the day, therefore, John had the theme for the October 2013 LiHE symposium: learning spaces in higher education. Within a month, Steelcase had agreed to become the official sponsor, underwriting some of the symposium's costs and co-hosting one of its four days at Steelcase University. And Lennie, who was serving as Director of Education Environments within Steelcase Education Solutions, came on board as a co-editor. Paul, who is Director of Learning Innovation and Professional Practice at Aston University and who is a long-time LiHE participant, completed the editorial team.

The symposium

For the symposium, therefore, we (the editors) sought chapters which explored learning spaces… within the domain of higher education and with an emphasis on learning, as per the focus of LiHE. We hoped to advance our understanding of the nature, function, and impact of learning spaces in higher education. We welcomed chapters from all scientific disciplines and which followed any methodological tradition. Specifically, we sought chapters which explored learning spaces in higher education along three broad but interrelated themes:

1. Conceptual: What is a learning space? Are there different types of learning spaces? What are the different components of a learning space? Answering these types of questions will sharpen the definition of learning spaces in higher education. Proposals will be evaluated, therefore, on their contribution to our understanding of the *nature* of learning spaces in higher education.

2. Practical: How are learning spaces constructed? How are learning spaces used as an educational tool? How are learning spaces changing over time and with technological advances? Answering

these types of questions will increase the application of learning spaces in higher education. Proposals will be evaluated, therefore, on their contribution to our understanding of the function of learning spaces in higher education.

3. Theoretical: What are the effects of different learning spaces? How does the learning space moderate other pedagogical factors? How does a learning space lead to learning? Answering these types of questions will raise the significance of learning spaces in higher education. Proposals will be evaluated, therefore, on their contribution to our understanding of the *impact* of learning spaces in higher education.

The call for chapter proposals resulted in submissions from around the world which explored a variety of different aspects of learning spaces in higher education. The subsequent review and resubmission process, however, whittled these down to the 14 chapters which follow in this anthology. The LiHE symposium at which the chapters were revised and the anthology was assembled was held in October 2013 at the University of Michigan in Ann Arbor and at Steelcase University in Grand Rapids. In addition to the academic symposium activities, authors toured Steelcase University, learning more about the types of research which are conducted there. They strolled the campus of the University of Michigan, seeing the spot at which President John F. Kennedy announced the American Peace Corps programme. And they watched the home team Wolverines beat the visiting Indiana Hoosiers in American football at Michigan Stadium – a.k.a. *The Big House* – the nation's largest and the world's 3rd largest stadium.

The editors and learning spaces

As editors, of course, we bring our own perspectives to the role, which are based on our own experiences with learning spaces. We each have our own disciplinary backgrounds, which come with their own specific approaches to learning spaces. And we have our own philosophical assumptions about human nature that, in turn, influence our views about learning spaces.

Lennie

I went back to graduate school as a 'mature' student. I think that my creative side was looking for a more pragmatic side. As a practising professional designer, my work had been focused on healthcare design and therefore I thought that it would be important to understand more about how to design for the most vulnerable populations. Thus, I got my Master of Science in Interior Design, a minor in Gerontology with a cognate in Human Factors Engineering. My Ph.D. studies focused on Environment Behaviour Theory [EBT]. The more my studies opened the world of EBT, the more I got annoyed. How in the world could all of this really important information remain 'dormant' on the shelves of academe, when architects and designers really need it in order to design more intentionally? My first aha.

In these Ph.D. studies we were also taught how to map human behaviour using qualitative research protocols. Another aha. Again, designers really ought to make it normal practice to see human behaviour within the context of a particular setting, and then use this knowledge to compare and contrast against information which is gathered in surveys and/or focused interviews (the latter two being the typical means of gathering client-related information).

What to do with these two aha's? I made a promise to myself as a design educator to ensure that: 1. I would incorporate behavioural mapping experiences into any design courses which I would teach, and 2. any research project would also be disseminated in practical terms so others could benefit. Two promises which I have kept. This background sets the stage for that which happened next.

My first design educator position was as an Assistant Professor at Virginia Tech University, where I was teaching the senior capstone course and some graduate seminars. The university architect discovered that I was teaching my students how to map behaviour, and approached me. "*Dr. Lennie, the Provost has launched a project to understand all of our instructional spaces on campus with the intention of generating some standards. Would you be interested in having your students help us out by understanding more of what goes on in these classrooms?*" Well, professors are always looking for 'real world' projects for their students, and so of course I jumped at the opportunity. Remember that to this point my professional practice had been in healthcare and my academic work – including grants, research, publications, etc. – had all focused on healthcare design.

As a studio design educator, I typically would only teach in design studio settings, so the remainder of the campus was like a foreign country. Of course, I had had my own student experiences with different classroom types, but the first classroom which we visited during the tour of campus with the architect was shocking. *"Oh my gosh! We forgot to design this space!"* The place was brutal… dark, over-crowded, and neutral in finishes, with no natural light. That experience was an epiphany, and changed my career.

My students became engaged in the project, and I organised a research group of like-minded designers and educational psychologists to focus on learner-centred spaces. I was also then asked to serve as co-leader of the Provost's special committee to evaluate all of Virginia Tech's instructional spaces using performance/design standards with evidence-based design principles as a focus; these are still in use today, and are a source of great personal pride to this day. What happened since?

I moved up the academic ladder multiple times, becoming chair of two different design schools, one in Canada and one in the United States. I continued my professional practice, but remained totally committed to learning-centred design spaces. My research also stayed focused on this topic, although often in the early years, I felt like I was on a soapbox, trying to get educators and designers alike to overcome their Industrial Age thinking, and to realise the importance of learning spaces.

In the early 2000s, Steelcase approached me to help the company begin thinking about learning spaces, and I was delighted to help. In 2011, I was offered the opportunity to become Director of Education Environments with Steelcase Education Solutions. I jumped. Why? Since about 2008, education in general has finally started to realise a need for change, and in the last 3 to 4 years, a tsunami of disruptors has hit standard educational practice. Consequently, the education and design communities are willing to listen to what research has to offer. In this role at Steelcase, therefore, I am privileged to conduct research which leads to the development of design principles which not only guide product specifications, but which also support the educational experience of both instructors and students. My team coaches architectural and design communities and end users about this research on a global scale.

My passion for educational design is almost 20 years old, and the world of education is now listening. How rewarding!

John

To be honest, I had not thought too much about the importance of learning spaces until 2009 when the new Ross School of Business facility opened. 'Weighing in at' more than 270.000 feet, the building boasts state of the art technology, LEAD Silver sustainability certification, and even an exercise and fitness centre. It was the classrooms, however, which triggered my curiosity about learning spaces.

The teaching wing of the new building consists of 12 u-shaped tiered auditorium style classrooms, 4 on each floor stacked on 3 floors. 9 classrooms have 85 seats and 3 have 95 seats. Tables are fixed, although seats roll on casters. A smart lectern is located at the centre-front, with all screens and white boards as the focal point for the students.

It is important to note at this juncture that the Dean, under whose leadership the new building was constructed, was formerly a professor at Harvard Business School. HBS, as it is known, pioneered the case method of teaching, in which students discuss, debate, dissect a situation about a company which is often in crisis. It is akin to a physician analysing a patient's chart, the process of which (hopefully) leads to the appropriate diagnosis and treatment of the illness. The case method 'requires' the case classroom— a u-shaped tiered space which holds one entire section of business students... between 85 and 95 at business schools with large M.B.A. cohorts.

Not all professors at the Ross School of Business, however, use the case method. At HBS, the case method is its 'shtick'. Every class of every course of the entire M.B.A. uses the case method. Indeed, by the time of graduation, students have read and analysed several hundred cases. No lectures. No in-class quizzes. No newspaper article discussions. Only the case method.

The irony is that the new building is less than five years old, and the administration is already looking for ways to renovate some of the classrooms. Indeed, that special Dean's committee on which I served recognised that many (most) professors were using other instructional methods – sometimes very innovative instructional methods – and that these case classrooms not only limited instructional innovation but were also detrimental to student learning. For example, it is very difficult if not impossible to do impromptu or even planned breakout discussions with students who sit on different tiers and who are largely tied to rows of tables in a u-shape. Fortunately, another major financial gift from the School's benefactor and namesake will allow for the renovation.

More recently, however, I also began thinking of learning spaces in higher education during a course on services marketing which I was teaching. I had assigned a seminal article by Mary Jo Bitner (1992) which models the ways in which the physical surroundings of the service environment (often called the *servicescape*) impacts both the customers and the employees who are in that service environment. While we were discussing Bitner's model during a course session, it dawned on me that the classroom was indeed a servicescape itself, and that the environmental dimensions must have an impact on my students.

Since then, I have been conducting an informal experiment with the ambient conditions of the classroom servicescape, playing music prior to the beginning of each course session. I arrive 10-15 minutes early, and fire up a selection of tunes on my laptop. I have received countless unsolicited comments, praising me for the use of the music. *"It really changes my attitude to the course,"* said one student. *"I love the atmosphere of this class,"* uttered another student. It also facilitates social interactions between students, many of whom are new acquaintances.

Perhaps more interestingly, however, I have also begun using the music with a kind of Pavlovian deviousness, in order to try to condition the students' classroom behaviour. A few seconds before the official starting time, I exit the classroom through the door on 'stage left', walking the 10 metres along the hallway and then re-entering the classroom through the second door. I return to my laptop, hit the mute button, and then begin my welcome. After the second or third iteration of this ritual, the muting of the music is sufficient to trigger student silence and focus. Oh, the power of learning spaces!

Paul

I had cause to start to think about learning spaces, and my use of them, in 2003. Keen to provide the students whom I taught with a richer learning experience, I sought to remove didactic delivery of information from the 'classrooms' of the programme modules which I had inherited so as to liberate face-to-face contact time for more discursive activities. I had aspirations for students to solve problems together in the classroom, drawing upon the information which was given ahead of the lecture. As we know, this mode of teaching is known as 'flipping the classroom' and although I was by no means a pioneer of this pedagogy (Maier *et al.*, 1998) had described this pedagogical approach five years before.), but I was nonetheless an innovator within my own institution. I recorded my lectures with *Microsoft Producer*, mass publishing CD ROMs and distributing them to students. Because of my relatively early adoption of this approach to teaching, I was in a single-numbered minority of people who stepped into the classroom each session having already delivered the lecture. As a consequence there were not many learning spaces designed to accommodate over one hundred students in a way which supported the peer collaboration activities which I wanted to facilitate and support. Indeed, the space I was allocated was always a tiered lecture theatre.

Undaunted by the less-than-aligned environment, I set out to reclaim the space from didactic intent and to recast it as a space for discussion and problem-solving. I did this by using the data projector to introduce tasks to students, expecting them to use their peers to their left and to their right to discuss the problems which were presented, and to negotiate solutions. As further technical options became available, I was able to bring laptops into the classroom and to complement the sessions with VLE-based activities. Eventually, these VLE-based technologies were implemented before, during, and after the sessions, with face-to-face and online learning opportunities being meshed together in a sequenced design which I came to refer to as 'woven learning'. Core to the philosophy of 'woven learning' is the provision of time and space for collaborative learning.

As my career progressed, I had opportunities to design learning spaces which would support peer collaboration to a greater extent than had the legacy lecture theatres which I had used previously. These new spaces were the 'flexible teaching spaces' introduced into the Faculty of Health at Birmingham City University as part of its Higher Education Academy funded Centre for Excellence in Learning and Teaching. These spaces were of course flat, with movable tables and chairs and embedded technology. Like many of the authors of the chapters in this book, I found that once these spaces were populated with teachers and learners, new approaches to teaching emerged. I also found that after teachers had developed pedagogical approaches which worked in these optimised spaces, they were far more likely to introduce similar (if slightly constrained) approaches in legacy spaces too. Thus, I would contend that institutional investment in new learning spaces leads to an impact which extends beyond the physical envelope of such new spaces through the (transformed) agency of the staff who 'cut their teeth' on the new spaces. As I have had the opportunity to learn from this anthology, and from the symposium that supported its creation, so my understanding of learning spaces as comprising a fusion of architecture, culture, furniture, people and pedagogy has matured. It is this fusion which characterises the anthology and it is this fusion which, for me, captures the true essence of an effective learning space.

Claus

My initiation to learning spaces in higher education came about 10 years ago when I was head of research at the then CBS Learning Lab of Copenhagen Business School. I was serving on a committee whose charge was to design a new teaching building for the School. We were introduced to the American architect Bruce Jilk, who is recognised for his innovative and flexible designs for schools and universities, and whom we engaged to conduct a workshop on the design of learning spaces.

Following that workshop, I co-developed a course on innovative teaching practices at Copenhagen Business School, in which learning space design was a dominant feature of the course. We were training professors to exploit the School's teaching spaces which had movable furniture... to make alternative use of floor space by setting up chairs and tables in different ways.

I was also lucky to meet American Professor Roger Putzel, who gave me his XB (eXperience Base) manual for running organisational behaviour classes. The idea is to treat the classroom like an organisation, allowing students to take control of the classroom and run sessions on their own (with guidance from the professor). This alternative approach to the flipped classroom also had obvious implications for the design of the learning space.

Today, I run professional training in my own company, cph:learning, in rooms with flexible furniture and round tables. I also have the ability to project images on three of four walls. The primary underpinning of the training is to refocus learning on the participants. They negotiate ideas at round tables, but of course can get input from the facilitator(s). For some types of training I use no tables, and for other types of training I use no chairs. My general philosophy is that the design of the learning space must follow the learning objectives of the training session. Flexible training rooms, therefore, are a prerequisite.

Co-editing the chapters in this anthology also reminds me how the drivers of learning are not always obvious. Indeed, in many cases they are buried. And sometimes they are even prevented as a result of traditional architectural design of lecture theatres, with their long rows of tables and chairs.

For me, visiting Steelcase University in Grand Rapids as part of the LiHE symposium in October 2013 was a truly unique experience. Steelcase is pushing the limits of our understanding of learning space design with its innovative research. And by experimenting daily with different learning spaces in the company, it is living what it preaches. I recommend everyone with an interest in learning space design to visit Steelcase.

A framework for the anthology

A significant challenge when editing an anthology is developing a framework for structuring its chapters, even when they all share a common theme. During the symposium, therefore, together with the authors we teased out a variety of frameworks by first juxtaposing a number of different dimensions around learning spaces: virtual versus physical spaces, active versus passive learning, practical versus theoretical emphasis, and mind versus body effects. We proposed learning spaces as sites of interaction – student to student, instructor to student, student to instructor, and so on. We tried two dimensional frameworks, Venn diagrams, circles, x-y plots, triangles.

In the end, however, we settled on a framework with three dimensions which to some degree parallel the three broad but interrelated themes of the call for chapters (see Figure 1.): 1. conceptualising learning spaces, 2. pedagogy in learning spaces, and 3. changing learning space. Each of the 14 chapters of the anthology, therefore, explores learning spaces in higher education, emphasising two of the three dimensions.

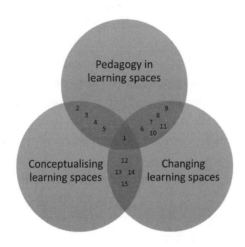

Figure 1: The framework for the anthology with chapter numbers.

The anthology, chapter by chapter

In Chapter 2 Ieva Stupans explores learning design within a distributed learning space at an Australian university. The chapter begins by describing the Australian context of higher education with respect to learning in the discipline of pharmacy. It then considers the affordances of online, face-to-face, and clinical placement learning. Finally, the chapter concludes with a case study of a programme which provides students with learning opportunities in a distributed learning space model. The key lesson from Chapter 2 is that through detailed consideration of learning design, programmes which are typically not available to students externally, can be provided within a distributed learning space.

In chapter 3 Jos Boys and Diane Hazlett investigate the relationship between learning spaces and student engagement and belonging. The chapter begins by exploring how unpacking the idea of relational learning

reveals verbal, non-verbal, and affective dimensions of student perceptions and experiences. It then outlines a framework for examining the
contribution of space to improving student engagement, based on case
study evidence. Finally, the chapter suggests some important variables
linking what matters about space and students' feelings of belonging and
identity. The key lesson from Chapter 3 is that better understanding
of the interactions between relational learning and space can improve
student engagement.

In chapter 4 Jennifer Rowley raises awareness of the need to adapt
curriculum and learning tasks to match the learning space. The chapter
begins by looking at why a learning space is redesigned and why academics
need to redesign curriculum to become better teachers of students in the
space. It then looks specifically at the effect that a new learning space
had on students' learning – specifically on the collaborative nature of
learning and engaged inquiry. Finally, the chapter advocates for understanding the learning space and its impact on the learner, and for the need
for curriculum remodelling to accommodate 21st century learner needs.
The key lesson from Chapter 4 is that the need exists for a match between
curriculum, instruction, and space.

In chapter 5 Nicola Bartholomew and Paul Bartholomew explore the
social and cognitive affordances of physical and virtual learning spaces,
and offer a case study of how this exploration has informed the redesign
of space-use in an undergraduate diagnostic radiography programme.
The chapter begins by identifying a problem context of teaching in a challenging physical space. It then explores theoretical perspectives relating
to the use of physical and virtual learning spaces. Finally, the chapter
concludes by showing how the theoretical exploration has informed a
solution for the problem discussed in the introduction. The key lesson
from Chapter 5 is that a hybrid learning space which embeds technology
within a physical space can repurpose it, leading to new opportunities for
the enhancement of learning.

In chapter 6 Silke Lange and John R. A. Smith examine the impact
of migration of students and staff between learning environments and
positions (teachers, researchers, and producers) on students' learning
experience. The chapter begins by distinguishing between physical
(geographical), virtual (online), and conceptual (state of mind) learning
spaces. It then describes Broad Vision, the art/science research and

learning programme on which this chapter is based. Finally, the chapter discusses the emerging themes, reflecting on a range of perspectives of Broad Vision participants. The key lesson from Chapter 6 is that spaces will only become learning environments with suitable activities and when groups or individuals are in suitable conceptual spaces.

In chapter 7 Steve Drew and Christopher Klopper investigate the perceptions and conceptions of teaching and learning spaces in higher education. The chapter begins by developing a framework of contextual affordances of teaching and learning spaces. It then applies the framework to data which were collected through PRO teaching observations and from a survey of the teachers' conceptions of teaching and learning spaces. Finally, the chapter concludes with a discussion of the heterogeneous disciplinary use of homogeneous learning spaces. The key lesson from Chapter 7 is that teaching and learning spaces moderate pedagogic practice.

In chapter 8 Kayoko Enomoto and Richard Warner inform the design and implementation of educational blogging as a reflective learning space. The chapter begins by conceptualising learning spaces and reviews the related literature on educational blogging for informing the design and implementation of reflective spaces. It then presents a study which explores the use of blogs as a virtual learning space for developing both discipline-specific skills and reflection skills. It continues by describing two specific projects, using quantitative and qualitative data analyses, which research the effectiveness of the design and implementation of blogs as a learning space in a 3rd year upper level Japanese language course. Finally, the chapter concludes with key recommendations for creating a learning space for developing both discipline-specific and reflection skills through the use of blogs. The key lesson from Chapter 8 is that a key element in the success of a reflective blog learning space lies in how appropriately and adequately blogging activities are scaffolded.

In chapter 9 Lennie Scott-Webber discusses the impact of change agents on higher education. The chapter begins by highlighting three change agents: 1. historical influences, 2. rate of technological change, and 3. the redesign of the classroom's physical learning environment. It establishes a framework for conceptualising and examining what an active learning ecosystem might contain. Finally, the chapter provides insights from learning research and brain science on the learner, the learning process, and the learning place. The key lesson from Chapter 9 is that when change is disruptive and impacts existing norms, a robust decision model promoting inclusive decision-making across stakeholder constituencies is necessary.

In chapter 10 Gary M. Pavlechko and Kathleen L. Jacobi illustrate the need for, and provide an example of, an effective faculty development programme for instructors selected to participate in the Interactive Learning Space Initiative at Ball State University. The chapter begins by describing the physical remodel of two classroom spaces on the Ball State campus which required moving from traditional lecture-based teaching to an engaged learning environment. It then discusses the need for preparation of a faculty member to assume a new role in the higher education teaching and learning experience. Finally, the chapter proposes a model of faculty development which was created to prepare faculty members prior to and during their time in the new learning space. The key lesson from Chapter 10 is that the preparation of faculty members, as they transition from traditional instructor to facilitator of learning, is necessary to ultimately change the teaching and learning culture across campus.

In chapter 11 Ryan Daniel and Katja Fleischmann explore the extent to which computer laboratories and other formal and informal learning spaces offer a viable alternative to the traditional design studio in supporting student learning and collaboration. The chapter begins by reviewing the literature on the design studio as a physical learning space, and on the pedagogy of design education. It then reviews the main features of learning spaces which support successful cross-disciplinary and creative collaboration. The chapter continues by exploring the perspectives of undergraduate media design students on the effectiveness of various formal and informal learning spaces, including a specialist computer lab which was constructed to replace the traditional design studio. Finally, the chapter provides insights into which particular aspects of learning spaces students identify as most important in terms of supporting and enhancing their capacity to be creative. The key lesson from Chapter 11 is that pedagogies and learning spaces need to be adjusted and adapted in order to facilitate the different ways in which students collaborate, are creative, and learn, be this face to face on campus in computer labs or virtually.

In chapter 12 Aileen Strickland heightens awareness around the active agency of learning spaces in shaping our social systems. The chapter begins by reviewing the social theory of structuration, establishing the concept of spatial agency. It then discusses its relevance to education and the direct application to learning spaces. Finally, the chapter presents implications for theory and practice for educators and students operating in these environments and the designers designing them. The key lesson from Chapter 12 is that, by understanding that learning spaces have active agency in the production of our social systems, we become empowered to see, act, and impart the values which are needed in the 21st century.

In chapter 13 Clive Holtham and Annemarie Cancienne explore the constraints on academic excellence which can arise from collective learning spaces which are not owned by any one discipline. The chapter begins by considering theory which highlights the different perspectives of designers, everyday users, and proactive users of learning spaces. It then compares that theory to actual experience in a single institution. Finally, the chapter reviews the implications for the process of learning space design. The key lesson from Chapter 13 is that the evolution of learning spaces is, and ought to be, a contested area which cannot be resolved only through a formal building commissioning process.

In chapter 14 B. Liezel Frick, Eva M. Brodin and Ruth M. Albertyn propose the relationship between doctoral supervisors and students as a co-constructed negotiated learning space. The chapter begins by exploring the unique nature and challenges of the student-supervisor relationship in the context of the doctoral learning space, arguing that both doctoral supervisors and students take part in negotiating their relationship, but that supervisors often take the lead in establishing this relationship which forms the foundation of the learning space which is created. It then uses transactional analysis theory as a point of departure from which possible identity positions are construed, which can lead to either negotiated or non-negotiated learning spaces. Finally, the chapter offers a framework for conceptualising the doctoral learning space and for characterising the main elements in the doctoral supervisor-student relationship. The key lesson from Chapter 14 is that students and supervisors need to understand their identity positions, and the implications thereof, if they want to negotiate a constructive and productive learning space.

In chapter 15 Eva Dobozy explores the concept of 'built pedagogy' from theoretical and practical viewpoints. The chapter begins with an introduction of the concept of 'built pedagogy', linking it to the development of learners' 21st century competencies. It then discusses the concept of formal, non-formal and informal learning from the perspective of Bourdieu's dispositional theory of action, and connects learning to learner agency and decision-making power. It continues with a real-world case example from a teacher education programme at an Australian university which illustrates how the traditionally disparate learning spaces have been re-conceptualised to facilitate the ideas of border-crossing and learner agency. Finally, it outlines some implications for future designs of the continuum from physical to virtual learning spaces design, focusing on the need to plan for non-formal learning and for the design of social learning spaces. The key lesson from Chapter 15 is that there is a need to make explicit the nexus between educational philosophy and architectural design of physical and/or virtual learning spaces, especially if the aim is to increase student agency, interaction, and collaboration.

In Summary

The NBC television network aired 79 episodes of the original Star Trek series over three seasons before it was cancelled. The captain and crew of the starship *Enterprise*, therefore, were only able to explore a limited number of strange new worlds... their contact with new life and new civilisations was cut short by the series' demise.

As editors, we feel that the page limits of the anthology have likewise restricted exploration of learning spaces in higher education. It was clear from the number of submissions to the symposium that this theme, like the universe, is boundary-less. This anthology, therefore, might be considered more of rallying cry for a mission to explore learning spaces in higher education. We hope that its chapters inspire you to embark on your own voyages of scientific discovery. Happy exploring!

About the Authors

Lennie Scott-Webber is Director Education Environments of Steelcase Education Solutions at Steelcase Inc. in Grand Rapids, U.S.A. She can be contacted at this e-mail: lascottwe@steelcase.com

John Branch is Academic Director of the part-time MBA programmes and Lecturer of Marketing at the Stephen M. Ross School of Business, and Faculty Associate at the Center for Russian, East European, & European Studies, both of the University of Michigan in Ann Arbor, U.S.A. He can be contacted at this e-mail: jdbranch@umich.edu

Paul Bartholomew is Director of Learning Innovation and Professional Practice at Aston University in Birmingham, England. He can be contacted at this e-mail: p.bartholomew@aston.ac.uk

Claus Nygaard is executive director of LiHE and executive director of cph:learning institute. He can be contacted at this e-mail: lihesupport@gmail.com

Chapter Two
The Design of Distributed Learning Spaces

Ieva Stupans

Introduction

This chapter contributes to the anthology on learning space design in higher education by describing and analysing a case study of the design of a programme taught in a 'distributed learning space'. I define learning space as: *'those sites across which formal learning is organised and distributed'.* For the purposes of my analysis I define three types of distributed learning spaces: 1) online learning spaces, 2) face-to-face learning spaces (on campus), and 3) learning spaces in the form of clinical placement sites. Consequently, this chapter provides empirical design considerations for programme development in three types of distributed learning spaces. I illustrate these design considerations through a case study drawn from experiences in an innovative Pharmacy programme at the University of New England in Armidale, NSW, Australia. Importantly, this programme is the only higher education institution in Australia offering an undergraduate degree in Pharmacy in a distributed learning space and one of only few such programmes worldwide. Reading this chapter, you will:

1. see how different conceptualisations of learning opportunities across various distributed learning spaces have implications for curriculum design;

2. gain insight into ways in which learning space design can be proactively linked to requirements for student learning outcomes; and

3. get to know more about the alignment of learning opportunities and assessment in distributed learning spaces.

Conventional programmes with time-honoured teaching and learning spaces, such as lecture theatres, seminar rooms and laboratories, are derived from long-standing, teacher-centred, teaching and learning models. These programmes, by necessity, cater to a relatively homogeneous student population who are able to commit to attending face-to-face classes in predefined spaces on campus throughout the academic year. In Australia, there have been many explicit calls for widening participation in higher education, both in terms of numbers entering higher education and in terms of greater participation of students from lower socio-economic groups (Heagney, 2009). These potential participants in higher education include mature-age students with families, and students living outside zones of convenient daily commuting distance to universities.

Alternatives to traditional classroom-based teaching, such as programmes available by what has been described as 'distance' models, are the only option for students restricted through mobility and/or financial constraints. In health disciplines, apart from nursing, distance programmes have not been widely available. It has been suggested that distance education that leads to independent study in isolation from other students may not provide the optimal environment for health-professional socialisation, which in itself is considered to be a critical element of education of students in health disciplines (Austin & Rocchi Dean, 2006). Additionally, development and assessment of clinical skills, interpersonal and communicative competencies have been regarded as requiring face-to-face interaction (Austin & Rocchi Dean, 2006). It is important to distinguish that a programme offered in a 'distance' mode may be enhanced by face-to-face contact between students, and between students and staff, and through opportunities for experiential learning such as those described in this chapter.

The University of New England in Armidale, NSW, Australia, has responded to the need for accessible programmes and is currently the only higher education institution in Australia offering an undergraduate degree in Pharmacy in a distributed learning space. In this programme, face-to-face opportunities for students studying in a 'distance' mode are provided through mandatory intensive schools, of generally three or four days' duration for each subject, undertaken on campus. The programme is supported by the University's online learning management system (LMS), a customised *Moodle* platform — a flexible learning platform that allows incorporation of forums, quizzes and wikis as well as progressive assessment. Additionally, all students studying in Pharmacy programmes across Australia are required to undertake experiential (placement) learning in environments such as community or hospital pharmacies as part of their programme of study. Each subject of the programme at the University of New England is situated within a coherent integrated framework for student learning – face-to-face, online and experiential and the learning space distributed across the University, online spaces within students' personal learning environments and clinical placements. This model is comparable to what has been described as a 'face-to face' event blended pedagogical template (Jara & Mohamad, 2007) where most learning activities are conducted online but where practical skills practise is on campus. In the programme described in this chapter, all students also undertake experiential (placement) learning in clinical environments within community or hospital pharmacy contexts.

In this distributed model, our programme has moved *"well beyond the concept of bolting a website onto a traditional classroom-based course"* (Skill & Young, 2002:25). The pedagogical challenge in this programme has been addressed by designing a curriculum where on-campus and placement learning opportunities are integrated with the online learning opportunities afforded through the LMS, thus providing an integrated comprehensive learning space for students within which the achievement of learning outcomes can be demonstrated.

In the rest of this chapter we share the detail of a learning design model in which learning outcomes are met within a distributed learning space model. The learning design is potentially transformative, offering the opportunity to fundamentally revitalise teaching and enhance learning through a *"transformative redesign process that rebuilds courses"* (Smythe, 2011:3). Through the chapter I briefly discuss learning design and learning outcomes in the context of Australian higher education; I then consider the distributed learning space curriculum model and examine the significance and options for co-location of learners and teachers and the achievement of learning outcomes. Aligned assessment approaches are also considered within the overarching framework I offer. Thus, the chapter provides coherent, pragmatic guidance for others who may be considering learning design in a distributed learning space.

Learning design and learning outcomes in the context of Australian higher education

In the learner-centred paradigm there is focus on the intended (and pre-declared) outcome of students' learning. Subject or programme learning outcomes describe that which learners are expected to know, or be able to do, after having completed that subject or programme of study. In Australian higher education there have recently been significant initiatives to focus attention on the meaning of academic standards, and on how the academic achievements of students and graduates are established, measured, monitored and reported. To this end the Australian Learning and Teaching Council (ALTC) has supported the Learning and Teaching Academic Standards project which aimed to define and describe learning outcomes in selected specific discipline areas. The ALTC (now Office of Learning and Teaching) has also provided funding for an Australian Pharmacy Network focused on Learning Outcomes for the Pharmacy Curriculum. The Network has established that the following programme-level learning outcomes should be evidenced at graduation (Stupans, 2013):

1. demonstrate professional behaviour and accountability in the commitment to care for and about people;

2. retrieve, critically evaluate and apply evidence in professional practice;

3. demonstrate team and leadership skills to deliver safe and effective practice;

4. taking account of the patient perspective, make, act on and take social responsibility for clinically, ethically and scientifically sound decisions;

5. communicate in lay and professional language, choosing strategies appropriate for the context and diverse audiences;

6. reflect on current skills, knowledge, attitudes and practice; planning and implementing for on-going personal and professional development;

7. apply pharmaceutical, medication and health knowledge and skills

i) within their scope of practice, in the assessment of individual health status and medication needs, and where necessary, develop, implement and monitor management plans in consultation with patients/clients and other health professionals to improve patient outcomes;

ii) to promote and optimise the health and welfare of communities and /or populations;

8. formulate, prepare and also supply medications and therapeutic products.

As this set of examples show, learning outcomes include more than being able to recall knowledge and include the evidencing of diverse outcomes that include skills and attributes in addition to the acquisition of knowledge. With respect to curriculum design, it has been shown that learning outcomes produced in a constructivist environment are not simply the accumulation of information but are congruent with the acquisition of an ability to apply knowledge (Tynjälä, 1999).

There is no single definition of effective higher education teaching, however it is *"broadly understood as teaching that is orientated to and focused on students and their learning"* (Devlin & Samarawickrema, 2010:112). In a student-centred model of teaching and learning, there is emphasis on active student engagement resulting in deep learning (Biggs & Tang, 2007). During active learning *"students move from being passive recipients of knowledge to being participants in activities that encompass analysis, synthesis and evaluation as well as the exploration of values and attitudes"* (Sivan et al., 2000:381).

Learning design decisions need to be made in the context of learning theories that attempt to describe how learners learn. The behaviourist view is one of changes in observable behaviour; approaches to promote learning include repetition, varied stimuli and careful sequencing of materials. The cognitivist view is associated with memory, motivation and thinking. Cognitivism focuses on gaining and organising knowledge, hence reflection plays an important role in the cognitivist view of learning. Lastly, in the constructivist view, learners learn through observation, processing, interpretation and construction of their own personal view (Ally, 2004). Social constructivism implies that this 'construction' process is aided through collaborative social interactions. Student-centred learning is related primarily to the constructivist view (Carlile & Jordan, 2005) however in practice it is acknowledged that learning design may incorporate elements of these three learning theories (Ertmer & Newby, 1993). Recognising the continuum of student learning from knowing to understanding to applying (Hailikari *et al.*, 2007) behaviourist, cognitivist and constructivist approaches may be used to design learning opportunities for the "what" (facts), "how" (processes and principles) and "why" (higher level thinking) of learning materials (Ertmer & Newby, 1993; Ally, 2004).

Two aspects of learning theories, reflection and collaboration, need to be highlighted in the context of health professional education. University preparation for careers in many health professions includes developing students' reflective practice to build skills for lifelong learning, thereby supporting professionals to remain up-to-date in their knowledge and abilities. The 'reflective practitioner' (Schön, 1983) is one who uses reflection to revisit experience both to learn from the experience and to plan for future action. Reflection may be viewed as a learning strategy, assisting learners to connect and integrate new learning to existing knowledge and skills. A review of health sciences literature indicates that capacity for reflection may be developed over time and with practice (Mann *et al.*, 2009).

Collaborative learning strategies and small-group work are reported to have a significantly positive effect on student attitudes toward learning and lead to the development of in-depth understanding, leading to significant gains in academic achievement (Osman *et al.*, 2011). Secondly, teamwork and co-operation are increasingly important in health care with teams being seen at many levels in health care organisations (Reeves *et al.*, 2011); university curriculum needs to ensure student preparedness for future practice.

Distributed learning spaces

A course where students are present on campus for only three or four days in an individual teaching period requires reconceptualisation of the design of face-to-face opportunities and supplementary resources provided through the LMS. Courses taught in distributed spaces differ considerably from those in traditional university environments in which the term 'blended' learning may be used to describe the provision of supplementary or complementary resources, such as lecture recordings, discussion boards and readings, for courses through the use of an institutional LMS such as *Moodle* (Sharpe *et al.*, 2006). Blended learning implies the use a mix of online and face-to-face learning. Face-to-face learning opportunities within this context are most frequently situated in lecture theatres, seminar and tutorial rooms and laboratories and require student attendance for some of these activities at on campus across the teaching period. Helms (2012) has reviewed and described a number of issues which have been evaluated for blended learning – face-to-face and online scheduling, communication approaches, course content and student motivation. There is little literature that provides guidance regarding distributed learning. Further research regarding best practice is required; however this needs to be in the context of the span of students' learning spaces i.e. blended- or distributed learning spaces.

Two critical questions have guided our curriculum design:

1. "what learning outcomes require students to be located in the same learning space at the same time?"; and

2. "how is face-to-face time optimally used?"

With these questions as our guideline, we have developed a student-centred approach to teaching in 1) online learning spaces, 2) face-to-face learning spaces (on campus), and 3) physical learning spaces in the form of clinical placements. Figure 1 shows the distributed learning space-model we used to design our undergraduate degree in Pharmacy.

	Synchronous learning events	Asynchronous learning events
Co-located learning spaces (physical)	Space: face-to-face learning spaces (physical, on campus). Learning activities: lectures, discussions in classroom, team work.	Space: clinical placements (physical, not on campus). Learning activities: learning through reflected practice during clinical placement
Not co-located learning spaces (virtual)	Space: online learning spaces (LMS accessed from any computer) Learning activities: live streaming of lectures, interactive online discussions	Space: online learning spaces (LMS accessed from any computer). Learning activities: vodcasts, podcasts, quizzes, collaborate to write wiki's.

Figure 1: Our distributed learning space-model.

Our distributed learning space-model conceptualises learning opportunities on two axes. The first axis deals with synchronous/asynchronous learning events. Synchronous learning events see all students participate in the learning event at the same time. Asynchronous learning events see students participate at different times. The second axis deals with co-located/not co-located learning spaces. Co-located learning spaces are physical learning spaces such as classrooms, lecture theatres, etc., where all students are located at the same time. And physical spaces for clinical placements, where each individual student is placed during the programme. Not co-located learning spaces are learning spaces which can be accessed from any physical location, such as virtual learning space devoted for student learning. Students can access a LMS (learning management system) from any computer, either at home, in a library, in an office, etc. Using not co-located learning spaces students can participate in either synchronous learning events or asynchronous learning events.

Learning opportunities and assessment in distributed learning spaces

Regardless of learning space, good instructional design which includes aligned learning outcomes, learning opportunities and assessment can promote student learning. In higher education, particularly in the health sciences, and the focus of this chapter in pharmacy programmes, a number of teaching approaches are used. In face-to-face pharmacy programmes active student-centred teaching approaches have been surveyed and reported (Stewart *et al.*, 2011) as typically including discussion-based learning, use of web-based modules to deliver content and assess student understanding, use of patient simulation, problem and case-based learning, team-based learning and traditional laboratory experiences to provide hands-on learning experiences.

The role of coursework assessments in the constructivist view has been commented on extensively in the context of assessment *for* learning (Gibbs & Simpson, 2004-05). The link between learning and assessment is acknowledged: *"By aligning assessment with the expected learning outcomes of students and the teaching and learning activities, and by choosing proper assessment methods and tasks, teachers can effectively guide students' study practices and enhance deep, meaning-oriented learning"* (Postareff *et al.*, 2012:84). Examples of student centred assessment include diaries, logs and journals, portfolios, peer/self-assessment, projects, group work and skills and competencies (Gibbs, 1995; Postareff *et al.*, 2012).

Lectures are typically described as providing for passive student learning. In a traditional university programme lectures are most frequently synchronous, face-to-face events, although across all universities lecture recordings are now often provided and accessed by students through university LMS; as a consequence, both the purpose and approach to lectures in a distributed learning space model, and indeed in all learning models, needs to be evaluated. In many disciplines, including health sciences, students need information (facts, concepts and context) to meaningfully engage in active learning through, for example, problem solving, case studies and experiential opportunities (see Bartholomew, 2014). Instructional design needs to include considerations as to how best to provide information in such a way that it is consistent with a student-centred design.

In our programme delivered in a distributed learning space information is provided online through our LMS in a variety of formats which students may engage with, and utilise, in a variety of ways to meet their needs. Information is most often not presented face-to-face during on campus residential schools. These online formats include traditional 50 minute lectures and short ten- to twelve-minute segments focussed on a few main concepts, recorded in a number of different ways such as vodcasts and podcasts that the students can access asynchronously with the ability to stop, fast forward, or rewind and to navigate to any point. Materials are also provided as annotated slides, web links and open resource animations. Again students work through these individually, in their own time and in their own leaning space. Our LMS is also used to provide access to computer-assisted assessment for either/both formative or summative purposes, generally in a quiz format, for example, for assessment of calculation skills. Students may also engage with other students and staff through asynchronous discussion. Although students work through these resources at their own pace, they help students 'stay on track', as the depth and breadth of resources are clearly indicated.

The practice of using the information, and assessment of the learning of information, is most frequently conducted through case study or problem solving activities which link information to real life cases. In case based learning, students are typically presented with issues or problems. The scenarios are usually taken from real life and presented from the viewpoint of a need to solve the problem. Cases frequently require research, elaboration, further analysis and synthesis together with decisions. Case discussions in a distributed environment may occur in a number of ways – synchronously, co-located in a tutorial type environment in residential schools, online, synchronously online through the use of technologies such web conferencing software and asynchronously online in discussion pages. Additionally, synchronous web-conferencing software provides online access to a shared screen, text and voice discussions. Students and staff can, through the use of these technologies, connect in real time.

Project work, which in turn provides artefacts for assessment, is an asynchronous active learning opportunity; the responsibility for learning is shifted from teacher to the student. Students learn to work independently, devising their own learning plans and actively finding information. Students may also carry out projects in teams – interaction and learning can be facilitated by Web 2.0 technologies such as blogs (see Enomoto & Warner, in this volume) *Twitter, Facebook, MySpace, Wiki's* and *Google Docs* which provide tools enabling communication, collaborative authoring and knowledge building by multiple users.

Role-play is widely used in the health sciences and social sciences disciplines. Students perform tasks that are based on the application of prior learning and human interactions. In pharmacy programmes, learning opportunities based on simulated pharmacist-patient interactions are provided so that students can develop and practise counselling. Patient counselling requires highly sophisticated levels of communication in order to meet its goals – which include achieving safe and appropriate use of medicines and therapeutic devices to optimise therapeutic outcomes. Counselling scenarios are assessed directly, but are also a component of Objective Structured Clinical Examinations (OSCEs) (Harrhy *et al.*, 2003; Sturpe, 2010). In an OSCE the assessment focus is the integration of higher levels of knowledge, skills and attributes. By their very nature, counselling learning opportunities are synchronous, but they may occur in face-to-face classes or be supported through use of technologies such web conferencing software, thus allowing students to be in their own personal online learning spaces. We have also used web conferencing software to facilitate assessment of simple student counselling skill scenarios (Stupans & Orwin, 2012); however, the complexity of OSCEs necessitates that both practice and actual assessments are conducted face-to-face.

Laboratory practical classes that focus on skill development, for example in compounding, i.e. extemporaneous product preparation of creams, lotions, mixtures etc. are synchronous learning events requiring students to attend predefined spaces on campus. In the sciences, virtual laboratories offer an opportunity for students to develop skills without accessing physical laboratories; however to date there are no examples within compounding (Robertson & Shrewsbury, 2011). Laboratory work is fully structured, and task-based, rather than seeing students taking an open-ended approach. Students are provided with hands-on experiences of handling apparatus and materials used in their future professional lives. Additionally as an informal teaching situation, practical classes are a venue for building student-student and student-staff professional relationships (Forret *et al.*, n.d.). The assessment of compounding skills is authentic and laboratory based.

In accordance with the principles of experiential education, clinical placements provide significant opportunities for student pharmacists to actively engage in learning within the clinical environment off campus on a daily basis – much of it as a part of wider learning. In our programme, placement opportunities are part of the student's study plan. Assessment of these placements is through assessment of student placement workbooks and preceptor assessment of student generic and occupation-specific skills. Students also use clinical placements for fieldwork. Learning opportunities that are essentially enquiry-based have been integrated into the programme. These are face-to-face off-campus experiences see students interacting and observing in a pharmacy. Each of these field trips has different foci. Assessment is generally through preparation of short reports.

Learning design and the distributed learning space: exemplars

Prior to considering individual units, it is pertinent to point out that individual-unit learning outcomes build the programme's learning outcomes. The levels of achievement i.e. standards for the learning outcomes increase incrementally through programme. The dimensions of breadth, depth, utility and application to practice and proficiency describe the standard.

Within learning design literature a 'castle top design' for learning has been developed (Fink, 2005). This 'castle top design', which presumes traditional classroom based teaching, potentially supplemented through online support, focuses on assigning learning opportunities to either 'in class' or 'out of class' activities with consideration being given to the development of learning activities which build on each other.

The first example is detailed examination of a second year Pharmacy Practice unit. (In Australian universities one unit represents, one eighth of a full time annual load and corresponds to approximately 150 hours of student effort). Adapting this 'castle top design' (Table 1) is a useful starting point for further discussion and presentation of how our learning design, including coursework assessments *for* learning (Gibbs & Simpson, 2004-05), is executed. Learning outcomes (albeit at a beginner level), the key points of learning opportunities and the assessment for this unit are displayed in Table 1. In Table 1 the general arrangement of learning opportunities and assessments is displayed. In our distributed learning space model for this second year Pharmacy Practice unit, learning opportunities such as laboratory practical classes and classes which focus on skill development – synchronous and co-located – are the only fixed event for students attending three or four day residential schools.

Other units are organised according to their own individual requirements. For example, other units include two face-to-face residential schools in one semester. The research units are distributed entirely in students' personal and clinical spaces with no requirement for on campus attendance. Mentoring for students is provided online.

The second example is a learning opportunity/ assessment in one of the third year Pharmacy Practice units. Learning outcomes addressed are: retrieve, critically evaluate and apply evidence in professional practice; demonstrate team and leadership skills to deliver safe and effective practice; communicate in lay and professional language and apply pharmaceutical, medication and health knowledge and skills. Through this learning opportunity students firstly undertake fieldwork to identify health promotion activities carried out in community pharmacies. They then work in virtual teams, researching and collaborating asynchronously and synchronously to develop several additional potential activities. Web 2.0 technologies allow multiple students to contribute content, to edit text and negotiate with other team members to produce their final assessment work, asynchronously – all the while with students situated in their own learning spaces.

The third example is a learning opportunity/ assessment in the fourth year Applied Pharmacotherapeutics units. Learning outcomes that are addressed are: retrieve, critically evaluate and apply evidence in professional practice; communicate in lay and professional language and apply pharmaceutical, medication and health knowledge and skills. Both practise for and OSCE assessments occur on campus, during residential schools. Students also complete individual reflection exercises, which are submitted online.

Learning outcome	Learning opportunity (synchronicity & location)	Assessment (Assessment number)
Retrieve, critically evaluate and apply evidence in professional practice	Resources which demonstrate different levels of health literacy, tools for determining health and prose literacy provided (asynchronous, not co-located)	Assignment in which students compare journal articles written at different levels of health literacy (Assessment 1)

Learning outcome	Learning opportunity (synchronicity & location)	Assessment (Assessment number)
Communicate in lay and professional language	Resources which demonstrate different levels of health literacy, tools for determining health and prose literacy provided (asynchronous, not co-located)	Assignment in which students compare journal articles written at different levels of health literacy (Assessment 1)
	Simulated pharmacist-patient interactions between students and tutors/actors where students can develop and practise counselling (Both synchronous, not co-located and synchronous, co-located utilised)	Simulated pharmacist-patient interactions between students and actors (Assessment 2)
	Observation of pharmacist on clinical placement (asynchronous, co-located)	Assignment in which students compare and contrast pharmacist behaviour to "best" practice (Assessment 3)
Apply pharmaceutical, medication and health knowledge and skills	Resources which cover key points of differential diagnosis of the symptoms most commonly seen by community pharmacists (asynchronous, co-located)	Simulated pharmacist-patient interactions between students and actors (Assessment 2)
	Simulated pharmacist-patient interactions between students and tutors/actors where students can develop and practise counselling (Both synchronous, not co-located and synchronous, co-located utilised)	Simulated pharmacist-patient interactions between students and actors (Assessment 2)
	Observation of pharmacist on clinical placement (asynchronous, co-located)	Assignment in which students compare and contrast pharmacist to "best" practice (Assessment 3)

Learning outcome	Learning opportunity (synchronicity & location)	Assessment (Assessment number)
Formulate, prepare and also supply medications and therapeutic products	Resources regarding calculations and calculations exercises Practice online calculations quizzes (asynchronous, not co-located)	Online calculations quiz (Assessment 4)
	Practical classes where students practice preparation of extemporaneous products (synchronous, co-located)	Practical Examination, preparing and supplying extemporaneous product (Assessment 4)
Integration of all specified learning outcomes	(synchronous, not co-located)	Written unseen, closed book invigilated exam (Assessment 5) Note: The main purpose of the final examination is to assess consolidation.

Table 1: Learning outcomes, opportunities and assessment: exemplar unit (In Australian universities one unit represents, one eighth of a full time annual load and corresponds to approximately 150 hours of student effort).

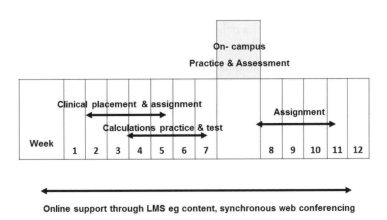

Figure 2: Learning Opportunities and Assessment within a Distributed Learning Space— detailed examination of a second year Pharmacy Practice unit.

Conclusion

This chapter describes and analyses an innovative student focused curriculum in which students are provided with learning opportunities such that they can achieve the Pharmacy learning outcomes in a distributed learning space. Three types of distributed learning space were discussed: 1) online learning spaces, 2) face-to-face learning spaces (on campus), and 3) learning spaces in the form of clinical placement sites. Together they provide the impetus for the design of this programme which provides opportunities for a more diverse base of students than a conventional campus based programme. Student comments, such as those below, align with our aspirations regarding opportunities for studying such a programme – even though they cannot commit to attending face-to-face classes, throughout the university year, in predefined on campus spaces, .

> " Having a family means that I cannot move and live on campus, so without this degree I could not be a pharmacist." (Student 1)

> " I had been waiting for years to continue my education and still maintain employment and without this programme I would not be able to study Pharmacy." (Student 2)

> "Enrolling in (this) Bachelor of Pharmacy externally has allowed me to continue my studies, regardless of my location." (Student 3)

Delivery of the programme has required detailed design work – the most critical decisions have been around requirements of synchronicity and co-location to enable students to achieve learning outcomes within a distributed learning space.

About the author

Ieva Stupans is Professor of Pharmacy at the University of New England. She can be contacted at this e-mail: ieva.stupans@une.edu.au

Chapter Three

The Spaces of Relational Learning and their Impact on Student Engagement

Jos Boys and Diane Hazlett

This chapter contributes to the anthology on learning space design in higher education by developing a rich understanding of what matters about space, particularly for enhancing student engagement and belonging. We suggest that this first requires an exploration into the relational aspects of learning in order to begin to model the often complicated and diffuse inter-relationships between its cognitive, experiential and emotional dimensions. Second we explore in more depth how these impact on, and are impacted by, material space. As our definition of learning space, we propose a relational understanding of material space, aiming to locate learning environments within the larger 'space' of learners' perceptions and experiences more generally. Working with this relational under-standing of material space, we first outline what we mean by relational learning, and by student engagement and belonging. This will be further explored through analysing a case study that suggests some helpful pointers. Finally, we offer an outline conceptual model that aims to locate some of the differing qualities of material space across the various dimensions of relational learning. Whilst this model is proposed not as a solution but as a means of encouraging debate, we argue that devel-oping learning spaces that support engagement and belonging as well as effective learning are an important issue for the higher education sector. This is because evidence shows that students' sense of belonging has a direct impact on their retention and success (Thomas, 2012). Reading this chapter you will:

1. get an understanding of the interplay between conceptual and material spaces;

2. gain an appreciation of how relational space can impact upon students' sense of 'belonging'; and

3. learn why we believe space 'matters' when considering relational learning.

Relational learning, belonging and engagement

Like Frick *et al.* (in this volume) we take a relational approach to learning; but here we focus more on how to articulate and evaluate the intersections *between* conceptual and material spaces. A relational perspective in higher education was initially proposed by Ramsden (1987:275) who argued that *"it involves inquiry into and reflection on how students learn specific subject matter in particular contexts"*. This means opening up the 'spaces-in-between' both tutor(s) and student(s), and between all participants and their situation – that is, what they bring to it, how they behave, what power relationships exist, how they process their experiences, how this connects with the wider educational context etc. Murphy and Brown (2012) also explore a more relational approach to HE pedagogy based on a synthesis of critical theory and psychoanalysis. They argue that by emphasising the inter-subjective nature of learning and teaching and the importance of emotions within it, a relationally centred approach can take seriously questions of trust, recognition and respect at the heart of the academic–student relationship, while also making space for doubt, confusion and relational anxiety.

If such a framework locks together the cognitive, experiential and emotional dimensions of learning, where does belonging and engagement fit? The Higher Education Academy (HEA) defined these qualities when they became key factors for a research project entitled *What Works?* to improve student retention and success: *"At the individual level 'belonging' recognises students' subjective feelings of relatedness or connectedness to the institution (...). Goodenow (1993b) described sense of belonging in educational environments as the following: Students' sense of being accepted, valued, included, and encouraged by others (teacher and peers) in the academic classroom setting and of feeling oneself to be an important part of the life and activity of the class. More than simple perceived liking or warmth, it also involves support and respect for personal autonomy and for the student as an individual".* (Goodenow, 1993b:25, quoted in Thomas, 2012:13).

The report's authors then put this in the wider context of one's 'place' in society using Bourdieu's concept of the habitus (the deposition to act in particular ways based on upbringing) (see also Dobozy, in this volume): *"Students whose habitus is at odds with that of their higher education institution may feel that they do not fit in, that their social and cultural practices are inappropriate and that their tacit knowledge is undervalued, and they may be more inclined to withdraw early."* (Thomas, 2002, quoted in HEA 2012:13). Within this, engagement is about the development of relationships with others and the connectedness it promotes: *"The engagement literature... uses a number of lenses to investigate influences on engagement. These focus variously on student motivation, teacher–student interactions, learners interacting with each other, the role of institutional policies, sociopolitical factors and the role of non-institutional influences such as family, friends, health and employment. While there is no unanimity about what motivates learners to engage, a strongly represented view is that education is about students constructing their own knowledge".* (Krause & Coates, 2008, quoted in Zepke *et al.*, 2010:2).

As Frick *et al.* (in this volume) also note, it is in subject areas such as health, that deal explicitly with therapeutic and professional relationships, we can see examples of making explicit what students should expect to get out of their learning relationships; in opening up key, but often unspoken aspects of that relationship, such as trust; and in putting in place specific protocols for assessing the effectiveness of engagement. In health and therapeutic contexts for example, the concept of 'working alliance' aims to describe the means by which a therapist and a client hope to engage with each other, and effect beneficial change in the client. It acknowledges the practitioner's active role in establishing, shaping and maintaining relationships throughout the process of facilitating change. The concept was defined by Bordin (1979) as a collaborative partnership comprising the emotional bond between patient and therapist, agreement on tasks and agreement on goals. A related study by Webb *et al.* (2011)

indicated that stronger alliances were associated with greater symptom reduction. An earlier study noted that client assessments of the therapeutic alliance are more predictive than therapist or observer ratings (Krupnick *et al.*, 1996). This suggests the analogous but crucial importance of taking the multiple dimensions of the learning experience into account; and of seeing learning as centrally a negotiated process through time. If our role in tertiary education is to enhance learning, develop cognitive independence and enable students to make connections, we need to develop ideas like the working alliance, as a potential set of approaches and attitudes – of explicit protocols – that intersect between and across pedagogies and the spaces in which they take place. To capture the wider aspects beyond particular formal learning encounters outlined here Figure 1 offers a basic outline of the different dimensions of relational learning.

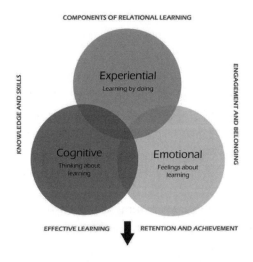

Figure 1: The components of relational learning.

Here though, we also need to understand better what it is that about the material environment that impacts on these forming relationships. For example, the HEA *What Works?* project (already mentioned), makes a more general analysis of the specific process through which improved belonging and engagement can be achieved. Thomas (2012:14-15) argues that this requires:

+ *"supportive peer relations;*

+ *meaningful interaction between staff and students;*

+ *developing knowledge, confidence and identity as successful HE learners;*

+ *an HE experience that is relevant to interests and future goals."*

Thus, while many of their examples (of different projects, run across a number of UK HE institutions) include a spatial dimension, the project conclusions do not map where or how material (or virtual) space impacts on these suggested areas of focus. This will be what we examine next; first by exploring how to conceptualise relationships between space and the activities that go on it; and second by reviewing a case study that helps us to see precisely what characteristics of space impact on students' perceptions and experiences of their learning. Finally, we will bring together relational learning and its material space characteristics into an outline model, suggesting what matters about space for enhancing engagement and belonging.

What matters about space for learning?

We began with a brief outline of relational learning, and how student belonging and engagement 'sits' within it, in order to consider some of the richness and complexity of our learning interactions with each other. We have already suggested that this centres on what happens in the *spaces in-between* the learner and tutor, the learners and each other, and the learners, tutors and their environment (its resources and material characteristics). Second, the chapter seeks to share an understanding of these 'spaces' as an entangled mix of verbal, non-verbal and affective relations, across cognitive, experiential and emotional dimensions, where belonging and engagement are as much 'felt' as consciously articulated. Third, it conveys learning as a dynamic and on-going process of negotiated relationships build through time and space, across the whole student experience.

Next, then, we want to explore what kind of conceptual framework and research methods might enable us to understand better what matters in particular about space in these processes. In this chapter we want to complement the work of other authors in this anthology who are using methods from across behaviourism and proxemics, (Scott-Webber, in this volume), human-computer interactions and affordances, (Bartholomew & Bartholomew, in this volume) and from theorists in the social sciences such as Giddens (Strickland, in this volume) Wenger (Enomoto and Warner, in this volume) Bourdieu (Dobozy, in this volume) and Lefebvre (Holtham and Cancienne, in this volume). We are especially interested in contemporary methods that articulate space as a relation and as completely entangled between personal, social and material dimensions. This approach is becoming increasingly central in work going on in science and technology studies, in anthropology and in geography (Latour, 2007, 2013; Ingold, 2000, 2011; Thrift, 2008). These theorists start from the understanding that we engage with the material world dynamically and continuously, through our individual perceptions and beliefs and everyday enactments in 'ordinary' social and spatial practices – that is, the un-thought about routines and assumptions about 'how things work.'

Within this framework, tertiary education – like other specialist groupings – has its own particular set of routines, referred to by Wenger (1998) as a 'repertoire', Latour (2013) as 'modes of existence', by Barnett and Coate (2005) as the 'hidden' or 'implicit curriculum' and by Bourdieu (1984) as a habitus. These everyday socio-spatial practices are performed, re-produced, adapted and contested by its many different participants in the educational context through, for example, the curriculum, teaching methods and equipment, patterns of assessment and timetabling. The material environment is one key way (among others such as body language, rules and regulations etc.) through which such on-going practices become routinised and made concrete. We change space through our affective encounters (Thrift, 2008), just as space changes us, through a process of continual, embodied negotiations. This frames different aspects as interacting with varying degrees of intensity and focus through time as a patterning of cross-flowing currents. Rather than a stimuli-response or cause- effect model that aims to clarify specific variables acting on each other, such an approach sees our relationships with space, objects and others as endlessly negotiated, reinforced and/or adapted through time and space.

Like Holtham and Cancienne (in this volume), we have turned to the work of Lefebvre (1991) to help shape a means to explore this complexity. This builds on previous work by Boys (2010, 2011) proposing a layered research method. In this version of Lefebvre's 'spatial triad', analysis takes place via the parallel investigation of three partial, non-comprehensive and overlapping processes that underpin learning spaces. These are:

+ educational encounters, practices and repertoires (both conventional and innovative);

+ the design of specific learning spaces;

+ participant experiences, perceptions and negotiations of both the encounters, practices and repertoires of learning and of the specific spaces in which it takes place.

To add to the complexity, these processes are affecting, and being affected by, the inter-locking dimensions of cognitive, experiential and emotional learning already outlined. What is more, the specifics of a particular learning encounter and learning context must themselves be intersected not only with the 'normal' routines of education (at an institution, within a particular society, culture etc.) but also with the wider educational and life experiences of the individuals involved. These relationships are outlined in Figure 2.

Figure. 2: Components of relational learning as a socio-spatial practice.

The aim of the model and method offered here is to capture the richness of such complicated and diffuse inter-relationships, whilst also enabling robust and usable results. Each of the aspects it opens up are always situated relative to both particular places and people; and no aspect is obvious, congruent or complete, either on its own terms, or with others. These never align (or do so only momentarily) so that the resulting pattern is what Geertz (1973) famously called a 'thick description'; that is, it is a rich and layered account that does not result in a 'solution' or conclusion, but can illuminate (Parlett & Hamilton, 1972) decision-making.

Exploring the impact of space on belonging and engagement

An example of the kind of insights this can offer is illustrated by the findings of a case study undertaken by Clare Melhuish (2011a) that investigated three new, specially designed spaces at two UK universities. We would like to suggest that work of this kind can help elucidate:

- the concepts and terminology participants use in connecting their personal, social, educational and material experiences;

- what it is that matters about space for students' feelings of belonging and engagement; and

- what kinds of changes to university space can improve student belonging and engagement.

In her study Melhuish started from a grounded theory approach (Glaser & Strauss, 1967). She aimed to uncover appropriate categories *from* the data she collected through a process of rigorous data sorting, coding and analysis. Through focus groups and observations of both teaching sessions and the material spaces themselves she concentrated on the spatial, material and sensory qualities (furniture and spatial layout, lighting, smells, colour and sound), technological infrastructure, and perceived status and image. Crucially each of these aspects was interpreted by students and staff in terms of what they brought to the experience, together with their expectations of learning, and of the spaces in which it was assumed to take place.

The material characteristics were *relational* to both people's perceptions/

experiences, and their simultaneous cognitive, experiential and affective modes of learning. For example, Boys has suggested elsewhere that the beanbag – and similar bright, relaxed types of furnishings – has come to 'stand for' (be a symbol of) informal learning (Boys, 2009). New learning spaces that use these kinds of fittings are then assumed to be collaborative and innovative.

But Melhuish's study showed that our interactions with built space are much more complex than this, even in response to the simple act of changing how you *sit* to learn. One of the spaces (Figure 3: InQbate Creativity Zone, University of Sussex) was a pure white technology-rich space, furnished mainly with white beanbags. As Melhuish (2011:87) writes: "*They seem to prompt more spontaneous and playful behaviour during teaching sessions, perhaps because of the smooth floor surface which makes them good for sliding on… In this case, the student group in question is described by a tutor as having a 'macho dynamic', and 'almost not grown-up enough to use the beanbags'.*" (Melhuish, 2011: 87)

In another of the spaces (Fig 4: CETLD, University of Brighton), the furniture was set out in a café layout, with designer chairs. Here, rather than 'playful' the space was perceived as 'civilised', generating a different kind of informality: "*When I first saw the space my impression was it looked like a cafe or something because of the tables and the mix and the funny chairs, and I thought, that's a bit strange. But… it does actually encourage you to relax.*" (Melhuish, 2011:88). Yet at the same time, furniture that clearly looks designed, and not typically academic/institutional, was experienced as both aspirational and intimidating by the users interviewed: "*One student describes it as 'so modern… I want to come up with innovative ideas here', and another concurs, 'it seems more modern here, not just the interior, but also the way of working here seems more millennium-ish'. But another perceives it as daunting: (…) "it seems very sort of modern and creative and innovative… I sometimes feel slightly pressured into being creative and I'm not really…*" (Melhuish, 2011:88)

What different students 'read off' these spaces depended crucially on what they thought learning should be 'like'. In some cases, beanbags were seen as inappropriately childish, in others as nicely comfortable. Both kinds of furniture aimed to support informal learning, but embodied various kinds of psychological impact for different students, across both negative and positive emotions. Some students were made to feel more connected (belonging, engaged), others less so. Studies like this therefore show first that the effects of a learning space cannot just be 'read off' its design but must always be examined through the spaces-in-between environment and participants; and second, that there is no 'correct' learning environment; rather that decision-makers need a better understanding of the interplay between participants in a space, and the cues they take from it.

Figure 3: Centre for Excellence in Teaching and Learning through Design (CETLD) learning space, University of Brighton, UK. Photograph: Clare Melhuish.

Figure 4: InQbate learning space at University of Sussex, UK. Photograph: Clare Melhuish.

The second important point from Melhuish's findings is that the students she interviewed were well able to 'read' space through sophisticated and multi-layered perspectives. They seamlessly integrated the cognitive, experiential and emotional dimensions of their learning experiences in their responses; and made comments that simultaneously dealt across

their local learning encounters, their educational experiences more generally, and their interpretations of both institutional identity and the wider
educational context. For example, students were well aware that the
learning spaces being researched in this study were special and different
to the 'normal' environments of lecture hall and seminar room; and were
part of an institutional as well as pedagogic agenda, that is, were also
about how the universities were attempting to 'position' themselves in
the wider world: "*The students reveal that InQbate was used as a key selling
point when they came to look around the university: 'they said, oh there's this
amazing room... you know, the really white, white room'. They believe, 'that's
the main sort of draw to the university now'. The sheer whiteness of the room
sets it apart, and makes it stand out from its surroundings, both physically and
institutionally. But, on open day, 'it was locked and so no-one got to see it. A
lot of people were like, oh, we heard about this amazing space that you spent
loads of money on and we can't see it'.*" (Melhuish, 2010:32)

Students and staff also 'read' the locations of these spaces within the
campus itself – how far away from the main entrance, how well sign-
posted, what kind of décor – as a component in assessing the (often
contradictory) 'value' of the facility, and its relevance to them. These
kind of complexities in interpreting a particular material space – in this
example, bringing together institutional identities and missions, timetabling issues, university and outsider interactions, power relationships,
patterns of exclusion and inclusion, size, location and atmosphere of the
space, and concepts of 'specialness'– show us two important things. First,
space is just one of the intersecting aspects that affect whether and how
people feel they belong, and can become engaged in, a particular situation; and second, that the actual qualities of material space *do* have an
impact on perceptions and experiences, but that this will vary with who
is in the space, and what they are doing there.

Relational learning, student engagement and learning space design

As we have already noted, whilst the work of the HEA has produced
some important evidence-based recommendations on how universities
and colleges can improve student belonging and engagement – some
of which relate to aspects of physical and virtual spaces – the role of

space in this process has not been explicitly examined. In this chapter we have suggested that it is valuable to develop models of learning that integrate its cognitive, experiential and emotional dimensions, and to begin to unpack where space matters; and in particular how it relates to the difficult, dynamic and on-going processes of belonging and engagement. We have used the findings of Melhuish's (small, pilot) study to outline potential modes of analysis that can capture the considerable richness and complexity of students' perceptions and experiences, yet still provide coherent, robust and comparative terminologies for more explicitly describing and understanding better the inter-relationships between these and the detailed design of learning spaces.

We have suggested that this involves both what students (and tutors) bring to their learning and teaching situations, and the kinds of cues and meanings that different kinds of pedagogies and spaces provide. We have further proposed that in order to make improvements to university and college learning spaces we need to develop conceptual models that start from relational learning, and use research methods that can simultaneously examine learning encounters, institutional identities and wider contexts. We want to be able to capture the multiplicity and multi-layered nature of both our 'readings' of, and enactments with, material space; and to locate what matters about material space as one – sometimes important sometimes marginal – component in the whole repertoire of learning.

In addition, if learning and student engagement in tertiary education is increasingly understood to include not only personal, peer and institutional but also beyond-institutional activities (Zepke and Leach, 2011; KWP, 2010), then we need to have better ways to assess these 'soft' outcomes of successful student engagement (Zepke and Leach 2010a), that can then be integrated with, and tested against, the hard data of student retention and completion figures, their levels of achievement at each level, and overall academic success.

The model offered here (Figure 5) is our first attempt to locate the different qualities of material space and its perceptions and experiences in relation to the three overlapping aspects of relational learning as well as to wider socio-spatial practices, informed by our interpretation of Melhuish's findings. Each of these elements is seen as being deeply inter-related, here artificially separated out to enable some degree of rigorous and useful analysis.

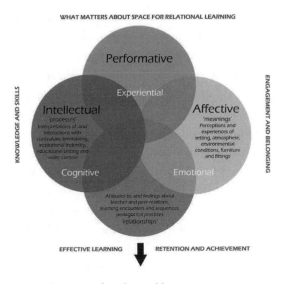

Figure 5: What matters about space for relational learning.

In this model, we show how material space can both support more effective learning and can enhance belonging and engagement, across its intersections with the affective and performative, as well as with more explicit – thought-about – understandings of the world. We propose that the affective (emotional, attitudinal) and performative (learning by doing, enacting social and spatial practices) dimensions of learning connect most directly with engagement and belonging. We also suggest that the affective and performative qualities of learning will be most directly impacted on by qualities of the setting, atmosphere, material conditions and resources of space/spaces – that is, they are the cues material space and its contents gives and what *meanings* these communicate to different participants. At the same time, students will mainly perceive and experience the wider context – the repertoire of education, it's curricula, timetables, course, faculty and institutional identity, institutional and educational position within the wider world – at the intersection of their performative and intellectual modes of engagement; that is through enacted and thought-about educational *processes*.

Finally, students will interpret their learning encounters and connections between peers and with tutors predominantly through their cognitive and affective *relationships*. Melhuish's work begins to show, we would argue, that what matters about material space is first, the meanings it communicates as a set of non-verbal, physically experienced 'cues'; second, it's framing of particular processes (repertoires) in specific ways; and third, the explicitly thought-about intersections between our understandings of the world and how it is experienced in everyday life.

There is, of course, need for more research and debate, of which this anthology is a part (see also Boys *et al.*, forthcoming). In addition, we also need to add the 'third' dimension of time to our model; as the student becomes a long-term participant of an institution. We need to understand more about how these intersecting processes change as the learner becomes more experienced, autonomous and research and/or profession oriented. Weller (2012:25), for example, examines how to lead students to a deeper understanding of their subject and its pedagogy, *"to enable students to perceive the transition of their identities as they engage with a field of knowledge that is continually reshaped by a community of practitioners, including their peers and lecturers"*. This requires us to learn more about how people's feeling of belonging and engagement change through time, and what this implies not only for the explicit configuring for each level of study of (discipline) curriculum design, teaching strategies and resources, but also for learning space design.

As we have already outlined, this issue is of considerable importance to universities and colleges. Students perceptions and experiences of their learning environments will affect how they much they feel they 'belong' and feel engaged with a university, starting from application open days and freshers' weeks, through to beginning study, socialising and accessing student support and other services, and so their development towards becoming a self-directed and independent learner. New students are often not prepared for the diverse range of contexts and learning relationships within their new environment. How does the learner know what, when and how to engage with these new conceptual, physical, virtual, social and personal spaces? Equally, how do we know that learning is being managed, facilitated and mediated to need at all stages of that development? If identity and expectations for engagement are not clearly articulated or explicitly managed, the unspecified interactional and relationship style is likely to lead to uncertainty and miscommunication. If students early in their learning encounters misread or misrepresent the relationship and interactional tone, this psychological disconnect is likely to be reinforced in subsequent academic and contextual learning encounters. By explicitly attempting to articulate belonging and engagement as a crucial element of learning, and to show how space can have an impact, we hope that higher education will explore further what kinds of learning spaces can enhance the whole student experience.

About the Authors

Jos Boys is Faculty Director of Student Enhancement and a Teaching Fellow at Northumbria University, England. She can be contacted at this e-mail: jos.boys@northumbria.ac.uk

Diane Hazlett is Director at Centre for HE Research and Practice, University of Ulster. She can be contacted at this e-mail: de.hazlett@ulster.ac.uk

Chapter Four

Enhancing Student Learning through the Management of Technology-rich Physical Learning Spaces for Flexible Teaching

Jennifer Rowley

Introduction

This chapter contributes to the anthology on learning space design in higher education by exploring the management (*not* the design) of technology-rich physical learning spaces in higher education and required modification in teaching practice and curricula to improve the teaching and learning process. I argue that good pedagogic practice requires that teachers in higher education understand the role that the learning space plays in student learning and that learning space should foster an environment where teachers are encouraged to engage in good curriculum design and to create appropriate learning tasks for enhanced student learning. I define learning spaces as the physical and online space within which learning occurs.

Teaching in a different physical learning space encourages academics to review current curriculum and their teaching practice to align with the affordances of that learning space – e.g. technology-rich, open plan spaces being used to facilitate collaborative and blended learning. This chapter shares how initial observations, made by academics teaching in a fairly typical but non-traditional learning space, revealed that a student-led learning model had emerged. This encouraged academic peers to consider reviewing current teaching practices and curriculum to actively align with the learning space in order to enhance further students' learning. Reading this chapter, you will:

1. identify how blended and collaborative learning can offer a more student-led, engaged enquiry-based approach to learning and teaching in technology-rich, open plan, non-traditional learning space;

2. see how redesigning curriculum to include a blended learning and collaboration for an engaged inquiry approach to learning (e.g. students creating *Wikipedia* pages; mobile apps etc.) results in a student-centred approach to teaching; and

3. understand the scaffolds that assist in assessment and learning activities to create a learning space where students are engaged in the learning as active participants.

A need to understand the connections between built learning environments and student learning outcomes has emerged out of concern for what pedagogies, curriculum, assessment and organisational forms are necessary to develop the capacities in students for the 21st century (State of Victoria, 2011: iv). Evaluating curricula for flexible learning to ensure optimal use of technology-rich physical learning spaces is leading higher education teachers to re-assess their current teaching practice. Current literature contends that learning experiences are enhanced for students who learn in technology-rich, flexible learning spaces. This chapter investigates the impact newly installed; technology-rich physical learning spaces have had on teaching and learning at an Australian University. The impetus by the University to re-design traditional teaching spaces (such as fixed seating lecture style rooms) was for improved collaborative student learning. The chapter, therefore, discusses collaborative learning, knowledge management and the changes higher education teachers are required to make in their pedagogic practice to ensure an enhancement of students' learning in a 21st century teaching and learning space. The outcome of re-designing curricula and learning activities/assessment for flexible teaching and enhancement of student learning in technology-rich, collaborative learning spaces is a student-led, engaged inquiry approach to learning and teaching.

Enhanced teaching and learning

According to a view held at the University of Sydney, effective learning spaces are characterised by *"highly innovative and imaginative pedagogies and curriculum, and leading-edge design of learning spaces, that significantly enhance student learning"* (Office of the DVC [Education]; May, 2013, page 1) and promote engaged inquiry through integration. Jisc (formerly the JISC) (2006) defines effective learning spaces as those able to *"motivate learners, promote learning as an activity, support collaborative and formal practice provide a personalised and inclusive environment and be flexible".* The learning spaces referred to in this chapter are not complex in nature and vary in how they have the potential to enhance students' learning. They include the physical space and an online space providing a blended approach to learning and teaching. In addition, learning studios created for student-led collaborative learning were commissioned. A learning studio in this instance is defined as a room with 90 seats or less with configurations of seating and learning technologies on a flat floor where pods are offered providing different configurations of furniture and student computing to promote enquiry, collaboration and problem solving with the use of technology (Office of the DVC [Education]; May, 2013, page 3). In an evaluation of the physical learning spaces in 2012 it was noted that the purpose of the learning studios was 54% group work and 25% for enhancement of learning whereas the actual approach comprised 42% group work and 23% technology interaction.

Teaching spaces were changed from traditional (fixed seating, lecture style) to open plan, technology rich spaces. This change in the physical learning space gave academics an opportunity to 'flip' the classroom and to redesign curricula, teaching and learning activities and assessment. The result was a blended learning approach as students engaged in both online learning as well as the face-to-face learning. Therefore, the 'flipped' classroom became one where students undertook some of the more traditional, content-driven learning (lecture material) online *before* the class and then engaged in collaborative learning activities (using that content) whilst in the class with the teacher or in the learning studio in a peer-supported environment.

To understand how the spaces work for enhanced teaching and learning, this chapter discusses the expected ways that students engage with both revised curricula and learning tasks. Learning therefore, in the new space was predicted to encourage a more inquiry-based learning approach leading to students engaging in collaboration to create new knowledge (for example) in teams or groups. To ensure that teamwork is successful the curriculum should concentrate on pedagogical techniques that assist collaboration that is appropriately supported by the technology.

This chapter aims, therefore, to assist teachers in higher education to incorporate the use of technology-rich, open plan learning spaces, blended learning and engaged inquiry into their learning and teaching practice through appropriate curricula design. It will directly and indirectly assist academics through the transferability of outcomes such as curriculum renewal and blended learning and thus students' enhanced learning as a result.

What, therefore, are the practical implications of re-designing curricula to optimise newly created physical learning spaces for enhanced student learning and how are blended learning spaces used as an educational tool with technological advantage? Through this chapter I present literature and some commentary on teachers' pedagogic changes to maximise students' learning (NB: the teachers were supported through the curriculum design process by the University's e-learning Unit).

Learning space, therefore, is understood as a series of intersecting aspects:

+ *engagement and adaptation*: how people understand and are affected by their environment, and how they use space and transform it through their use;

+ *spatial routine*: those everyday social and spatial practices which affect, and are understood by, others within a community;

+ *design*: established repertoires of spatial designs and the process and outcome of attempted innovation (Boys, 2011:81).

This chapter discusses the design and implementation of blended and collaborative learning for developing enhanced learning experiences for students. It draws together the various uses of collaborative learning, learning with technology and a technology enhanced curriculum to identify best practice, assess differences in teaching in a technology-rich learning space, and design methods for future learning spaces implementation.

Learning and teaching challenges in re-designed learning environments

When surveyed in 2011 and 2012 students stated they wanted *"more group work with technology provision and more support for collaboration"* (Office of the DVC [Education]; May, 2013:1). The author realised the impact of such a student response and identified two challenges in learning and teaching. The first challenge was *how* the higher education teaching staff would revise their pedagogic practice to engage students in collaborative learning. This involved teachers ascertaining the nature of learning and how the learning would be supported. The literature stated that teachers teaching in technology-rich, open plan learning spaces engaged in less lecturing with a more student-centred approach to what was being taught (knowledge, skills, and competencies). This, therefore, would involve a transition for staff from current teaching practice to designing activities that engaged learners in an active learning model that was student-led. The second challenge was to design multi-modal methods of learning which encouraged an active rather than passive learning approach. For example integrating technologies that are 'beyond' disciplines, and using tools that give students a type of research project that they can work on collaboratively in their groups.

Academics should be creating opportunities for students to engage in learning that relates to their real world experiences. Today's youth are frequently creative, interactive, and media oriented (Greenhow *et al.*, 2009) and this leads teachers to cater specifically for individual learning preferences. The enhancement of a 'student' learning space in higher education is commonly implemented through the integration of technology use (e.g. with social networks, mobile technology etc.) – ensuring that it is always available. It is essential that the learning space allows students to explore the technology available and the possible learning activities that are student-generated products potentially created in virtual folders or in 'cloud' technology (e.g. a visual diary or an image gallery). Another example might be using a technology to allow students to choose people in a network and set up a study group while establishing direct links to social media such as *Facebook*, *Twitter* or to *Google* or virtual design studios (Bennett, 2012). The development of knowledge in these virtual and physical settings encourages teachers to produce a pedagogic design for non-traditional academic learning. For example, a blended learning approach, which means preparing for the class to be less lecture-focused and more directed towards students working in groups collaboratively (informally and formally) and away from the set class times.

At many higher education institutions physical learning space is designed to meet a range of student learning requirements. For example they could be quiet individual zones and private group spaces; private rooms for group work or small meetings, with LCD flat-panel monitors; open collaborative areas with access to power and wireless for laptop users; or a café, for example, with indoor and outdoor seating. Most spaces will have also computers with printing facilities available so that it is not completely reliant upon students and the BYOD (bring your own device) option. In essence, learning spaces that are technology rich and encourage collaboration amongst students in a range of group work configurations are now the 'norm' in higher education. Often the spaces are designed with white boards surrounding the walls, which is an invitation for students to come forward and write, share and brainstorm ideas in response to material being presented by the lecturer. This physical adjustment to the learning environment encourages students to work in groups and to collaborate.

There are challenges in organising the students in such physical spaces so that they do not lead to a chaotic, disorganised learning experience. As teachers, we are experiencing an era of student-led curricula, research, teaching and learning. Students will take what they want from where they choose – whether it be knowledge, practice or research. Our role, therefore, as teachers in higher education is assisting students' choices and helping them to organise and make sense of the content by relating content to real life experiences. Academics should be providing authentic learning environments and designing their practice to include rich learning that engages higher order learning skills, not just passive learning such as watching a video and answering questions (see Bartholomew & Bartholomew, in this volume). In any curriculum renewal process teachers are obliged to alter learning tasks to reflect the learning outcomes and for this, guidance is needed (Biggs, 1999). A solid connection can be established between learning and teaching through appropriate use of blended learning. For example, by encouraging continual student discussion about what is sustainable learning and by building on the evidence-based learning story students engage in during class time.

Below, the modification three teachers made to curricula, learning tasks and assessment as a result of being scheduled to teach in the newly designed open plan, technology-rich learning space is reported. The teachers' comments highlight the path they took to understand the fundamentals of blended learning, collaborative learning and technology-rich learning design. The emphasis on collaborative learning (through a blended learning approach) emerged as a natural choice. Academics reported, after the first semester of teaching in the new space, that students were encouraged to collaborate because of the way the learning environment and curriculum was structured. From the perspective of higher education learning and teaching, this raised concerns regarding the need for academics to reconsider their pedagogic practice to drive forward with flexible/technology supported learning because of its inherent benefits. How then, do we as teachers, place the pedagogical changes required to teach the 21st century learner within an academic programme of learning and how are learning programmes designed by the academics in tandem with the students to engage them in the new types of learning space?

Acceleration in academics' knowledge

It is essential that teachers make room in curricula for students' informal learning as traditional learning in higher education rarely allows for reflection by students on material that is presented (see Dobozy in this volume). The newly designed physical space allowed informal learning and conversations to take place as students worked together in groups on a task set in the *traditional* lecture time. Conversational learning (Kolb & Kolb, 2005) relies on the experiential learning philosophy and allows for true reflection-on-knowledge (Schön, 1995) that promotes deep learning. The knowledge produced by students during this informal learning is often through informal dialogue, innocently offering spontaneous solutions to discussed problems without any explicit reference to the theoretical knowledge presented by the lecturer. It is reported that students adapt to new technology quickly when integrated purposely into curriculum and pedagogic practice (Taylor *et al.*, 2012).

It may not be realistic, however, to expect the same of higher education teachers who may require some scaffolding to adapt to the re-designed teaching space, so it could be argued that students must lead the way in a reformed 21st century learning model. As teachers, we should listen and watch what students are doing in the spaces; with the technology, and through collaboration (see Enomoto & Warner, in this volume). Student learning, in other words, must become the criteria by which we judge our pedagogic innovation. In the transition phase for academics it is vital that there is educational design support provided to the development of appropriate pedagogies incorporating the tools provided in these spaces so that suitable process and products are incorporated for students. In the case reported in this chapter, specific learning designs were formally trialled and evaluated at the end of 2013 by the e-learning educational designers who endeavoured to facilitate a community of practice whereby academics involved in the project met collectively to share experiences and theoretical perspectives and to support each other in the design and use of the collaborative spaces for teaching and learning. This level of peer support for teachers using the space along with technology experts was a valuable mechanism for professional academic development.

Teaching in the learning spaces

As previously stated, an outcome of the introduction of the learning space was to develop a community of practice among the teachers who were new to teaching in technology-rich learning spaces. In addition, educational design support was offered to enable the teachers to develop pedagogies. Specific learning designs were trialled and evaluated at the end of 2013 based on the principles of productive pedagogy. It is expected that that these designs will provide exemplars for other academics interested in using the spaces and complement the professional development work-shops being offered by the University's e-learning unit. These designs will not be discussed in this chapter, however responses from the teachers about what they perceive as the changes made to students' learning tasks and academics' workload will be presented. Specifically, academics were asked if they had to change their teaching in anticipation of the technology and the physical learning environment and the nature of the impact this had on their teaching preparation workload.

In general, teachers re-assessed their whole curriculum in anticipation of the response by the students' engagement with the space and this meant there was a constant management of transferring a known traditional teaching style to one where the students were leading the learning. The curriculum roles of content, pedagogy, assessment and technology in learning are outlined by Dede (2010), who proposed that information and communication technologies (ICT) may aid in representing content, engaging learners, modelling skills and assessing students' work, thus resulting in prosperous higher education institutions. Dede (2010) also suggests that students' assignment work might involve new media productions that express understanding, rather than the traditional writing of papers synthesising expert opinion.

The teachers were designing learning activities and content for the technology-rich and blended learning environment opening up the opportunity to create a curriculum centred on engaged inquiry. For example, one academic asked students to create a *Wikipedia* article from the first day of class and so students had to learn *how* to access *Wikipedia*, add information, edit, add links etc. and the activity was student-led. The focus was for students to improve their research and writing skills. As a student-centred activity it was a collaborative process as students had to agree before posting to *Wikipedia* about the content that was to be kept and used for the publicly shared space. The wiki tool on the University's Learning Management System was used as a workspace for students before they posted to Wikipedia.

So, what other new teaching strategies were used? Below are answers from three higher education teachers who answered the question: What was the specific CHANGE in your teaching practice to improve the teaching and learning process?

"I've had to really work to make sure the blended approach was communicated clearly to students, to make online discussions relevant, and to ensure that the in-class activities take advantage of the collaborative and technology-rich space of the Learning Studio" (Teacher #1).

"I suppose the major changes were along the lines of a more prescriptive set of agendas for each class. The balance I have tried to strike between a detailed class agenda and a more flexible one that can take into account the contingencies of the actual experience in the class room was upset

somewhat and I'm still trying to reforge that balance in a new way" (Teacher #2).

"During the course of a semester in a conventional learning space, I might have students break out into groups to work during a lecture only once, perhaps twice at best. In the new learning space group work took place in most lecture hours. I think probably 8 out of 12. So it was necessary for me to think of things that students could work on collaboratively that had some formative benefit" (Teacher #3).

It can be seen from these three responses that the technology rich learning space has the potential to encourage professional learning for teaching and a model for others interested in using the collaborative learning spaces in their future teaching. The teachers' re-designed curricula centred on the best way for students to use the spaces in the discipline context and to use enhanced student-led and peer-to-peer learning and declarative learning content accessed online to prepare students for the subsequent classroom activities. There will be ongoing exploration by the University e-learning unit (through student evaluations) as to whether the use of the learning spaces facilitated networks and communication.

There is concern amongst higher education teachers that change challenges current practice and therefore increases workload. Sadly, a few see this change as a negative and fail to recognise the professional learning opportunity for academic development. The three teachers were also asked: Did preparing classes for the learning spaces increase your workload? Below are the responses.

"Yes. I've made 10-15 minute videos with Articulate Storyline for students to watch and take an embedded quiz; coupled with the online discussion, this equates to their one-hour weekly online tutorial. Preparing for the classes has also been complicated by infrastructure – we've had significant Wi-Fi and sound issues. And I learned that Skype and Jabber are not installed for video conferencing [in the new teaching space] – nor is there any camera to facilitate Adobe Connect. Trying to navigate which department has jurisdiction over the IT in the room has been a complicated process. Because I'm also using Blackboard [the University LMS] and Twitter in the class, it means that I'm having to stay on top of more tasks during the week too" (Teacher #1).

"It did increase my workload, but that is hardly surprising. Learning about all the different possibilities of Blackboard and trying to work those out with the designer was pretty labour-intensive. Also, each week, I have a fair few tasks that need to be carried out, some of which are quite detailed" (Teacher #2).

"Yes, at first. In the early weeks I tried to organise students/groups for equity reasons so that we could have even numbers at [learning] pods. This was time-consuming and, despite my best efforts, students didn't consult lists before lecture hours and ended up sitting wherever they wanted and forming groups on the day. On consultation with e-learning designers I relaxed the rules and allowed students to sit where they wanted, which was usually with the same group each time. We had hoped they might like to vary the groups they worked with but I found they preferred to keep working with the same students. This may actually represent a way of offsetting the uncertainty of the new environment. So to get back to the point, I stopped trying to organise their groups for them after about week 3 or 4 and so preparation time reduced" (Teacher #3).

Did this change in learning tasks enhance the students' learning experience? There was evidence of active student-centred activities and so a renewed curriculum incorporated a more formal engaged inquiry approach to teaching and learning. From a teacher perspective, the next evaluation will explore how teaching in the spaces affected their teaching experience and whether they felt confident in facilitating student-led teaching.

Knowledge management and reflective practice

Beneath the surface of this discussion lies a fundamental debate regarding the role of the tertiary sector and the role of education in relation to the wider society. What is knowledge production and how does this relate to conceptions and ways in which the academic can ensure the academic puts the theoretical knowledge into practice? Knowledge of e-learning and technology is usually domain specific to the academic's discipline (O'Dea & Rowley, 2009). Once placed in the new learning space the academic has to search for a type of pedagogy that will serve the purpose of the learning environment, the content and the level of the students who they are teaching. A well-designed 'lesson', therefore, in a new *physical* learning space can change an academic's approach to teaching and alter the students learning experience by challenging their understanding of traditional learning and lead them towards a path of research and inquiry that engages a range of other learning contexts and impacts on the next phase of their development as a learner and practitioner. What engaged enquiry means in practice is the way knowledge is discovered, constructed and disseminated in any discipline and is influenced by technology for knowledge work.

Recently, some Australian studies identified a change in undergraduate students' use and preference for a range of technologies and identified a wide range of technology-related competencies (Taylor *et al.*, 2012). However, another study noted that, *"we cannot assume that being a member of the Net Generation is synonymous with ways of knowing how to employ technology strategically to optimize learning experiences in university settings"* (Kennedy *et al.*, 2008:10). Yet another study surveyed fifty-one students about their use of reflective practice and challenged reported assumptions about students' use of and confidence with digital technologies (Brooks & Rowley, 2013). The students' reflections were intended to provide insight into the students' skills in reflective practice and whether reflective practice might be utilised to benefit students and avoid constraints through informing future curriculum. The opportunity for students to use technology in their knowledge management showed engagement in higher level thinking which is mandatory for meaningful reflection. The students' responses suggested *"embedding technology into their learning in a meaningful way encourages empathy with the process and heightens an awareness of the learning product"* (Brooks & Rowley, 2013:56).

That technology-rich learning might facilitate critical thinking through the creation process; on going, collaboration between peers, and eventual communication as a result of writing and analysing reflective practice is just the tip of the iceberg for teachers in higher education to consider when designing learning activities in technology-rich learning environments. The rapid development and globalisation of digital technologies has seen demands placed on higher education institutions to provide learning experiences suited to students born after 1980, who are deemed to have sophisticated technology skills, new cognitive capacities and learning styles, fluency in multiple media, the ability to process information quickly, be adept at multi-tasking, have low tolerance for lectures and prefer active to passive learning. Yet, Bullen *et al.* (2011) found that post-secondary students enrolled at a higher education institution used a limited set of ICTs, the use of which was driven by issues of familiarity, cost, and immediacy. They found no evidence of students having deep knowledge of technology. This attempt by students to 'manage' knowledge through technology-assisted learning can lead to them operating a higher level of thinking but this requires scaffolding.

The act of producing knowledge relies not only on accessing existing knowledge but also building context-dependent knowledge through reflecting on practical situations. Schön (1995) states that students who are able to act knowledgably, effectively, deliberately, strategically and reflectively are deliberately developing a desired competency (like ICT skills) through active reflection on both the theoretical and practical facets of learning. Acting reflectively is not a taught skill but a developed competency derived from the nexus between theory and practice (Schön, 1995). However, the production of knowledge through reflection does not necessarily happen automatically and both theoretical and practical learning needs to be structured through the design of well aligned learning objectives, learning tasks and teaching. Through the reflective process, students create new knowledge and practices based on their actions (see Dozby, in this volume).

Students' genuine learning processes through well designed curricula and online learning tools

This chapter now builds on comments from academics' teaching for the first time in the new learning space. Educational designers assisted academics with course development and collected observational data of students' engagement with the learning during the classes and audited the online learning space. This recently-collected (at the time of writing) data will provide an opportunity for teachers' professional development in student-led learning and will add to the knowledge for all higher education teachers on learning spaces.

Mason (2011) conceives reflection as a process integral to a range of learning activities such as inquiry, communication, editing, analysis and evaluation. He notes that while reflection is viewed as important, it tends to be viewed as an activity that takes place after a learning activity or experience, but not intrinsic to that experience. Mason's (2011) investigation reveals that tools for scaffolding reflection in e-portfolios are under-developed. Mason (2011) argues that reflection, discourse and knowledge construction take place through questioning, and that reflection is deepened beyond a consideration of factual materials, supported by use of "why?" questioning techniques.

An e-portfolio built around curricular requirements may encourage deeper reflection on programme goals and objectives. Individuals can quickly and easily *"add content, manage resources and establish clear connections between customizable learning outcomes and portfolio work samples"* (Reese & Levy, 2009:4). Faculty may use e-portfolios to introduce themselves to students, showcase accomplishments, or present content in classes. Instructors may use teaching e-portfolios to document teaching philosophy, instructional expertise or experience, and lesson plans (Reese & Levy, 2009). The digital format of the portfolio allows for possibilities in interactions, relationships and connections that are possible beyond the regular classroom.

Recommendations include that e-portfolio practice should become an integral part of pedagogical and curricular reform through design in accordance with four principles: the aligning of learning goals with curricular content and structure; reflection of the implementation context enabling exploration of a range of opportunities and approaches; provision of multi-dimensional scaffolding for both teacher and learner; and sponsoring of teacher and learner investment through the provision of built-in facilities that take into account their unique socio-historical development of a sense of self and identity.

Barrett (2007) advocates the use of e-portfolio for enhancing collaborative learning as it encourages reflection. The potential of e-portfolios to support the types of reflection that help students understand their own learning, and provide a richer picture of the growth in students' work over time is evident; Barrett (2007) argues that evidence in an e-portfolio is not only measured by the artefacts that a learner places there, but also by the accompanying rationale that a learner provides. She notes that careful scaffolding is required to promote critical reflection

Findings from Chan and Cheng's (2010) qualitative study carried out with 63 undergraduate students at Hong Kong's Polytechnic University, suggested that e-portfolio practice facilitates a three-phase cycle of independent learning through planning, monitoring and reflecting. Challenges were identified in three areas: the 'clone' performance of students through their desire to meet evaluation (assessment) criteria; teachers' struggles to shift toward a learner-centred paradigm without appropriate or adequate scaffolding; and the risk of students 'dressing-up' their achievements in e-portfolio presentations to meet institutional policy focus on graduate competitiveness.

It is clear that the e-portfolio as a technology tool is connected to the use of a technology-rich, blended learning space in this instance as students were being asked to create tools to enhance their learning. Many learning activities encourage student-led learning and the e-portfolio (as a personal learning environment) allows for reflection on and in the knowledge generated in the specific discipline.

Conclusion

The chapter explores the management of physical learning spaces in higher education (*not* the design) and how it required modification in teaching practice and curricula to improve the teaching and learning process. As the academics stated above, using the newly designed space and their renewed curriculum to include a blended learning approach encouraged students to engage collaboratively in learning. Teacher #3 noted, "*To ensure a successful lesson delivery in the learning spaces I would need expert advice or further training in the future but I think that all students should experience this and overall, I think the teaching in the learning spaces was a positive experience*". The discussion presented contributes to our understanding of the potential *impact* of learning spaces in teaching and learning in higher education today. In fact, it is evident that a pedagogic focus of sharing in a technology-mediated learning environment and the role technology plays in the revised teaching activities in engaging the 21st century learner.

An underlying theme across literature related to students' technology use asserts the need for empirical evidence to establish student use, skills and attitudes toward technologies, and the contexts within which this technology may support learning within higher education institutions (Kennedy *et al.*, 2008). This chapter has analysed current literature about the change in teaching practice in the technology rich learning space, the need for academics' curriculum renewal; it has examined the potential uses of collaborative learning by students; and how teaching in technology-rich learning space has the potential to act as a catalyst for development of technological skills in students.

About the Author

Jennifer Rowley is a Senior Lecturer in Music Education and Academic Director of Professional Experience at The University of Sydney. She can be contacted at this e-mail: jennifer.rowley@sydney.edu.au

Chapter Five

Social and Cognitive Affordances of Physical and Virtual Learning Spaces

Nicola Bartholomew and Paul Bartholomew

Introduction

This chapter contributes to the anthology on learning space design in higher education by offering theories relating to the social and cognitive affordances of physical and virtual learning spaces. The chapter then shares a case of how these theories informed a change in use of a learning space resulting in the inclusion of technology to enhance the student learning experience. For the purpose of this chapter we define a learning space as an environment; either physical, virtual or hybrid that is designed to motivate students to learn, to provide a framework for active learning and to support collaboration (adapted from Jisc (formerly the JISC), 2006). Reading this chapter, you will:

1. be familiar with theories that relate to the social and cognitive affordances of physical and virtual learning spaces;

2. come to read an account of how the application of theory can help to inform the repurposing of a physical space; and

3. learn of an example of how the hybridisation of a physical and virtual learning space has led the enhancement of student learning opportunities.

As information and communication technologies (ICT) continue their permeation into modern life, teachers at all levels of education; primary, secondary and tertiary, have the option of deploying ICT applications to some degree to support their students. Very often this does not result in simply choosing between the physical learning space or the virtual learning space but in deciding how to create the right mix. This is fundamental during the curriculum design process when academics are considering how to make use of the learning spaces available to them. Naturally, this consideration includes the best use of physical spaces – but designers of academic provision also have a wide range of online tools from which to choose in order to enhance delivery.

Educational settings that combine ICT applications with face-to-face learning are often referred to as blended learning models, though terms such as hybrid and woven learning are also encountered in this context. This blended approach may combine the affordances inherent in both learning space domains; later in this chapter, following our introduction of underpinning theory we present a working example of just such a hybrid approach.

Whether a unit of a programme of study (a course or module) is delivered through 'traditional' teaching methods or through the medium of an ICT application, the same stated learning outcomes of the course/module need to be achievable by the students. Many researchers have investigated whether there are differences in the performance of students in relation to the achievement of intended learning outcomes when supported through online study compared to traditional teaching methods (Hale et al, 2009; Hrastinski, 2008; Kekkonen-Moneta & Moneta; 2002) and broadly, little in the way of difference in potential has been found.

Of course, student performance as measured by the achievement of learning outcomes is manifested through the results of (summative) assessment and where such teaching (and thus learning) is instruction-heavy, assessments are often deployed simply to test whether information has been effectively transmitted and effectively received. In this context the comparison of domains is quite straightforward, but if we believe that learning is a social activity, inextricably linked to co-construction of knowledge and collaborative sense making, then we must accept that claims of successful learning experiences should go beyond simple verification of the student receipt of information.

This social nature of learning is often and appropriately exploited in educational sessions and whether it is referred to as collaborative learning, co-operative learning, peer supported learning or simply group work, it is common for academics to deploy techniques that invite, or sometimes force, students to work together to achieve a common outcome. If social learning is our aim, how might we be able to exploit the affordances of learning spaces to help us achieve that aim?

Social and cognitive affordances of learning spaces

The term 'affordance' refers to the particular properties of a system that make it facilitating of a particular process. This use is attributed to Tolmie and Boyle (2000:2): *"Affordance means the properties of a system which allow certain actions to be performed and which encourage specific types of behaviour"*. A social affordance may be considered to be a learning space design feature that fosters collaboration. Such collaborative processes are necessarily dependent on some interaction between participants within that space. These processes, whether within the physical or the virtual space, are dependent on some form of multilateral or bilateral discussion. Effective learning spaces will be designed to enable discussion through, for example, flexible seating in the physical domain or online forums in the virtual domain, but participants must also be prepared to engage in discussion to reap the benefits the designed space can afford. Through meaningful discussion, learners develop and share a common understanding (of a given topic) leading to co-construction of knowledge; thus the social affordances of a space cascade into a cognitive affordance whereby space-supported discourse leads on to bolstered opportunities to learn.

Although our everyday lives support the development of our (informal) discussion skills, it is a mistake to think that effective spontaneous discussion between students in an educational setting is just waiting to happen. Brookfield and Preskill (1999) warn us about assuming that students even understand what discussion means in an educational context, let alone value it as a teaching tool. They go on to speak of students' mistrust of 'supposed democratic discussion' and state that attempts to engage students in such a way can be interpreted (by students) as merely a way of reinforcing academic power in a non-traditional way.

Where students perceive that facilitated discussion is in some way a mechanism for deploying academic power, the situation often leads to the mere appearance of learning and understanding where little may actually exist (Bartholomae, 1986; Zamel, 1993). Sommers (1992:28) makes this point as a personal observation: *"I, like so many of my students, was reproducing acceptable truths, imitating the gestures and rituals of the academy, not having confidence enough in my own ideas, not trusting the native language I had learned. I had surrendered my own authority to someone else, to those other authorial voices".*

The risk of such superficial discussions occurring is dependent on a number of things, not least of which might be the extent to which specialised language is used within a particular academic community or discipline. Bourdieu *et al.* (1996:5) refer to such specialised language as code and discuss the difficulty 'apprentices' have in making sense of it: *"The code cannot be learnt except through a progressively less unskilled decoding of messages"*. This seems to imply that initiates are expected to learn this language in a somewhat osmotic way. It could be suggested that good learning design should include ample opportunity for students to not just be exposed to specialised language, but to be given opportunities to actually use it – both in conversation and as a tool to apply the concepts coded within language to real 'problems'.

Perhaps we should not be surprised by students' suspicion to classroom discussion, since although the act of discussion itself is a part of everyday life, the physical context of the learning space may apply an overlay of expectation on the players involved in the social act of communication that takes place therein.

This is reinforced by research that explores students' expectations of lectures; Maunder and Harrop (2003) conducted a study that, in part, investigated the factors that students feel contribute to productive lectures. Twelve recurrent factors are identified with peer-to-peer discussion not emerging as a recurrent factor at all. Though interaction with the lecturer was an emergent factor, this was ranked eleventh out of twelve as a contributing factor. The most recurrent factor was the supply of a 'handout' that contains the main points – reinforcing the argument that the lecture as an educational transaction is perceived as having an instructional not a discursive purpose. If we are to transform these learning spaces into social domains of collaborative learning, we need to first overcome the expectation of didacticism.

There is plenty of other evidence to suggest that to do anything else but lecture didactically within a lecture theatre is to meet with disapproval from students regardless of the benefits in achievement of learning outcomes from more discursive teaching methods. Huxham (2005) cites a number of authors to support this view (Van Dijk *et al.* (1999); Lake (2001) and Goodwin *et al.* (1991)). In addition to the expectations of our students, there are additional difficulties in attempting to facilitate 'classroom' discussion, since there is little agreement amongst academics as to what actually constitutes 'discussion': Brookfield and Preskill (1999) write that some authors attempt to make distinctions in verbal exchanges by differentiating between 'conversation'; 'discussion' and 'dialogue', with 'conversation' being portrayed as less formal and 'discussion' necessarily leading to an advancement of an idea – a collective creation of new (shared) understanding.

If we accept this view of 'discussion' then this is not significantly different from collaboration or collaborative learning. Dillenbourg (1999:2) gives a definition of collaborative learning as *"a situation in which two or more people learn or attempt to learn something together"*. There are dangers in assuming that discussion equates to collaboration though; as Blatchford *et al.* (2003:155) offer *"...there is more to group work than sitting students in groups and asking them to work together. There may be talk between pupils of course but this can be relatively low level and not about the work in hand, and rarely in service of a joint activity."*

Though we should not expect rich discussion to spontaneously emerge from such teaching situations, it is possible to initiate sustainable discussions within lecture theatres through judicious use of structure and a high degree of facilitation. Fry *et al.* (2000) summarising the work of Lacoss and Chylack (1998:77) recount the views of American students in higher education: *"Particularly appreciated were lecturers who incorporated responses from students, by soliciting questions during lectures...They welcomed attempts to jolt them out of the passive role in lectures and agreed that such interactive advances were 'well worth the initial awkwardness they felt'"*; though this is more along the lines of tutor-peer interaction than peer-peer interaction that characterises collaborative learning.

Huxham (2005) reports on a technique of introducing 'interactive windows' into lectures to stimulate discussion, he provides evidence as to how both the lectures themselves and the 'interactive windows' within them have consistently proved to be popular with students, but he was unable to demonstrate any statistically significant learning benefits that can be attributed to the inclusion of interactive windows – though the small changes measured were towards the expected trend of the intervention.

Comparison of learning domains

What are the distinctive features that make the physical space a successful collaborative domain? In the real world it requires little effort to establish a social presence within a group setting. Our physical existence places us within the social domain and facilitates the possibility of our interaction with others. This can be contrasted with the virtual domain whereby we need to make an effort to interact with others; typically this will take the form of initiating or responding to a dialogic (or multilogic) transaction through a medium such as an asynchronous online discussion forum.

In many important ways, if a student does not actively take part in an online discussion they do not exist within the discourse transaction at all. Garrison *et al.* (2000:94) support the notion that creating a social presence in the virtual domain requires proactive efforts. They define social presence in this context as *"the ability of participants in the Community of Inquiry to project their personal characteristics into the community, thereby presenting themselves socially and emotionally as 'real people'"*. Murphy (2004) when drawing from Henri (1992) and Garrison *et al.* (2000: 422) suggests that social presence is the critical factor in moving from discussion to collaboration *"When a sense of community is formed through communicating on a social rather than just an informational level, interaction can move to a higher level and become collaborative"*. However, this position of active participation as being the route to learning is not uncontested, Beaudoin (2002) makes mention of 'witness learners', those who learn from more passive engagement in online seminars and verifies the phenomenon in his own practice context – classifying the learning as 'auto-didactic'.

In the physical world (in contrast to the virtual world), social presence is implicitly and inextricably embedded, since even those who do not actively pursue discussion take up physical space and are therefore within the transaction frame – there is the opportunity to offer back-channel feedback such as nods, smiles, frowns and other gestures that convey participation in the discourse even without making explicitly active contributions.

Agencies within an interest in learning and teaching (Jisc for example) uphold an expectation for modern learning spaces to be designed to motivate students, to promote learning activities and to support collaborative practice. For many teachers in higher education however, the physical space in which they teach is often a traditional lecture theatre, which places constraints upon the pattern and process of interaction. This is largely due to the physical arrangement of the participants whereby students sit in serried rows facing the tutor; thus when limited discussions are initiated, students only have discursive access to one or two other people. On reflection, it would appear that the lecture theatre teaching space offers very little potential to foster peer-to-peer communication, discussion or collaboration – but the explicit social affordance of physically 'being there' does weigh heavily in its favour and actually offers a number of more implicit cognitive and social affordances over collaboration in the virtual space as a result.

Affordances of physical learning space

Firstly, the mode of communication within a physical space is largely naturalistic – we talk to one another every day and the temporal dynamics of discussion are such that talk flows naturally. This may be contrasted to an online situation where hours or days can occur between turns in a discursive transaction (as in asynchronous computer mediated communication for example). Thus, the physical space offers an opportunity for a very rapid dissemination of ideas that may result in a much quicker construction of shared meaning than may be possible in a virtual space.

Secondly, voice emphasis, physical gesture and facial reinforcement can enrich the meaning of any given communication act in a way that cannot be replicated by text based online interaction (though emoticons such as :-) do get used to try and reproduce some of the context lost in text-based communication).

Thirdly, it could be contended that even passive players within the communication act are not really passive; they supply back-channel feedback to whomever is speaking through a process of active listening, giving reassuring nods when in agreement and frowning or shaking the head when in disagreement. These pseudo-passive cues can have a profound effect on the way a discussion evolves, introducing what amount to positive or negative feedback mechanisms into a debate or discussion.

As mentioned earlier, teachers in higher education (and doubtless in other sectors) have a choice in how to mix collaborative learning opportunities from both the physical and the virtual domains. Given this and the social affordances that are on offer to support discussion and collaboration in the domain of the physical world, what affordances does the virtual domain offer to support collaborative learning?

Affordances of virtual learning space

When considering discussion and collaboration in the virtual domain, this almost always means considering asynchronous text-based communication applications and although other technologies such as synchronous text communication and synchronous video communication are fairly easily deployed, they are only now beginning to grow in popularity (Hrastinski, 2008). It has been suggested that the asynchronous nature of online courses attracts learners to study online (Hrastinski, 2008). What then, are the social and cognitive affordances offered by asynchronous online discussions (AOD) that make it a suitable candidate for fostering collaborative learning?

Firstly, the 'anytime, anyplace, anywhere' affordances of AOD can be used to support an argument for deploying it to facilitate broader opportunities for student discussion. This argument becomes especially persuasive for distance education where students have very limited opportunity to physically meet; though we would not disagree with this, the argument is weaker in the context of a hybrid learning environment since we can *choose* between the physical world and the virtual world for any facet of the educational experience.

Secondly, and taking our previous argument forward, some of the affordances offered in the physical world domain can, in some cases be a *dis*-affordance. The naturalistic temporal dynamics of discussion as outlined above can promote inequity in student discussions, disadvantaging those who are introverted, those who are expected to converse in a non-native language; or where students would simply benefit from some time to think about what is being said before responding. In these situations, the non-naturalistic temporal dynamics of an online asynchronous discussion is actually an affordance that, we could argue, produces a deeper, if slower, mode of discussion. Pilkington and Walker (2003:42) support this argument stating: *"In face-to-face classrooms non-native speakers (NNS) often struggle to keep up with the flow of discussion or have difficulty in expressing ideas in writing"*. They go on to cite a number of authors who have suggested that online discussion can be highly motivating and more inclusive for such students (Chun, 1994; Pennington, 1996; Warschauer, 1996; Beauvois, 1998). Although their perspective is of value, Pilkington and Walker's paper focuses on *synchronous* online discussion, where the effects of the non-naturalistic temporal dynamics affordance are likely to be minimised since response times are in the order of seconds rather than the hours (or possibly days) of asynchronous discussions; though there are still some instances where the affordance of text-based communication itself is enough to allow NNS to participate more fully – an example of such a scenario would be where an NNS was fluent in the group language but was inhibited by a strong accent.

Thirdly, one of the key affordances of AOD comes as a consequence of the act taking place on computer networks, meaning that participants are only ever a couple of clicks away from being able to access any file on their computer or the Internet. This offers a great deal of potential for enriching discussion and promoting collaboration. Participants can 'send' web-links to one another; append files such as extracts of previous work, pictures or other media files. This ability to spontaneously include a citation to support an argument or to show another participant what you mean with pictures or video clips is a very powerful way to enrich discussion and is not generally possible in traditional face-to-face discussion domains. Kekkonen-Moneta and Moneta (2002:423) support this view stating *"The World Wide Web provides a platform for…downloadable files, graphics, animations, audio, and video….e-Learning tools and techniques have the potential to capture and even enrich and individualize the communications and interactions that normally take place in the classroom"*.

Affordances from a teacher-perspective

So far we have discussed the affordances that the physical learning space and the virtual learning space offer students to facilitate discussion / collaboration but we should not ignore the affordances that we as teachers enjoy by exploiting the affordances of each domain:

In the physical learning space, when we attempt to initiate and sustain small group classroom (or lecture theatre) discussion in this context, we do so in the knowledge that we can see and hear our students, we can pick up on the 'buzz' of the parallel conversations and we can walk the room sampling the discussions and joining in where we want or need to. Things are very different in the virtual domain of AOD, but this mode of collaboration still offers some useful affordances for teachers. Firstly, we see *all* of the discussions; since we can review the succession of threads at our leisure we can 'hear' (read) each student who contributes to the debate. This contrasts strongly with the real world model when the best we could do was to sample the ongoing discussions through real-time selective eaves dropping. Once we realise fully the power of the technology in this regard, we do not miss a word or a student (or indeed the lack of a student). This degree of oversight suggests some obvious analogies with the social concept of the panopticon as introduced by Jeremy Bentham and invoked by Michel Foucault (1975).

Foucault used the panopticon principle as a metaphor for social surveillance in that human behaviour may be modifiable through the explicit possibility of surveillance at any given moment. Foucault applied this principle to social institutions arguing that, through a constant stream of information (knowledge), the state is able to exercise power over individuals and thus influence their behaviour towards compliance. Foucault believed so strongly in this link between knowledge and power he would refer to it as a single concept: knowledge-power.

As society has continued to develop since Foucault's death in 1984 so has our ability to carry out surveillance on our population with increasing degrees of sophistication. In a significant way, virtual learning environment software such as *WebCT*, *BlackBoard* or *Moodle*, represent perfect panopticons. Such applications offer us the opportunity to survey our students' interactions in detail, we can find out who has logged on to the system, when, for how long, what did they say, who did they talk to, what other resources or activities did they access?

Some authors raise concerns in exploiting the panoptical potential of technology in this way, for example"...*the concern we have tried to raise in this paper is that the 'surveillance-capable' nature of these technologies may mean that they are used in ways, which, we feel, are inimical to the underpinning philosophies of education in general and nurse education in particular*" (Epling *et al.*, 2003:417).

We contend that the perspectives articulated above in respect to panoptical technologies in the context of education, telecommunications and to an extent wider society are slightly skewed, in that they seem to suggest that the concept of the panopticon as Foucault describes it is a wholly unwelcome phenomenon, ignoring the panoptical principle as a product or cultural artefact of a benevolent society not a despotic one. Bentham's original prison concept should be considered in reference to the prison system it was proposed to replace, where discipline and compliance was enforced by brutality and conflict.

Advantages of being able to use (for example) *Moodle* logs benevolently include being able to track the usage of particular resources or being able to check the scores of formative tests so as to verify whether the group is learning effectively from the programme; this latter example allows for timely and targeted intervention by way of support to students prior to summative assessments. In this regard the panoptical potential of these technologies is deployed in a beneficial way for the group as a whole. This, we contend, may offer sufficient justification for use of this knowledge-power.

Hybridisation – an example from practice

We offer now an example from practice that demonstrates how the merging of physical and virtual domains offers an effective solution to teaching within a challenging physical learning space. The case identified, by way of explanation of the issues raised previously, relates to a second year undergraduate radiography module at Birmingham City University. In 2011, a restructure of the Faculty of Health saw the Department of Radiography physically relocate to merge with other health professions in a single dedicated Health campus. The main campus building was a relatively new construction and traditional lecture theatres were in short supply there. As the second-year radiography cohort was fairly large in terms of numbers (approximately 120) the module was duly allocated a learning space, which was in effect, three classrooms combined into one through the opening of temporary walls. Prior to relocation, the module had been delivered within traditional lecture halls but subsequent to the relocation was to be conducted within a large classroom containing a podium and data-projector at either end of the 'room' with a third in the centre of the long non-windowed wall – with desks and chairs sprinkled liberally across the expanse. Learning spaces have evolved over recent years to support a more learner-centric pedagogy and the campus itself, being new, was designed to support this approach. Indeed, Boys (2011) notes that the shift away from formal lecture halls towards informal learning spaces has been a driver in recent building design (in addition to the pragmatics of space utilisation and cost).

Ordinarily this transition from formal lecture hall to flexible learning space might be viewed as a positive step by all but the most ardent traditionalists; however, the challenge in this context was one of scalability. Individually, each classroom should offer a suitably flexible environment for smaller group teaching but when conjoined, the three rooms could pose a significant challenge in terms of space management. Anecdotally, Health colleagues had suggested that this expanded space was 'impossible' to teach in and this perception may have manifested from their expectation to continue their delivery of formal lectures within the new large, informal space.

The configuration of tables within the teaching space meant that, for many students, their backs were directed toward the tutor and data projectors so visibility was compromised. Furthermore, for many students at the periphery of the room, the quality of sound was significantly diminished even though roving microphones were available for use. Student evaluation comments from those who had previously experienced lessons within these conjoined rooms are representative of their levels of dissatisfaction:

> "If you aren't sitting close to a projector screen or facing the lecturer it makes it more difficult to follow"

"The set up of the room makes viewing of images on the display screen very hard as one might not be sitting at a table with a good view"

"The seating arrangement is a bit poor because we can not always see the teacher"

"The room is not ideal for formal lectures"
(2nd year undergraduate radiography students)

It is generally accepted that the average concentration span during lectures is approximately 15 minutes. Gibbs (1989) acknowledges this phenomenon and shares potential management strategies; for example, advocating the incorporation of visual aids into lectures to focus attention. Ordinarily this may be a simple and effective solution yet many students within this large learning space simply could not view the projection screen and as suggested, this made the session 'difficult to follow'. Delivering a formal lecture within an inappropriate environment would lead to student detachment and subsequent dissatisfaction with the learning experience as a whole.

The solution was to re-design delivery of the module, realigning it to take into account the affordances (and constraints) of the allocated learning space. Through that work, an opportunity to develop the classroom into a hybrid learning space was realisable as the room offered flexibility in terms of seating arrangements and could support both connected and mobile learning due to wireless connectivity and readily available power sockets.

Misaligning space-use with the affordances and constraints of the space by conducting teaching sessions as one might within a lecture theatre leads to two interrelated problems. Firstly, the aims of a lecture are not well served – information is not effectively transmitted; and secondly the affordances of the more socially orientated space are not well exploited with opportunities for discussion and collaboration being overlooked.

Once the equation of 'teaching + large group = lecture' was challenged, an alternative option to augment the physical space with virtual space within the classroom was enacted. This, in turn, led to approaches that fostered collaboration and active learning within this large group context.

The pattern of classroom activity, in essence, became problem-based in nature interspersed with occasional windows of tutor instruction and was concluded with a formative online assessment. However, as discussed earlier, the acquisition of a language or 'code' (Bourdieu *et al*, 1996) and opportunities to apply this code were to become an influencing factor in the subsequent levels of learner engagement. The module's virtual learning space (*Moodle*) was designed in advance of the classroom sessions and was designed to prepare students for the classroom activity; to support classroom discussion and to support further self-study. The *Moodle* space presented the session learning outcomes from the outset to help focus learners on key elements that ultimately would be assessed in accordance with the principle of constructive alignment (Biggs, 2003). Students began their learning sequence through their receiving access to a series of pre-session learning activities in the form of podcasts. These short podcasts with associated handouts covered foundation material that would be built upon further within class; and, importantly, they provided the means of acquiring a rudimentary language for discussion. In this way, the learning of the language was not being left to osmotic chance but was strategically delivered in manageable chunks with opportunities for application in-class. The podcasts, available for download were also designed to help to satisfy the student expectation for instruction as suggested earlier by Maunder and Harrop (2003). This pre-session material was made available online a week before the scheduled classroom session and could be accessed at a time and space to suit the individual learner. Using *Moodle* as a repository for this material enabled learners to access information repeatedly to build understanding – an additional affordance of the virtual domain when compared to traditional didactic delivery methods used in the physical world domain.

Following online delivery of information, the physical classroom could be (appropriately) used as an informal learning space wherein small groups of students would access problem-based activities via laptop PC's and work through solutions collaboratively through peer discussion. The classroom-based learning activity was then made available for download from the *Moodle* site, helping to reinforce the relevance of the virtual space to the module as a whole. One of the key benefits of teaching within this informal open space was that the tutor is liberated from the constraints of the podium and is better able to interact and converse with individual student groups. Fry *et al.* (2000) previously showed that students valued being questioned in class but this was still clouded by their sense of 'awkwardness' when answering. It could be contended that this awkwardness would be heightened within the formal quiet of a lecture hall but alleviated within the hubbub of an informal classroom where student-tutor interactions occurred within small groups. The shift from lecturer to facilitator, moving between groups while cross pollinating ideas, also helps to build a sense of community as a prerequisite to collaboration as suggested by Murphy (2004).

If we return to the viewpoint of Blatchford *et al.* (2003) who contend that talk within student groups may not necessarily be about the work in hand, the introduction of an online assessment to conclude the learning activity helped to focus in-class discussions. The questionnaire tool within *Moodle* was used to build an anonymously-responded 'quiz' relating to the session topic that included closed, short and open questions. Student groups would discuss the questions, collaboratively build their responses and would input them to the questionnaire/quiz online. Any potential reticence in responding due to awkwardness through answering incorrectly was addressed by the anonymous nature of the questionnaire. Another key feature of the teaching model was that once the questionnaire was closed during class, the tutor was able to review the responses of the whole group. The *Moodle* questionnaire tool generates aggregate scores per closed question type and through this; the tutor can establish the percentage of student groups answering a closed question type correctly. For open (essay) questions, the tutor was able to review the written responses on screen, which offered an opportunity to engage in clarification of misunderstandings, the promotion of further discussion and simple summation of key points.

Using the virtual learning space in this way demonstrates an affordance of the panopticon principle in practice. Although Epling *et al.* (2003) may disapprove of learner surveillance, the questionnaire/quiz allowed for timely and targeted interventions by the tutor to benefit the whole group and to foster further discussion. It also encouraged learner engagement within a large group setting where the risk of discussions veering off course would be greater if students were not aware of the surveillance regime. It is worth noting that the closing remarks in the paper by

Epling *et al.* (2003:417) indicate that they are not entirely disapproving of surveillance techniques as they state: *"It may be that their use can, in certain circumstances, be justified"*. The hybrid learning space as described is perhaps an example of such justified use.

On conclusion of the module, student evaluation proved to be extremely positive which may be considered in sharp contrast to their previously held perceptions of being taught in this large classroom using conventional teaching methods:

> *"I actually liked the classroom layout, gave more space and relaxed atmosphere to learn in"*

> *"I liked how there were quizzes and interactive lessons with the laptops. Broke it up from being stuck watching a PowerPoint in a lecture theatre"*

> *"I like how the laptops are incorporated. In other modules it is difficult to concentrate but with laptops it is much easier to focus"*

> *"Liked the sessions with quizzes that we can work through ourselves and then go through the answers together. Challenges my brain rather than being spoken at for 2 hours!!"*

> *"I think that the use of the laptops in lectures for group work was really good as it enabled groups to work through things and discuss at own pace then the images reviewed by the lecturer after"*
>
> (2nd year undergraduate radiography students)

Conclusion

This chapter has identified the distinctive features of physical and virtual learning spaces that render them suitable for collaborative learning and discussion. Facilitating discussion, whether in the physical world or online, is not without its challenges as students entering higher education are shown to anticipate instructive lectures; rendering them passive recipients of information. When this expectation is not realised and students are encouraged into seemingly forced collaborations then the situation may be met with suspicion and disengagement.

Although physical and the virtual learning spaces each have their affordances, to mix these domains within a classroom setting as a hybrid space is perhaps the key for successful learning. The physical domain, particularly when established as a more informal learning space can enable the tutor to facilitate learning in real-time, picking up on visual cues and back-channel feedback within the room. Here is an opportunity for students to learn within a more relaxed environment where they may feel less awkward when questioned by the tutor within their smaller groups. A problem-based approach can also help to build further this sense of community, as students and tutor work through activities together. Using technology as a means to facilitate dialogue and thus augment opportunities for knowledge construction and application also helps to focus the learner on the given activity. Additionally, networked computers offer the additional affordance of rapid information retrieval to support this knowledge construction.

For the physical space to work effectively, the virtual learning space was structured in such a way as to prepare students for the ensuing in-class activity. Initiate students must first establish a common language for a given topic of study before they are able to engage in meaningful discourse on the subject. The virtual space can be used to instruct students on the basic foundations of this language at a time and place to suit them.

Virtual learning platforms such as *Moodle* host a wide range of interactive learning activities that can be deployed to actively engage the learner both within the classroom and during periods of self-study. Furthermore, using virtual platforms for in-class assessment enables the class to be monitored in real-time by the tutor. Student awareness that the tutor is expecting responses from each group, verifiable via *Moodle*, helps to ensure that each group engages fully with the given activity. This in-class surveillance also gives tutors the capacity to evaluate the overall understanding of the group so that timely and targeted interventions can be made from the online responses given. We contend that the hybrid domain can offer an ideal in terms of learning space management since the social and cognitive affordances of both physical and virtual spaces are exploited to deliver rich, and more complete, cycles of learning.

About the Authors

Nicola Bartholomew is the Senior Learning and Teaching Fellow in the Faculty of Health at Birmingham City University. She can be contacted at this e-mail: nicola.bartholomew@bcu.ac.uk

Paul Bartholomew is Director of Learning Innovation and Professional Practice at Aston University. He can be contacted at this e-mail: p.bartholomew@aston.ac.uk

Chapter Six

Promoting Collaborative and Interdisciplinary Learning via Migration between different Learning Spaces

Silke Lange and John R. A. Smith

Introduction

With this chapter we contribute to the anthology on learning space design in Higher Education by considering learning spaces as physical, virtual and conceptual spaces in which opportunities for collaborative and interdisciplinary learning are fostered. The chapter uses the migration of students and staff between various learning spaces and positions (teachers, researchers and producers) as an example of an educational model for the future. We define a learning space as a space in which learning happens, providing that suitable activities take place and that participants are in a responsive state of mind. The chapter is based on the findings of *Broad Vision*, an ongoing art/science research and learning project based at the University of Westminster, London, UK. We conclude that spaces will only become learning environments when groups or individuals are in suitable conceptual spaces with activities that promote learning. Reading this chapter, you will:

1. see how conceptualising learning spaces as either physical (geographic), virtual (on-line) or conceptual (state of mind) allows for different approaches to teaching and learning;

2. know more about the anthropological and sociological effects of students' migration between these three types of learning spaces; and

3. learn from the *Broad Vision* project, how students' change in learning space, leads to change in role, and how these changes impact their learning experience during the project.

Learning spaces and migration

There is no consensus as to what the term *learning space* applies (Jisc (formerly the JISC), 2006; Scottish Funding Council, 2006; Temple, 2007; Boys, 2011). It may refer to a physical space such as a classroom or it may be a state of mind. On-line resources such as *Blackboard* and *Facebook* complicate further the task of classification. We have found it useful to at least try to distinguish between physical (geographic), virtual (on-line) and conceptual (state of mind) learning spaces and to consider that *space* is not synonymous with *environment*. Learning space implies a space in which learning happens but in order for learning to take place other conditions are necessary, for example suitable activities and a responsive state of mind, with the combination of all contributing to the learning environment. These distinctions are useful for various reasons. They allow us to discuss on-line learning environments and physical learning environments in similar terms even though, in practice, the former also requires the latter; they permit us to consider almost any physical space as a potential learning space; and they enable an understanding of a significant theme that has emerged from our work: migration. By providing this understanding we encourage the reader to consider how migration between learning environments may provide others with similarly rewarding results. *Migration* may be defined *as "The [...] temporary removal of a person, people, social group, etc., from one place to another"* (OED, 2013:np). In this study, we explore migration between both physical and conceptual learning spaces and consider its effects in anthropological and sociological contexts, addressing questions such as *"how does migration effect cultural change, affect identity, and explain incorporation and exclusion?"* (Brettell & Hollifield, 2008:4). A major review of the literature on learning spaces excluded all *"literature dealing with space as a metaphor"* (Temple, 2007:19) dismissing it as *"unrelated to physical spaces"* (Temple,

2007:22). We contend that learning environments require metaphorical as well as physical learning spaces. Hence a learning environment demands the co-location of a conceptual learning space with at least one of the physical or virtual learning spaces.

The *Broad Vision* Project

Broad Vision is an art/science research and learning project at the University of Westminster, London, UK. At its core is an optional undergraduate taught module, which is augmented with extracurricular opportunities. The project began in autumn 2010 as a way of bringing together students and staff from various subject areas to improve communication and understanding between different disciplines. The development of the project, from the initial idea to the validation of the module, took two years of reflection and analysis, partly because a taught module was not initially an intended result, but largely because of the emergent nature of the project's outcomes. The module is designed to expose students to a diverse range of research methods and resources, thereby supporting the development of student-led interdisciplinary projects. *Broad Vision* is informed by experiential learning theory (see, for example, Kolb & Kolb, 2005): in simple terms, students are assessed within the module on process rather than product, but the majority of students follow through to the extracurricular activities, where their products are realised. The University of Westminster is organised administratively into faculties, departments and courses and is organised geographically over several sites, mainly in city centre locations. Each site houses a single faculty, with one exception housing two. It is a practical inevitability, increased by geographical circumstance, that these metaphorical islands develop different organisational cultures and languages. Schein (1992:12) defines organisational culture as a *"pattern of shared basic assumptions that the group learned as it solved its problems of external adaptation and internal integration, that has worked well enough to be considered valid and therefore, to be taught to new members as the correct way to perceive, think, and feel in relation to those problems."*

The lecturers who instigated the *Broad Vision* project did so because it had become clear to them, when discussing a shared interest in microscopy, that they spoke different languages, even when they were using the same words. Language and meaning are greatly determined by culture, and the three lecturers came from different cultures: Imaging Science, Photographic Arts and Life Science. The lecturers applied successfully to an internally advertised Interdisciplinary Pedagogic Learning and Teaching Fund and the project commenced. Excited by opportunities to cross cultural divides, and exploring further the theme of microscopy and image interpretation, a team of undergraduate students and academic staff was recruited from Photographic Arts, Imaging Science, Illustration, Computer Science, Psychology and Life Science.

The University is metropolitan and cosmopolitan with a diverse student body. Students who were in the second semester of their second year, exactly half way through three-year undergraduate programmes, were predominately those recruited to both the initial extracurricular project and the current taught module. It was considered important that students would have developed a strong sense of their own discipline's language and culture, allowing identification with peers from within their discipline at the same time as providing a contrast with those from outside.

From the outset it was assumed that the language barrier that existed between academic staff also existed between students. In actuality language was less of a barrier between students from different disciplines, who swiftly resorted to simile and metaphor to aid understanding. What had not been envisaged was the significance of *place*, a significance that became increasingly apparent throughout the life of the initial project, and which is now central to the module.

Various different places were used for their intended purpose or subtly subverted, both within the various university sites and outside. The influence of different environments on the behaviour of individuals and groups was noted contemporaneously by project participants but only analysed later by the educational researcher.

Current Educational Landscape

The *Broad Vision* project is taking place during a challenging time in higher education in England and Wales. Government initiatives, such as *Securing a Sustainable Future for Higher Education* (Browne, 2010), *Students at the Heart of the System* (Department for Business, Innovation and Skills,

2011) and the *UK Quality Code for Higher Education* (Quality Assurance Agency, 2011), focus predominantly on economically viable structures and systems with the aim of creating a market-led model of education based on competition between (and within) institutions in response to 'consumer demand'. Some educationalists contest this model by proposing an alternative future for education. Coffield and Williamson, for example, introduce the concept of 'communities of discovery' in their publication *From Exam Factories to Communities of Discovery* (2011). According to Coffield and Williamson, the main features of such communities include educators and learners as partners (not providers or consumers) with interchangeable roles; the availability of intellectual and physical spaces in which to grow; and a mode of learning that is collaborative and based on dialogue. In contrast to recent government initiatives in England and Wales, the concept of 'communities of discovery' proposes a more egalitarian model, inviting all participants of education to shape the learning landscape in which they wish to work, collectively and democratically.

The ethos of *Broad Vision* is one of a community of discovery, where the hierarchy of lecturer-student relations is reduced to a minimum. Rather than *lecturer* and *student*, the terms *researcher* and *student researcher*, or the non-discriminatory *participant* are used. The project employs student-centred approaches to learning and teaching, for example consultation, collaboration and sharing skills within and between disciplines. In order to develop and support interdisciplinary projects, the choice, interpretation, structure and use of learning spaces play crucial roles.

Project Structure

Each iteration of the project follows a different theme (year one: microscopy; year two: the Images from Science 2 exhibition (Rochester Institute of Technology, 2008) was the stimulus; year three: the simple terms, Data, Truth and Beauty). Each iteration is structured in three phases: "*disciplinary exchange, interdisciplinary research and audience engagement*" (Barnett & Smith, 2011).

The three phases are characterised by different types of migration and different types of learning environments. In the first phase, a group of students and a lecturer from each discipline devises and runs a short, interactive, workshop introducing some aspect of their discipline to the others. This phase sees the first instances of migration within the project when students and lecturers enter physical spaces that are new to most of them (but 'home' to the group running the session) and as students become teachers and lecturers become students. The second phase sees an explosion of students' ideas, enthusiasm and ambition being tempered by lecturers' experience into proposals that are potentially realisable within the constraints of ethics and available time and resources. This phase sees the transformation of a disparate array of individuals into a somewhat more cohesive community, which then becomes a group of outsiders migrating between various learning spaces. The third phase remains extracurricular and is optional, providing personal and professional development opportunities, the exact natures of which are dependent on the students' proposals, negotiated and assisted by the lecturers. Migration in the third phase, which is outside the module structure, sees participants occupy spaces differently, with more freedom than is possible even within the loose structure of the module. Realised outputs have included exhibitions, publications, websites, symposia and conference presentations. In due course there is the process of reverse migration, whereby participants return to their programmes of study or teaching, enriched by the experiences and knowledge gained.

Physical and conceptual learning spaces are augmented by the virtual space of an online social network, namely *Ning*, allowing participants to engage from different places and at different times. Furthermore, the virtual space has developed into a rich archive for both future participants and for pedagogic research.

Within this chapter we aim to reflect the distinct and different perspectives inevitable in a project such as *Broad Vision* and include contributions from the educational researcher, lecturers and student researchers. The chapter concludes with the consideration of how educational institutions can support progressive pedagogies within an educational model underpinned by the notion of migration of staff and students between learning environments.

A Pedagogic Perspective

In 2010 I (Silke Lange) was invited by the *Broad Vision* team to participate in the project as an educational researcher to provide an informed perspective on pedagogical aspects of the interdisciplinary venture. Since then I have had many opportunities to observe the movements across the borders of each discipline and the interactions between participants in each other's territories, as well as spaces external to the University premises, such as galleries, conferences and libraries. The project has provided a case study to research interdisciplinary learning, generative curriculum and collaborative creativity. As the project progressed, the importance of the learning environments, the physical and virtual spaces, as well as the community and the changing identities of participants within that community became increasingly significant and worthy of further exploration. Theories of social constructivism (Vygotsky, 1978), communities of practice (Wenger, 1998) and interdisciplinary learning and teaching (Chandramohan & Fallows, 2009) shaped the framework of the educational research.

Recent literature highlights that research into learning spaces often focuses on campus design and management; the development of new spaces; using different layout, design and furniture; use of new technologies; and using student-centred approaches as supposed to teacher-centred approaches (Jisc (formerly the JISC), 2006; Scottish Funding Council, 2006; Temple, 2007; Boys, 2011). Furthermore, the importance of intellectual spaces seems largely dismissed in the context of the discussion of learning spaces (Temple, 2007; Boys, 2011). The focus in *Broad Vision*, however, is about moving between spaces, exploring the novel and unfamiliar, using existing spaces in ways different from their original purposes. Here then, an explorative case study approach has been adopted, examining the nature of participants' learning, the environment in which this was happening, the identities participants have developed in the process of learning, as well as *"exploring the creative potential that is emerging in the spaces between disciplines"* (Blair, 2011:36). A number of methods have been used to collect data, including observations of the learning environment, semi-structured discussion groups, and online exit questionnaires collecting both qualitative and quantitative data.

Research Design

Throughout the three year life of the project, twenty-four sessions have been observed – focusing on the physical learning environments, the range of learning methods, the social interactions between students and lecturers, and students and their peers, associated with the learning spaces. The type of learning spaces used, and sessions happening within them, varied greatly – for example: a planning meeting in a cafe to discussions of photographic aesthetics in an illustration studio; project presentations in a classroom; demonstrations of digital photography in a microscopy laboratory; student presentations at public and a gallery residency. Sessions observed resembled *"the way in which a migrational pattern that involves several sites of settlement can invite different modes of engagement with the various national cultures encountered"* (Dewdney et al., 2011:154).

Towards the end of each year of the project, semi-structured discussion groups with students and staff were conducted (nine groups in total, each with between four and six participants); these aimed to identify participants' perceptions and experiences of working within this alternative educational model; in particular how it compared to the conventional structures and uses of learning spaces in courses and modules within the University. Data gathering from multiple sources was followed by an in-depth analysis in relation to the different methods used. Recurring themes enabled us to identify similarities and differences between participants' perceptions and observations.

Insider Perspectives

Curiosity about exposure to discipline-specific facilities and equipment seems to be common to all participants of *Broad Vision*. This is not unexpected, particularly as participants are self-selecting: anyone choosing to work across disciplines will be curious of the 'other'. Unexpected emerging themes include: the migration between sites and positions; the significance of the community, including its impact on the motivation and aspirations of the individual; and engagement through novelty. In the section that follows, stories told by participants offer insights into their learning experiences, highlighting benefits and challenges of the physical, virtual and conceptual learning spaces.

Migration between learning spaces and positions

The movements between the different specialist facilities, internal as well as external, the use of formal and informal learning spaces, and the transitions from lecturer to facilitator, from student researcher to student teacher, changed general perceptions of physical spaces as well as creating conceptual learning spaces that had not been envisaged at the start of the project. Observations such as this by a Physiology and Anatomy lecturer are not uncommon on *Broad Vision*:

> *"I was struck at how one's discipline transcends one's physical environment; everyone looked the same [because of the lab coats] but approached their task so differently. The session was designed to introduce everyone to the scientific method and the use of microscopes [...] Working with people who are not afraid of asking 'dumb' questions, experiencing what we, as scientists, take for granted and seeing how people adapt to a new environment has been a significant pedagogical wake-up."* (in Barnett & Smith, 2011:33)

These kinds of observations by staff are clearly supported by student researchers:

> *"The physical space is also dynamic and changing. There is no set lecture hall or classroom or studio. The lab, illustration space, computer lab, in the museum. This is a logistical nightmare, students have to be updated regularly, but this keeps the students alert. I have a very visual memory. If I walk into the same classroom eight weeks in a row and get taught various lessons they are not going to stick."* (Student researcher in Lange & Dinsmore, 2012:np)

> *"My own experience with the project has been one that has afforded me avenues and experiences simply not available had I not have taken on the chance of working outside of my discipline. In terms of a space, Broad Vision offers not only physical changes of space for students, but also theoretical. We all become insular at times with regards to our own ways of working, when you are forced to confront them by someone who may not even have a basic grounding in your way of working, re-learning the basics becomes a good opportunity to re-evaluate your own working methods."* (Student researcher, informal discussion, 2013)

Whilst these two student researchers address slightly different issues of migration in their accounts, they both describe notions of change:

change in location, and change in one's role, and how these changes have impacted on their learning experience during the project. Savin-Baden (2008:13) refers to such learning spaces as *"smooth learning spaces, which are open, flexible and contested, spaces in which both learning and learners are always on the move"*. The idea of moving between learning spaces (face-to-face and virtual) when collaborating with peers has also been explored by Daniel and Fleischmann (this volume). In *Broad Vision*, students as well as lecturers are 'on the move', particularly in the way in which they switch between being a teacher, researcher, facilitator and learner; according to Savin-Baden (2008:20) through such transitional processes *"unexpected learning spaces emerge"*. These unexpected learning spaces are conceptual spaces, describing different attitudes, approaches or reactions to a task, space or situation.

A lecturer from Imaging Science (John R. A. Smith), shared his experience on *Broad Vision* and how he introduced the idea of using spaces external to the University campus, relevant to the curriculum of his module:

> *"It has been surprisingly liberating to be part of a project where the roles of student and tutor have been mixed up so much. Added to the mix, I was studying for a post-graduate certificate in higher education over two years of the project so apart from anything else I was a student studying my own pedagogy. Sessions run by others provided me with valuable peer-observation opportunities."* (Informal discussion, 2013)

A recent graduate from Illustration, now undertaking an internship on the project, describes such affecting attitudes in her learning experience in a more personal and situational way:

> *"My experience from all the changes of one space to another, both physically and conceptually, is that I usually change my way of thinking/ attitude in each space so I can take more out of it. For example, at the illustration studio I felt more free to be spontaneous and active, whereas in a lab I was more constrained and focused because of the safety regulations and so that I could understand certain information on science that was not familiar to me. Also visually we went from bright white studios to photography darkrooms. That again changed how I behaved in that space. But this is something subjective as I'm familiar with art studios, whereas a psychology student was telling me how the illustration studio*

was too white and bright that it made her feel a bit uncomfortable. The whole shift from one place to another is very refreshing and exciting though, it almost surprises you every time as you expect it to be one thing and it's something completely different." (Student researcher, informal discussion, 2013)

This comment highlights how migration between the different physical learning spaces encourages different behaviour and responses to each space, by different individuals, based on unfamiliarity and imposed regulations.

Other spaces to which *Broad Vision* participants migrate are virtual spaces. As stated by Lippincott (2006:12), *"developing spaces where students can collaborate outside class provides support for an increased emphasis on teamwork, both in and outside HE"*, and confirmed by one of the students researchers:

"The Ning site also formalises this community behaviour. Makes it 24 hours and open to everyone. It is also a language which students understand." (Student researcher in Lange & Dinsmore, 2012:np)

As noted by Temple (2007:35), *"physical space and intellectual space (for teaching and learning, and research) may, then, be connected through the operation of social networks"*. Virtual learning spaces play crucial roles in the future of education and the ways in which we learn and develop curricula. This has also been proposed by Savin-Baden (2008:81), *"digital spaces demand that we confront the possibility of new types of visuality, literacy, pedagogy, representations of knowledge, communication and embodiment"*, and by Enomoto and Warner (this volume). Furthermore this approach to sharing information and networking beyond one's immediate team extends to professional international networks as observed by one of the Psychology lecturers on the *Broad Vision* team:

"Immediately after the 'creative conversation' session in phase two, I blogged the following: "Broad Vision is opening up to me possibilities for different ways of working... it is demonstrating to me the potential for social networking as a tool to support asynchronous communication across geographically distributed teams. I must think of applications of this technology for my own work." [...] The Ning site indeed proved

> *vital to our interdisciplinary collaboration by supporting asynchronous discussions of how to implement our research questions across a team that was geographically distributed by more than 300 miles."* (in Barnett & Smith, 2011:115)

Modern technology allows us to network across the globe as well as within a classroom, as seen in Figure 1, in which a student is showing a video clip to one of the lecturers. Using electronic devices, such as smartphones in the classroom, has transformed the learning experience and increased the level of interaction between staff and students. Feedback for ideas and experiments is immediately available and the process of developing projects and learning seems a more collective undertaking.

Figure 1: Student researcher demonstrating an artefact of their research to a lecturer. © *Natalia Janula, Broad Vision 2012.*

Significance of the community

The notion of the collective is also evident in the significance placed upon the community (Wenger, 1998; Coffield & Williamson, 2011). Participants of the project belong to the community of their own discipline, whilst simultaneously contributing to the shaping of a new interdisciplinary community: one that is self-selected and built on similar interests and aspirations. The experience of being part of the *Broad Vision* community is summarised well by the Project Lead when speaking of a period during the first year of the project, when the team was able to take over the central gallery on campus for six weeks and treat it as a residency:

> "I have got a favourite moment which is [...] very much about that gallery residency, that was [...] my office for a few days, ...and students were working on their own stuff. So there were the illustration students that moved in, made it their studio and they are also the co-curators and we were making decisions about that... And then the photographers would come by and just say 'oh, I've got this' and 'I was printing this' and 'which image do you think?' and there was this collective emergence of the exhibition and [...] the longest [...] build up to an exhibition I think I have ever experienced. And then the imaging scientists would come by and there was this [...] chattering and everybody was helping each other out and it was a collective development. I wasn't in charge; I was part of a team. I had more experience than they did in building the exhibition, but it was just, it was a learning environment that was utterly informal, ...just naturally interdisciplinary, because these people by this stage really knew each other well. There was no disciplinary boundary." (Project Lead during discussion group)

The Project Lead emphasises the importance of physical or psychological removal from the conventional learning environment and the importance of working differently within a certain space. This is not about creating new environments but is about using existing environments in different ways to prompt new ways of seeing and working, as well as *"providing opportunities for reflection and presenting challenges to current thinking"* (Savin-Baden, 2008:8).

Simply being part of this community also creates challenges to one's thinking and encourages the development of ideas and research:

> "I think the most important part is the community. For Broad Vision meetings I want to have something I have produced, researched or stumbled across to share and talk about. I am pushing my project forward, not just for my own self will but because I want it in a form I

can share and show off to others. Broad Vision happens in the corridor on the way to a lecture, sat in the pub, on the Ning social networking site; it happens in a community and as an individual you are accountable to that community. The best part is you always have something to talk about with these people because they see you as an expert in a field they want to know more about. In this case expertise is relative, it is not to know everything about the subject. It is just knowing more than the person you are talking to." (Student researcher in Lange & Dinsmore, 2012:np)

This account by one of the student researchers resembles theories on how learning communities affect educational outcomes as expressed by Beach-board *et al.* (2011:853) in their study on cohorts and relatedness which proposes that "*environments that support perceptions of social relatedness improve motivation, thereby positively influencing learning behaviour*". We suggest that Figure 2 highlights such a notion of relatedness expressed by students through active engagement in each other's project developments during the interdisciplinary phase of the *Broad Vision* project. The lecturer remains at the periphery of the group discussion, offering an alternative perspective when necessary.

Figure 2: Student researchers engaged in project development, observed by lecturer (standing). © Natalia Janula, Broad Vision 2012.

Engagement through novelty

Novelty is experienced by most project participants, whether in the form of entering the different specialist spaces, working with unfamiliar equipment, exploring new methods of working or simply learning the language of a different discipline.

> *"If someone told me a few years ago that I would be teaching artists, photographers, psychologists and computer scientists how to perform blood grouping experiments I would not have believed them. Yet, on an autumn Wednesday afternoon that is what we did – we opened our doors to interdisciplinary research and I am rather glad we did. Teaching laboratories are always a great place to be, full of ideas and curious minds, yet I have never experienced the excitement of 30 (well-supervised) 'novices' being asked to put on a lab coat and a pair of latex gloves for the first time."* (Physiology and Anatomy lecturer in Barnett & Smith, 2011:33)

> *"When artists come into the lab they ask 'what happens if we do this, this and this' and I'd say, let's try it... Science students will go into a lab, see a certain type of equipment and use it for that purpose, whereas people from a different discipline come in and just want to have fun, not just for the sake of it, they are curious. Through doing the experiments you discover new things and so this is one thing that I take away from this project, to introduce more of curiosity driven research to the curriculum of my science students."* (Biotechnology lecturer during discussion group, 2013)

It is particularly interesting to consider these two observations, as both express surprise and enthusiasm for what has happened in their laboratory, describing the *"learning space as active agency"* (Strickland, this volume). Furthermore, both lecturers come across as open-minded individuals embracing ideas of teaching science in the 21st century as summarised by Narum (2004:10) as follows: *"recognise the social nature of scientific research, teaching and learning by facilitating interactions between and among students and faculty; reflect and foster the blurring of disciplinary boundaries that is a feature of contemporary science; and acknowledge the role of serendipity and story-telling in doing science – providing space for exploiting the unplanned and teachable moment, for sharing what is becoming known."*

In the context of *Broad Vision*, 'becoming known' relates to the concepts of social learning and the community of discovery in which all participants, migrating between positions and spaces, construct knowledge collectively. Perhaps the most convincing example of migration between spaces and embracing novelty is expressed by a Human and Medical Science student carrying out a dissection of the respiratory tract of a pig at London Gallery West (Figure 3). He states:

> *"The lines that divide my student life and my professional life had started to disappear. I was no longer a student sat in a classroom listening passively to what my lecturers had to say. That moment I felt the pleasure of playing a more active role as a student. I was applying the knowledge gained during the past years of my studies and I was helping to build knowledge [...]. The experience gained reinforced my knowledge of my own discipline and of myself. I believe that there should be more space within our academic curricula for such active ways of learning."*
> (in Barnett, 2012:124)

Figure 3: Human and Medical Science student carrying out a dissection of the respiratory tract of a pig at London Gallery West. © Chiara Ceolin, Broad Vision 2012.

Broad Vision has not only provided students with new ideas and enthusiasm for their disciplines. Staff commented extensively on how they wanted to apply some of the ideas and teaching methods explored on the project in the teaching of their own disciplines and professional practices:

> *"I find myself bursting with new ideas on how to improve the teaching and learning for our students, ideas for transition and retention as well as wanting to engage with more interdisciplinary projects."* (Physiology and Anatomy lecturer in Barnett & Smith, 2011:33)

> *"I suspect that Broad Vision may provide a model not only of the learning opportunities offered by interdisciplinary practice, but how to initiate and support the interdisciplinary work conducted by professional researchers."* (Psychology lecturer in Barnett & Smith, 2011:115)

> *"I have adapted many of the things I have observed with Broad Vision and incorporated them into my other modules. One example is the use of different places. In the past I often timetabled a gallery or museum visit in the last week of term as an extracurricular treat. Now I have timetabled visits near the beginning of modules to add context and provide stimulus, and it is always possible to integrate into the module's assignment some aspect from the visit. Switching roles has most definitely increased my level of empathy with students, which has had knock-on effects in so many ways elsewhere."* (Imaging Science lecturer, informal discussion, 2013)

Visual Summary

In order to assist the reader to comprehend and apply our central thesis, we have sketched a diagram of the migration between learning spaces (Figure 4). In this we highlight the key aspects, interactions and exchanges within and across disciplines.

Within our conceptual learning space (state of mind) we include the multiple roles of researcher, teacher and learner. We group together physical learning spaces as well as virtual learning spaces; we connect the two groups to conceptual learning spaces via activities, and by doing so illustrate our concept of learning environments. Arrows between roles and spaces illustrate paths of migration.

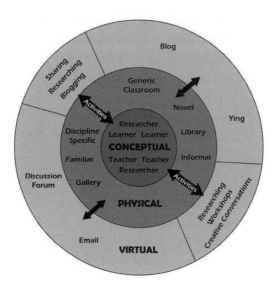

Figure 4: Migration between Learning Spaces.

Conclusions

The findings of the research presented in this chapter highlight different experiences of the project, yet the similarity in appreciation of having been able to participate in the project is clearly evident. The ways in which physical, virtual and conceptual learning spaces were designed and utilised have been crucial to the success of the *Broad Vision* project. The design of the project, its structure in phases, gave each participant the opportunity to gain an insight into the thinking and working of the others. The understanding of each other's territory was enhanced through the introductory workshops and the creative conversations as well as the collaborative development of ideas and projects.

The novelty of migrating between discipline-specific spaces encouraged flexibility in thinking and innovation in production of knowledge. Furthermore it provided transformational experiences to many participants, especially those who were open-minded and self motivated. A challenge for projects of this type is to cater for students at different stages of their degree and with different levels of readiness for the amount of self-directed learning required.

One of the challenges of resourcing *Broad Vision* is its requirement for discipline-specific spaces, e.g. darkrooms. The study confirms however, that rather than have static, flexible, learning spaces where students attend week after week, *we* can be flexible, and migrate to suitable conceptual spaces.

The disruptive nature of *Broad Vision* works well for the small community on which the case study is based. Disruption is good precisely because it is different and novel, but may be too chaotic for a larger programme.

The refined model that resulted after three years is robust and adaptable, underpinned by contemporary theories but built using local resources. The validation of an optional taught module provides sustainability within the standard programme structure. The module content is generative and the theme changeable, whilst the structure, learning outcomes and assessment criteria are predetermined.

As we stated at the beginning of this chapter, spaces will only become learning environments with suitable activities and when groups and individuals are in suitable conceptual spaces. It is the adaptation to a space, or migration to another space, that is key. It is these abilities of adaption and migration that are so desirable in preparing graduates for life beyond university.

About the authors

Silke Lange is Director of Learning and Teaching in the Faculty of Media, Arts and Design at the University of Westminster, London, UK. She can be contacted at this email: langes@westminster.ac.uk

John R. A. Smith is a Senior Lecturer in Imaging Science in the Faculty of Media, Arts and Design at the University of Westminster, London, UK. He can be contacted at this email: smithj1@westminster.ac.uk

Chapter Seven

Perceptions and Conceptions of Learning Spaces in Higher Education

Steve Drew and Christopher Klopper

Introduction

This chapter contributes to the anthology on learning space design in higher education by presenting how teachers' perceptions and conceptions of university learning and teaching spaces moderate their pedagogic practices. We define a learning space as a space being collaboratively constructed between teacher and students through linguistic means (Marton & Tsui, 2004:21, 30) and within which meaning is negotiated and shared through common language (*ibid* 28). In the chapter we present and trial a framework of contextual affordances for the analysis of learning space as part of our study. Reading this chapter, you will:

1. encounter a new framework arranging personal and organisational contexts of learning spaces;

2. follow the application of the framework to data from peer observations of teaching and surveyed academics' conceptions of learning spaces to show that while many learning spaces might be homogenous in design, varied use does occur between discipline areas; and

3. conclude that academics' conceptions of learning space do moderate pedagogic practice.

Learning and teaching spaces are complex states embedded within multiple contexts. Increasingly, students and teachers need to engage in environments that include physical, technical, and virtual aspects to support learning activities. Holtham and Cancienne (in this volume) elaborate this further through the discussion of the evolution of learning space. The learning space is not just about student learning, but also about the provision of a rich set of opportunities for reflective practice (Schön, 1983) and peer collaborations to assist situated professional learning for teachers (Billett, 1996; Lave, 1993; Lave & Wenger, 1991).

Learning spaces created within the traditional university learning environment have inexorably expanded from the didactic lecture hall presentations and focused active learning (Biggs, 1989) opportunities in tutorials and laboratories. Once designed for a predominantly on-campus in-person student, these spaces now include prevailing technology and communications to cater to different attendance and delivery modes. The role of lecturer as orator and motivator to create emotional and intellectual learning spaces to engage students with learning (Trigwell et al., 1999) still exists but is expanded to include pedagogy-leveraging information systems to allow learning beyond the classroom. Learning spaces for students are no longer limited to the synchronous interactions with teachers and peers and increasingly have become flexible, mobile and often combine communications over a range of information channels, media and devices. This provides a challenge for teachers as they come to grapple with understanding how learning spaces are created and mediated with technology to engage students with learning activities that effectively assist them towards desired learning outcomes.

Authentic learning spaces (Meyers & Nulty, 2009; Newmann & Wehlage, 1993) seek to emulate situated learning by creating intellectual spaces to undertake similar problems within the university classroom. Learning-research models from the praxis paradigm all involve a cycle that studies a real-world problem, designs an intervention to address it, implements the intervention, and then analyses the outcome before modifying the design and starting the process again. As goal-oriented strategies, they are of particular use in learning about and impacting upon complex social settings such as those in Higher Education (Lizzio & Wilson, 2004). The complex context in which university teaching takes place provides a significant influence on how teachers conduct their

craft (Cranton & Carusetta, 2002; Lea & Callaghan, 2008). The infer-
ence here is that many teachers will moderate their approach to teaching
according to the contextual affordances provided in the institution.

There is often a noticeable effect on how learning and teaching are
conceived by different disciplines and university cultures that exist
(Knight & Trowler, 2000). Under such influences it would be reasonable to expect evidence of moderation of pedagogic practice and its use
of space based on discipline area. Further influence exists where there
are discipline specific teaching contexts required such as laboratory and
clinical space. Specific teaching and learning contexts provide their own
challenges as in clinical study (Hoffman & Donaldson, 2004) and interprofessional education (Oandasan & Reeves, 2005). Moving into the
online learning and teaching realm further challenges teachers' existing
conceptions of teaching (Gonzalez, 2009; Oliver & Herrington, 2001).
There are links between teachers' perceptions of the teaching environment and the approaches to teaching that are adopted (Prosser &
Trigwell, 1997).

Defining a system, supporting learning spaces

The complex web of factors that influence how learning and teaching
in higher education occur is apparent in extant literature (Cranton &
Carusetta, 2002; Hoffman & Donaldson, 2004; Lea & Callaghan, 2008;
Sharma, 1997). Distilled from literature and observations of university
students and teachers, Figure 1 arranges the multiplicity of contextual
affordances that support the construction of a learning space. Notion-
ally these fall into two broad areas that relate individually to the teacher
and student. The shared zone depicted as the 'Teacher-Student Interaction Context' is where co-constructed learning space, as defined earlier,
effectively resides. As such, this diagram presents a conceptual model
relating learning spaces and contextual affordances in a way that provides
a framework to underpin the analyses to come. Each of the layers represent contexts within a teaching and learning system that influence the
layers above and beside, and which, in turn provide a feedback channel
to those below.

At the layer marked 'Organisational Learning Affordances' there are
three distinct sub-levels that include physical affordances, technological

affordances, and virtual affordances. The campus physical affordances are the tangible items like buildings, rooms, and equipment that exist to create an effective physical and intellectual environment supporting face-to-face interactions between students and with teachers. To further the learning experience a supporting layer represents the 'technical affordances' within the physical space such as computers, networking, software, lighting, and sound. Using the campus based technical affordances, representational spaces or virtual contexts can be created in which students may engage with each other, teachers, and representations of learning objects, processes and relationships. An example at this layer would be the Learning Management System (LMS).

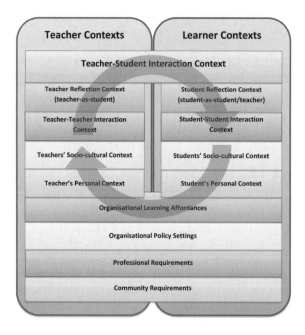

Figure 1: Contexts for Learning Spaces.

At the university-level are 'Organisational Policy Settings' that provide the rules and expectations influencing the nature and extent of the learning affordances at the layer above. Where learning outcomes are aimed at preparing students for transition into professions then various accrediting bodies may also influence the nature of learning affordances. This is reflected at the Professional Requirements layer. The 'Community

Requirements' layer reflects that every university operates with community expectations that graduates have necessary knowledge to support that community in turn.

The realm of blended or technology enhanced learning begins to blur the distinctions between layers when students' personal and mobile technologies are used in on-campus learning but also create opportunities for online learning and off-campus interactions to create digitally enhanced learning spaces. At the 'Student's Personal Context' layer a personal physical context and a personal technical context can be discerned. The personal technical context includes any devices with which a student can engage with or execute learning activities. A student's personal physical context for learning can be in class, on a train, in a home office or anywhere that their personal technical context allows them to facilitate a learning space. Socio-constructivist learning theory (Lave & Wenger, 1991) relates the role of learning communities where students are able to co-construct understanding through interaction. A 'Student-Student Interaction Context' is supported by a student cohort that embodies a culture or set of norms that includes and values interactions that support learning and this is represented in the supporting Students' Socio-cultural Context layer. Analogues of the personal technical, personal physical, socio-cultural, and student-student interaction contexts exist for teachers in the creation of teaching spaces that influence the creation of effective learning spaces for students. In this case the Teachers' Socio-cultural Context describes the norms and expectations around faculty discussion of teaching and learning with each other and with students to co-construct teaching spaces that enable learning.

Reflective practice creates another layer for both students 'Student Reflection Context' and teachers 'Teacher Reflection Context' such that metacognition about learning and teaching can occur. Teacher reflection places the teacher into the learner role where they can review their experiences, those of students and peers, to create interventions that meet improvement goals. Similarly, student metacognition is about reviewing what was learnt and understanding how it was learnt. As soon as students take on a peer-teaching role then reflection underpins effectiveness of the student-as-teacher role (Boud et al., 1999; Rubin & Hebert, 1998).

All of the preceding contextual affordances support the interactions between students and teachers at the 'Student-Teacher Interaction

Context' that create 'learning spaces' and facilitate learning. At this layer it is the teacher as motivator, orator, challenger, narrator, collaborator, and demonstrator that creates the emotional and intellectual environment that engages students and moves them into their learning spaces (Trigwell *et al.*, 1999).

Perceptions and conceptions of learning spaces

We situate this investigation of learning space moderation of pedagogy at an Australian, multi-campus university. Like most universities it has a high investment in physical teaching and learning spaces, with significant information systems infrastructure for business processes, education delivery and support. Data sourced from observations of teaching in different learning spaces indicate a diverse range of capabilities and understandings that teachers possess about how learning spaces may be constructed in the university context. A unique account is given of how teachers at Griffith University moderate their pedagogic practice depending upon the features and facilities in the learning environment. Analysis of data collected during peer observations of teaching and augmented using surveys of teachers provide rich evidence of the ways that learning spaces moderate pedagogic practice.

Data for the first question comes from a survey of teachers (N=21) recording their conceptions of learning space and teaching space. The remaining questions are explored through the analysis of observers' notes (N=101) recorded during peer observations of teaching (Klopper & Drew, 2013, in press). At the study site there are four discipline groups: physical sciences, health sciences, business, and social sciences with data being collected from each. The next sections relate the framework for analysis of data and the sources of data used in this study.

A Framework for Categorising Use of Learning spaces

A review of frameworks that codify the use of learning spaces revealed little that can be adapted to the analysis of the collected observation or conceptions data. Different descriptors of effective learning spaces have been derived that reveal ideals, considerations or principles that describe the nature or design of the space (Mitchell *et al.*, 2010; Radcliffe, 2009;

Reushle, 2011) rather than the nature of its actual use for learning and teaching. Adaptation of Nielsen's (1994) ten usability heuristics to the study of usability of a learning environment constructs a framework for how a learning space might be evaluated in terms of usability rather than how it is actually being used. A similar treatment of Norman's (1986) study of the goal oriented cognitive structure of tasks and actions create a focus on the nature of the task rather than how it engages with the environment in which it is happening.

Revisiting Figure 1 it is apparent that "Contexts for Learning and Teaching Space Use" (CLTS) provide suitable taxa for uses of a learning environment. As such it provides a possible framework for the analysis of use of learning and teaching spaces (Table 1).

Taxon	Context
1	Teacher Reflection – teacher as learner
2	Teacher-Student Academic Interaction, Motivation, Collaboration, Stimulation & Emotion
3	Teacher-Teacher Interaction context
4	Teachers' Socio-Cultural context
5	Teacher Personal Physical context
6	Teacher Personal Technical context
7	Campus Physical Affordances
8	Campus Technical Affordances
9	Campus Virtual Affordances
10	Organisational Settings
11	Professional Influences
12	Community Influences
13	Student Personal Technical context
14	Student Personal Physical context
15	Students' Socio-Cultural context
16	Student-Student Interaction context
17	Student Reflection – student as learner / teacher

Table 1: Contexts for Learning Space Use.

Perceptions of Teachers' Use of Learning spaces

The PRO-Teaching observation dimensions enable most teachers to comment productively upon a colleague's pedagogic practice and student engagement with teaching and learning activities (Drew & Klopper, 2013; Klopper & Drew, 2013, in press). For the purposes of this study the two relevant observation dimensions were Dimension 8: "Does the teacher demonstrate effective use of the learning environment?" and Dimension 9: "Does the teacher demonstrate effective use of teaching aids and resources?"

The environment in which a class is executed provides constraints and affordances for effective teaching. Making appropriate and effective use of the learning environment speaks to the university teacher's understanding of the limitations that the environment places on the effectiveness of different teaching strategies. To be most effective, the teacher must understand how to make optimal use of the available tools and affordances in that environment to complement teaching strategies and to enhance student learning.

Dimension 8 as stated is clear and directly observable. However, an explicit emphasis on considerations of potential limitations and augmentations in the learning environment provides further enhancement. Such modifiers are expressed through relevant environmental controls and the responsiveness to student perceptions of the learning environment.

Dimension 9 expands upon control equipment used in the learning environment to include different teaching materials and aids. This dimension speaks to the effective presentation of ideas and concepts in a classroom. With appropriate teaching materials and aids the intent is to improve the quality of explanation and stimulate student interest in teaching and learning activities. In this matter teaching materials and aids offer some facilitation as they offer multiple channels of information for students with a range of learning approaches and styles.

There are different expressions of resources and aids available in different teaching and learning environments. Using them appropriately is a matter of adequately understanding them and the desired means of reaching the learning objectives. Design and preparation of the teaching materials is part of designing the activity that uses them appropriately. In the online learning environment many of the same materials and aids can be employed albeit in a different representation virtually.

Teaching materials and learning aids can be used in different ways to different effect. That effect can be limited by the approach (Trigwell *et al.*, 1999) and pedagogical content knowledge of the teacher (McNamara, 1991; Trigwell, 2011), combined with the given set of affordances and constraints within the learning environment. For an observer there are two discernible and observable aspects generated from this dimension. Firstly, the choice of teaching materials and aids; and, secondly, given the apparent constraints are they used to best effect.

Teachers Conceptions of Learning Spaces

A representative selection of teachers involved in peer observation of teaching was asked to provide answers to two simple questions relating to what they conceived a learning space and a teaching space to be. These were asked as separate questions in order to prompt some discrimination between the two constructs if at all possible. A survey was sent by email to participants in the PRO-Teaching project asking them for written responses to the following questions: "How would you describe your understanding of a learning space?" and, "How would you describe your understanding of teaching space?" Responses were anonymous with only school affiliation provided to capture discipline related themes.

Analytical Treatment and Outcomes

Treatment of collected data was completed: first, closed coding of text against taxa from each of the frameworks described; and second, open coding using thematic analysis of text. Analyses were divided into five groups corresponding to data from the conceptions surveys; and, one each for observed use of learning environment for teachers from each of the four discipline areas: physical sciences, health sciences, business, and social sciences.

Table 2 maps the constructs (taxa) in the CLTS framework against percentage of observations in which constructs were observed. The line with diamond markers represents Dimension 8: "Does the teacher demonstrate effective use of the learning environment?" and the line with square markers Dimension 9: "Does the teacher demonstrate effective use of teaching aids and resources?"

There are three major "peaks" or groupings of areas of use of features of the learning environment; and use of teaching materials and aids that observations reveal. The first occurs at taxon 2 to capture teacher-student interaction. The second and largest peak encompasses taxa 7 and 8. Taxon 7 relates to use of the campus' physical space while taxon 8 relates to technical affordances for learning and teaching. Given that this data is derived from observations of campus based teaching this is a reasonable expectation. The third peak is related to the student personal technical context and personal physical context and is expressed mostly through the use of materials and aids relating to computer accessed items. In some instances a fourth peak is observed for the use of space for student-student interactions. In particular these are features of use of the learning environment within Health Sciences and to a lesser extent in Business where problem based learning and group activities have been observed to be a more widely used aspect of teaching.

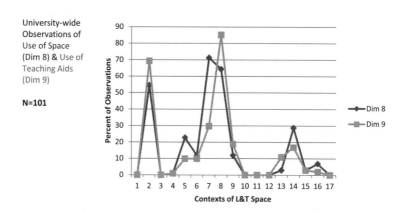

University-wide Observations of Use of Space (Dim 8) & Use of Teaching Aids (Dim 9)

N=101

Table 2: Observations of Use of Space and Use of Teaching Aids using CLTS Framework.

In the case of observation of teaching in music and fine arts, within the Social sciences group, classes were predominantly small groups in small rooms with the teacher demonstrating and involving students in experiential activities. This is representative of the "master-apprentice" teaching style characteristic of this learning context. It was noticeable in this context an equally high observation of use of space and use of learning aids and materials in these instances.

For comparison purposes the data from the conceptions of learning space and teaching space survey was also evaluated using the CLTS framework. The analysis pictured in Table 3 revealed a clear dichotomy in expressions of teachers' conceptions of learning space and teaching space. As with the analysis of the observed use of learning space there were distinct peaks; relating to teacher-student interaction, campus physical affordances, and student's personal physical context. Teachers' conceptions of learning space also included new peaks representing the perceived importance of the campus virtual affordances and the student's personal technical context needed to access these media and facilities.

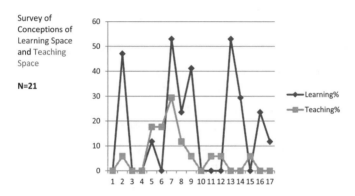

Table 3: Conceptions of Learning Spaces CLTS Framework.

With respect to teaching space, teachers' conceptions peaked at the taxa relating to campus physical affordances, and to the teacher's personal physical context. These reflect the classroom and campus-based space use that teachers operate within. Smaller peaks refer to the teacher's personal technical context (computers, network, etc.), and the campus technical affordances which relate to exactly the same items both on and off campus and spanning on-campus and online teaching requirements.

Observations from this comparison are that most teachers believed that teaching spaces and learning spaces were quite different conceptually. They placed a high significance on students' personal and technical contexts as well as their socio-cultural contexts in what constitutes a learning space. Perhaps the most important observation is differences in what teachers' conceive a learning space is, and what is revealed through their observed use of the environment. This is most apparent around the elevated significance placed on the campus virtual affordances (LMS) and reduction of emphasis on campus technical affordances as important for constructing learning spaces.

Open Coding Using Thematic Analysis

Thematic analysis of text was undertaken separately from observers' notes for each discipline group and from the conceptions survey responses. From the observation notes the constructs or expressions formed as specific verb statements relating to 'use' were recorded and entered into a spreadsheet to derive a crude list of twenty-nine constructs that applied across the discipline areas. For each discipline area, the list was sorted on descending frequency of occurrence with those constructs not appearing for that discipline area relegated to the bottom of each list. A similar treatment was given to the aggregate data for the entire academic population to get a university wide view of the outcomes. The top 5 codes for each academic group appear in Table 4. Separately, a thematic analysis of text, using the same process, was constructed from the surveys of teachers' conceptions of learning space and teaching space. As themes relating to 'use' and to conception subject are quite different so the constructs in each list are distinct.

Group	Construct	Physical Sciences	Health Sciences	Business	Social Sciences	University
1	PowerPoint / Slide-ware	✓	✓	✓	✓	✓
2	AV presentation /media use	✓	✓	✓	✓	✓
3	Students engaged / on-task		✓	✓	✓	✓
4	Teacher movement around room	✓			✓	✓
5	Appropriate lighting		✓			✓

Table 4: Top 5 Open Codes Relating to Observed Use of Learning Spaces.

It is apparent from the uniform observations of use of slide-ware, audio-visual presentations and media that the affordances of the technical aspects of the teaching space play a large part in the pedagogic choices of teachers in the teaching space. At the university where this study was undertaken there is uniform outfitting of every teaching space with the same technical affordances. Observed student engagement with learning activities suggests that the activities were mostly designed to suit the affordances of the learning spaces. For Physical Sciences, observed student engagement was just beyond the top 5 and may reflect a distribution of different learning activities amongst spaces that afford different levels of engagement such as laboratories and lecture halls. Teacher movement around the learning environment is afforded in larger spaces by the use of technologies such as radio microphones, laser pointers, and slide advance mechanisms which are important in the case of lecture recording requirements. In smaller environments, the affordances of the physical layout enable more frequent interaction between teacher and individual students. Each of these factors relating to teacher movement also features in the open codes.

Of interest are the particular codes that appear just beyond the shared codes for each group as these arguably represent the distinguishing features of space use for each discipline. For the physical sciences the application and qualities of technology in the learning environment played a prominent part in observed use. These codes included use of the "visualiser" allowing zooming in on documents; quality and nature of text in presentations; and, use of laser pointer and slide advance mechanism. In health sciences the focus of observations was on work-shopping and group work, interactions with and between students, ensuring appropriate lighting, and use of printed handouts to assist learning. Observations in business classes also highlighted a focus on interaction with and between students, but with a weighting of attention on the teacher's use of materials and aids, the whiteboard, computer, and access to the virtual learning environment as embodied by the learning management system (LMS). In social sciences there was shared focus between teachers' and students' uses of materials and aids and with a concentration on interactions with and between students.

Quite revealing of discipline specific teachers' socio-cultural contexts are particular uses of the learning environments that do not get observed at all in each discipline area. In physical sciences there is no observed inter-action with and between students; no engagement with physical space itself, and no use of students as active part of the learning experience. Given the inward focus of many proponents in this discipline area such an observation may not be unexpected. Observations in health sciences also did not mention use of physical space or active use of students, but of particular note was that there was no observed teacher use of tech-nology or equipment in the learning environment. As much health science learning takes place in clinical settings then it may be reasonable to assume that these sorts of activities might be observed there rather than on campus where most observations have taken place. Teachers in the business disciplines were not observed to have made much use of students, space, properties or demonstration in their use of the learning environment. In social sciences as a contrast, there was a noted lack of observed use of technical equipment and engagement of students with the virtual learning environment.

Open coding of responses of teachers to the survey capturing their conceptions of learning space and teaching space reveal interesting corre-lation with the observed use of the learning environment as captured by the CLTS closed coding of the same survey. Teachers' conceptions of learning space and teaching space share the codes: 'virtual environments' and 'physical space' as the top two responses in each category. Referring to the closed codes for observed use of space, these correspond to the observed use of campus physical affordances and virtual affordances.

As before, it is the popular responses just outside of the common areas that distinguish more clearly the differences in teachers' conceptions of the two forms of space. In terms of learning space, teachers see student use of information technologies, space and opportunities for exploration, interaction and collaboration, as well as space that extends beyond the classroom. By comparison, teaching space reflects opportunities for lead-ership of learning through expert delivery, mentoring and guidance; as well as creation of emotional and intellectual spaces in which to engage students.

What are teachers' understandings of how learning spaces may best be used to enhance student learning and engagement with learning?

Open and closed coding of teachers' conceptions of learning space indicate that they see important uses of space in influencing learning as being: academic interaction and stimulation between teachers and students; campus physical affordances; campus technical affordances, campus virtual affordances, student's personal technical context, student's personal physical context, and student-student interaction context (see Table 3). Each of the discipline groups provide learning experiences within their allocated space such that they assist student attainment of the particular learning outcomes required by the organisation, profession and community. Thematic analyses of notes on observed teaching suggest that in physical sciences this appears to involve a greater utilisation of technical aids to learning. In health sciences this is reflected in the enhanced use of interactive learning and group learning activities. In business a focus is on use of space for teacher-led learning activities that demonstrate and relate professional expertise. In social sciences there is more of a sharing in use of space between students and teacher for particular learning activities.

How effectively do observed teachers use the available features of the physical and technical context in classroom teaching?

Thematic analysis of observers' notes provided clear indications that technical affordances of the learning environment were a particular focus in each discipline. Closed coding using CLTS framework also indicated the physical affordances of the campus were an important part of the observed use of the environment. In each observed lesson observers were required to record levels of evidence supporting effective use of the learning environment and learning materials and aids. It is apparent that in the social sciences there is enhanced effectiveness of use of the learning environment, materials and aids. This was most noticeable within its sub-group of music and fine arts. Observers' notes have indicated that in these areas where many of the learning outcomes are in the psychomotor domain

(Ferris & Aziz, 2005) there is an enhanced engagement of students with activities that purposefully make use of space and materials.

In an engagement 'enabled' environment do teachers adopt more engaging activities that utilise the features of the environment?

The general answer to this question is 'yes' however it is challenging to discern this from the observation data itself. As related above, each formal learning space in the university is uniformly enabled with computer and audio-visual equipment including access to the Internet. Thematic analyses of observers' notes on use of learning space indicate a similarly uniform focus on the use of these features. This suggests that pedagogy is being moderated by the features of the learning space in this case. As suggested by Holtham (this volume) such uniformity acts to stymie the evolution of learning spaces. Access to activity-specific learning environments is timetabled in order to provide engagement with discipline relevant equipment. While adding to the variety of activities each space is designed to focus pedagogy on the features of that space. In physical sciences teaching within specialist wet laboratories, engineering and computing laboratories ensures that activities are aligned with the particular features of those spaces. Similarly, health sciences have problem-based learning, clinical learning, and placements in work integrated learning settings. Business make good use of small spaces for group based tutorial and workshop activities that are highly engaging with the actors being the applicable feature of the learning environment. Social sciences and in particular the Arts involving education, music, fine art, and drama all concentrate on use of the space itself rather than the features that exist in the space.

In less "enabled" environments how do teachers moderate their pedagogic approach and activities?

The uniform outfitting of every teaching space with the same technical affordances seems to be the key moderator of pedagogic approach. Where classes can be timetabled in a range of different locations it is apparent that many teachers design their teaching and learning activities with the expectations of the given minimum of common features. Teachers engaging in online delivery place similar expectations in terms of affordances of the teacher's physical and technical context whether personal or on campus; and students personal physical, technical, and virtual affordances. What become interesting are the differences in approach that are utilised given different affordances of particular physical spaces. For example, flat teaching spaces are good for group activities where tiered lecture halls are not. Tiered halls are excellent for performances and demonstrations where flat spaces often are not. What is noticed within the observed classes in the social sciences is that lesson design and preparation often involves the use of properties that are brought by the teacher or students to create an engaging learning experience that makes use of the space. Many physical sciences see teachers focus on theory and content dissemination in the tiered lecture halls informing related activities in more 'enabled' spaces to come.

Limitations and Future Work

There are inherent limitations in this study such that it is confined to a single organisation, albeit cross-disciplinary, but which shares the same organisational settings and uniform provision of features in learning spaces. Cross institutional studies would provide a clearer relationship between teachers' use of space and the standard of provisions for teaching and learning within that space. Student attendance patterns and require-ment for employment in order to meet fees and living expenses has meant an institution wide move to enable the delivery of online courses. Supporting this are a range of new features in the LMS, with which both staff and students must become familiar. As these changes progress, it will be interesting to see if the new affordances provide new limits on the use of virtual learning space.

Since organised peer observation of teaching has only been in exist-ence for a few years at Griffith University and in that time has only involved around 10% of the academic population. It is reasonable to say that participants in this study are all part of this minority group and so their pedagogic skills and knowledge may be distinct from those of the majority. As academic development opportunities through peer obser-vations within the organisation become linked to performance reviews, and as evidence it collects becomes an expectation of promotion and teaching award applications, then a broader range of observations of use and conceptions of learning space and teaching space may provide a more balanced organisational view.

A possible aspect that moderates teachers' uses of learning space extends from the expectations and learning cultures of students. To a large extent these are perpetuated by the teachers themselves. In line with Knight & Trowler (2000) teachers often resist adopting practices that do not fit within the accepted existing discipline repertoire. In a world where student evaluations are still an important discriminator of teaching quality for the organisation then there is little impetus to take risks by confronting student expectations. An exploration of development of discipline teaching practices beyond the historical and conservative starting with first year cohorts and course conveners may provide new understanding. This concept of academics' socio-cultural change is explored further by Pavlechko and Jacobi (in this volume).

Reader Debrief

In this chapter a study of perceptions and conceptions of teaching and learning spaces in higher education is described. A framework – Contexts of Learning and Teaching Space (CLTS) describes a system that supports the creation of learning spaces. It provides codes that are used to categorise the ways that teachers are observed to use learning environments and also their conceptions of what learning spaces and teaching space are. It was found that most teachers beyond the social sciences moderated their use of space by designing their learning and teaching activities to use the institution supplied generic features. Within discipline areas, distinctive difference in the observed use of space emerged with physical sciences favouring technology, health sciences engaging with group activities and interactions, business leaning towards teacher activity within the space, and social sciences featuring optimal use of spaces and students with a balanced blend of engagement of teachers and students with the features of the learning environment and associated materials and aids. It is suggested from this study that given a range of features within the teaching and learning spaces and training in order to effectively use them that most teachers will design and execute activities to take advantage of them as appropriate to their disciplinary context.

About the Authors

Steve Drew is Director Learning & Teaching in the Griffith Sciences Executive, Griffith University, Australia. He can be contacted at this e-mail: s.drew@griffith.edu.au

Christopher Klopper is Director Postgraduate Studies and Higher Degree Research in the School of Education and Professional Studies, Griffith University, Australia. He can be contacted at this e-mail: c.klopper@griffith.edu.au

Promoting Student Reflection through Considerate Design of a Virtual Learning Space

Kayoko Enomoto and Richard Warner

Introduction

This chapter contributes to the anthology on learning space design in higher education by informing the design and implementation of educational blogging to create a successful virtual learning space for promoting student reflection. We present a study which examines the use of blogs as a virtual learning space, where both discipline-specific skills and reflection skills were double tasked and developed in the students' blogging activities. We broaden our definition of learning space beyond traditional notions of lecture theatres, tutorial rooms and library. We share the view that a learning space encompasses *"the full range of places in which learning occurs, from real to virtual, from classroom to chatroom"* (Brown, 2005:12.4). Such a definition is indicative of a growing realisation, which we share, that most learning activities occur outside the confines of the classroom (Milne, 2006:11.7). Reading this chapter, you will:

1. learn more about which scaffolding measures are required to best exploit blogging as a medium for promoting students' reflection, as well as developing their discipline-specific skills;

2. gain insight into a variety of ways in which blogging activities relate to students' learning outcomes; and

3. learn which design considerations are important when the virtual learning space designed for blogging is seen as a community of

practice, which benefits students' engagement and their learning outcomes.

Cultivating student reflection skills is central to realising espoused graduate attributes in today's Australian universities. Dewey (1933), in his landmark study on the notion of reflection, noted that whilst thinking is not something we can learn or be taught, we can improve our thinking through reflective processes – which he compares to critical analyses of the self. Yet, in reality, one primary challenge *per se* in higher education is getting undergraduate students to reflect and to understand the value of exercising and incorporating reflection into their learning processes (Enomoto & Warner, 2013; Rowley, this volume). For example, those who issue vague instructions for a 'reflection assignment', such as *"Please reflect on what you learned in this project"* are liable to face student responses such as *"I learned a lot from this project!"*, which evidence little by way of reflection (Enomoto & Warner, 2013:188). To tackle this challenge, we consider it crucial to design a learning space which hooks into the curiosity of the students so that they naturally engage in reflection in their learning.

Integral to the development of more informal out-of-classroom learning spaces has been the emergence of Web 2.0 enabled participatory virtual learning spaces such as the blog. A blog is an online posting of personal experiences, thoughts and opinions, and blog readers can write their comment under any blog post that they read. Thus, if well designed and appropriately implemented, a blog can serve as an effective learning space for sharing knowledge and co-constructing content. Such Web 2.0 participatory technologies have become powerful drivers for transforming both delivery of content and where and how that content can be accessed and acted upon, thus creating new learning spaces in today's higher education.

Through this chapter, we explore what scaffolding measures are required to best exploit blogging as a medium for promoting reflection, as well as developing discipline-specific skills. Scaffolding as a concept derives originally from Vygotskian socio-cultural theory based on childhood learning (Vygotsky, 1978). This concept has been increasingly applied to educational contexts as a teaching strategy, which can be defined as the *"role of teachers and others in supporting the learner's development and providing support structures to get to that next stage or level"* (Raymond, 2000:176). Hence, in this chapter, we regard scaffolds as *"the support that a teacher can give learners so that they can work at a much higher level than on their own"* (Rose et al., 2003: 42).

The study presented in this chapter was undertaken in a research-intensive Australian university context – a 3rd year undergraduate course in Japanese delivered in a blended mode using a *Blackboard* platform. The findings of our study subsequently led to design considerations for developing both discipline-specific skills and reflection skills in a virtual learning space. We conclude this chapter by proposing research-based recommendations as key points for designing and implementing successful reflective blogging activities which can be applied to other disciplines and courses. However, before presenting our study, we begin by discussing the concept of what is meant by a learning space.

Conceptualising Learning Spaces

One of the roles of any learning space is to provide a learning environment conducive to the facilitation of learner success. Yet, in order to create such an environment, it is a prerequisite that the concept of what actually constitutes a learning space be interrogated. A recent definition of learning spaces as *"locations, physical or virtual, where learning happens"* (McPhee, 2009:1), typifies the contemporary shift in thinking about what characterises early twenty-first century learning spaces. Traditionally, the concept of the learning space in a higher education context has focused on the formal and the physical (Stupans, this volume). This includes the lecture theatre or the tutorial room, laboratory or library, all of which, as Johnson and Lomas (2005) note, are normally subject to parameters which determine their use. This can include seating arrangement, availability of room facilities, restricted opening hours and *"pre-determined learning activity patterns such as lectures and discussions"* (Johnson & Lomas, 2005:16), which carry with them a sense of the on-campus culture – the places and formats in which education occurs (Lomas & Oblinger, 2006).

Yet, such a limited learning space scenario is being challenged by *"the Net Generation (Net Gen)"* students (Brown, 2005), who now have the ability, through the ubiquity of digital, portable devices, to go beyond the classroom and turn any space into a learning space – where these students can often have a greater sense of confidence and control than in learning spaces in previous centuries. Therefore, it is imperative that higher education firstly recognises the increasing digital literacies of these Net Gen students. Secondly, such recognition needs to be demonstrated through the provision and support of not just physical but also virtual learning spaces (Johnson & Lomas, 2005) where these *"digital natives"* (Prensky, 2001) have the potential to inhabit. These virtual learning spaces form part of what have been termed *"Next Generation Learning Spaces (NGLS)"* (Wilson & Randall, 2012:1), whereby the concept of the classroom extends into a blend of physical and virtual learning spaces.

Theoretical Framework for Creating a Reflective Learning Space

We frame our approach to using a blog as a reflective learning space within Lave and Wenger's situated learning theory (1991; 1998), which argues that learning is situated and that it necessitates participatory engagement within a community of practice (CoP). We subsequently discuss the concept of situated cognition, a requisite for situated learning, as being central to the creation of a successful CoP within a blog learning space. We propose that, if designed successfully, a blog can bring about a CoP that affords not only a learning space for scaffolded individualised reflection, but also the offering of opportunities for the students to engage in the practices of their community (Picard *et al.*, 2011). Such a CoP allows the students both to practise reflection in their blog writing and to give input and feedback (as blog comments) on the reflections of other members of the community. If successful, this can also lead to and foster vicarious learning, a core facet of Bandura's social learning theory (1977; 1994). Vicarious learning happens when a person changes their own behaviour through observing and modelling the behaviours of others, as Bandura (1994:66) notes: *"Virtually all behavioural, cognitive, and affective learning from direct experience can be achieved vicariously [second-hand] by observing people's actions and the consequences for them."*

Therefore, this chapter also addresses how such a blog-based learning space can promote and nurture vicarious learning through observing and modelling other students' language use and reflective practices. However, before outlining our approach to blog design and implementation, we discuss further the concept of learning spaces, prior to providing the rationale behind our decision to explore the use of a blog as a reflective learning space in a higher education context.

A Learning Space for Utilising Students' Existing Skill Bases and Realities

Successful incorporation and adoption of any NGLS requires a radical pedagogical shift, on the part of both teacher and students, as not only are such spaces more student-centred than the more static, formal learning spaces of prior years, they are also student-driven to varying degrees. This is because Net Gen students bring with them technological 'savviness' and skill bases as digital natives, which they could quite reasonably expect to put to use in their university studies, both within and beyond the classroom – they are 'bringing more to the table'.

Yet, herein lies the challenge of promoting pedagogical interactions within these new virtual learning spaces, to ensure that students are, indeed, 'actively' engaged in 'learning' in an environment within which they might previously only have been operating in their social (as opposed to academic) lives. Furthermore, to engage fully with these students, it is also crucial to create NGLS that effectively incorporate 'virtual, yet real' interactions – a world with which these students are already familiar (see Lange & Smith in this volume). Such virtual learning spaces can bring about learning through experiences that are relevant to students' everyday realities.

One example of such a learning space is the blog, widely used in diverse higher education contexts for over a decade (Deng & Yuen, 2009); it allows students to (co-)construct content rather than just consume it. Blogs are "*distributed, aggregated, open and independent*" (Farmer & Bartlett-Bragg, 2005:197) tools that can empower both teachers and students to be more reflective and connected practitioners. Although they have been used with varying degrees of success (Krause, 2004), there is increasing interest in pedagogically optimising the potential inherent in their versatility (Deng & Yuen, 2009) in establishing learning communities.

A Blog Learning Community that Promotes Reflection and Connectedness

The versatile nature of blogs rests in their potential for use as tools for facilitating reflection in a learning community. Krause (2004) commented on the success of one of his student blogs, relating to critical student analyses of style manuals, in getting students to scratch below the surface to reflect upon the different authors' perceptions of style. Crucial to his study was the active construction of communicative content by the blog writers themselves and the blog community structures, allowing other community members to comment on each other's blog posts. Such feedback by and to student bloggers, in a designated blogging community, can help foster deeper thinking and learning development (Deng & Yuen, 2009; Ray & Coulter, 2008). As Krause (2004) observes, there is authenticity in terms of fitness for purpose in such actions, creating a sense of community within the learning space, where those blog writers can create, reflect and comment upon blogs relevant to their mutual interests.

Central to the success of a blog learning space is a sense of 'connectedness' in that its effectiveness is dependent on its ability to "*facilitate connections*" (Lomas & Oblinger, 2006:106). If students feel connected, then the learning space can both promulgate such connections and help develop a sense of connectedness and belongingness (Thomas, 2012). The culture of Web 2.0 enabled connectedness is part of the everyday world where the majority of our students inhabit. Such digital natives are accustomed to actively co-constructing communicative content via social media such as *Facebook* and *Twitter*. This forms part of their situated cognition (Brown *et al.*, 1989), generating the culture of learning, without which situated learning cannot take place.

Utilising Students' Situated Cognition in a Blog Learning Space

Core to the aforementioned situated learning theory (Lave & Wenger, 1991) is situated cognition, whereby "*knowledge is situated, being in part a product of the activity, context, and culture in which it is developed and used*" (Brown *et al.*, 1989:32). In this respect, the use of a blog enables students to develop knowledge and understanding in a culture where they are already situated in real life. Thus, to engage with these students and to design a learning space that builds upon their own existing social and cultural space, we need to incorporate media that allow for such social and cultural engagement into a space of situated cognition – a requisite backdrop to the development of a shared CoP.

A CoP is understood as *"groups of people who share a concern or a passion for something they do and learn how to do it better as they interact regularly"* (Wenger, 2006:1). Lave and Wenger (1991; 1998) proposed that the characteristics of a CoP are threefold: First, there must be a shared domain of interest; in the context of our study, met by being learners of Japanese, undertaking a specific course. Second, is the sense of community where community members are mutually supportive, allowing them to learn from each other. In this study, building such a sense of community is facilitated by scaffolds that encourage students to comment upon each other's blogs. Third is practice; members must be practitioners with the tools to do the job. In this study, practice is manifest in the students' participatory engagement in blogging activities. Importantly, core to our contention that blog-based learning space can be characterised as a CoP, is the integration of the aforementioned concept of vicarious learning. This is manifested through the continuous 'lurking' aspect of observing other users' blog posts, comments and their interactions – both before and after posting their own blogs and commenting on other students' blogs. Such lurking behaviour is one way in which the potential of a blog as an enhancer for connectedness within a CoP can be realised.

Issues in Exploiting the Potential of Blogs

The literature on educational blogging is characterised by cases of blogs that fail to address the potential of a blog as a learning space. Typical areas where the promise of blogs remains unfulfilled lie in focus deficiencies (Brownstein & Klein, 2006), the haphazard nature of contributions (Krause, 2004), ill-defined purpose (Efimova, 2003), lack of rationale (Kerawalla et al., 2008) and insufficient structure, particularly in relation to reflective blogging (West et al., 2006).

Of particular importance in the potential of blogging for double tasking generic reflection skills and discipline-specific language skills, is the provision of sufficient and appropriate scaffolds. Brush and Saye

(2002) refer to hard scaffolds as planned support structures embedded in advance by a teacher, foreseeing characteristic student difficulties with specific activities. In contrast, soft scaffolds are teacher or peer support made in response to situation-specific student needs during the learning process (Brush & Saye, 2002). Indeed, the above-mentioned literature on educational blogging indicates that it is the lack of these types of appropriate scaffolds that largely results in a loss of the 'buy in' potential of a blog as a learning space. Therefore, requisite scaffolds for successful reflective blogging activities will be considered in the design of our study as outlined below.

The Study

This study employs a mixed mode (quantitative and qualitative) research paradigm. We explore the use of blogs as a learning space for developing both discipline-specific language skills and reflection skills in the context of Japanese 3A (n=49), the 3rd year undergraduate Japanese course at the University of Adelaide. This course was taught by one course coordinator and three tutors in a blended mode; 75% face-to-face and 25% online learning through a *Blackboard* platform – MyUni, using its blog facility as the students' learning space. In this advanced-level language course, 80% of the cohort was studying for various non-Arts degrees across the University. Using MyUni, we created a 'class blog site' where the students were required to participate in the following three blogging activities, all in Japanese:

1. writing and posting their reflective blogs as a blog author;

2. commenting on other students' blogs as a blog reader;

3. replying to received comments from their classmates and tutors.

Whilst activities 1) and 2) were to be assessed, activity 3) was not. Table 1 shows the percentages of each blogging activity for which each student was assessed, adding up to 22% of the entire course assessment. Each student in the course was randomly assigned a group of four 'blog buddies'. We asked the students to comment on their four buddies' blog posts to receive a 1% participation mark, whilst they were also free to comment on any other classmates' blogs once they had finished commenting upon their blog buddies'. This ensured that all students received peer input and/or feedback on their reflections in their blogs.

	Posting	Commenting
Blog 1	3%	1% as participation
Blog 2	3%	1% as participation
Blog 3	3%	1% as participation
Video Blog	9%	1% as participation
Total	**18%**	**4%**

Table 1: Assessed Blogging Activities Percentages.

Objectives of the Study

In this study, we make two specific investigations into the effectiveness of our design and implementation of these blogging activities as our study objectives:

i) to examine learning outcomes in terms of skills development – whether language skills scores or reflection skills scores or both can be improved within this blog learning space;

ii) to examine learning processes in order to inform design considerations for (language and reflection) skills development – to ascertain what kind of categories of description emerge from the students' comments.

Constructing Blog Themes to Facilitate Reflection

To facilitate student reflection in their blogging processes, it was essential at the beginning of the course, to explain and make very clear to the students, the rationale, objectives and expectations of this blog assignment both orally and in writing. Similarly, it was crucial to construct each blog theme in such a way that it naturally prompts the students to reflect in the process of producing each blog. Table 2 presents the overarching themes for the three (written) blogs and the final video blog. When releasing each blog theme, we presented the following two scaffolds with it: 1) marking criteria, including language and reflection skills criteria, in the form of a rubric (Figure 1); and 2) starter questions to help prompt their reflections. For example, for the Blog 2 theme, such starter questions were:

- do I enjoy some types of class activities more than others? Do I have examples?

- do I feel nervous or lack confidence with some types of activities? Why do I feel so?

- when I study on my own, what methods do I use?

- when I study on my own, do I explore content beyond the course? Why or why not?

- how do I think this kind of information about my own learning style can help me?

- can I better improve my study habits, knowing my learning styles?

Notably, we constructed a reflection-facilitating theme for each blog, so that the three themes demanded an increasing degree of reflective complexity from Blog 1 to Blog 3.

	Theme
Blog 1	Why I am learning Japanese: What do I want to get out of the learning experience?
Blog 2	My learning style: How can I take advantage of my learning preferences in my study strategies? (based on the VARK Questionnaire on learning styles: <http://www.vark-learn.com/english/page.asp?p=questionnaire>
Blog 3	My life style: What makes me happy? (based on a video clip "The Economics of Happiness"): <http://www.youtube.com/watch?v=iqjvmV4qOe0>
Video Blog	Blogging in Japanese: Any benefits I have gained and any challenges I have faced?

Table 2: Blog Themes.

Category 1: Language Skills (0-5)				Score:	/10
1. Length (min of 450 – max of 600 characters) & Japanese typing skills including use of Kanji (1)	Appropriate in length & shows very accurate word processing skills, including use of Kanji (1)	Too short/too long in length OR shows several typing errors, including use of Kanji (0.5)	Too short/too long in length AND repeatedly shows typing errors including use of Kanji (0)		
2. Use of grammar & vocabulary (2)	Use of grammar and vocabulary is excellent (2)	Use of grammar and vocabulary is good (1.5)	Use of grammar and vocabulary is fair (1)	Use of grammar and vocabulary is poor (0.5)	Use of grammar and vocabulary is extremely poor (0)
3. Content (organisation & coherence for effective communication, eye-catching blog entry title) (2)	Content is very well structured for effective communication with blog readers; title is very creative and original (2)	Content is well structured for good communication with blog readers; title is sufficiently creative and original (1.5)	Content has limited structure for some communication with blog readers; title is fairly creative and original (1)	Content is not well structured resulting in poor communication with blog readers; title is not very creative and original (0.5)	Content has no organization and coherence resulting in extremely poor communication with blog readers; title is not at all creative and original (0)

Category 2: Reflection Skills (0-4)	1. Use of reflection to evaluate and analyse own learning styles for deciding appropriate study strategies (2)	Very good evidence of reflection undertaken to evaluate/analyse own learning styles for deciding appropriate study strategies, resulting in excellent descriptions of study strategies (2)	Good evidence of reflection undertaken to evaluate/analyse own learning styles for deciding appropriate study strategies, resulting in good descriptions of study strategies (1.5)	Some evidence of reflection undertaken to evaluate/analyse own learning styles for deciding appropriate study strategies, resulting in some descriptions of study strategies (1)	Little evidence of reflection undertaken to evaluate/analyse own learning styles for deciding appropriate study strategies, resulting in poor descriptions of study strategies (0.5)	No evidence of reflection undertaken to evaluate/analyse own learning styles for deciding appropriate study strategies, resulting in no descriptions of study strategies (0)
	2. Use of reflection for goal-setting and task-setting informed by own learning-styles (2)	Very good evidence of realistic goal setting and task setting (2)	Good evidence of goal setting and task setting (1.5)	Some evidence of goal setting and task setting (1)	Little evidence of goal setting and task setting (0.5)	No evidence of goal setting and task setting (0)
Category 3: Research Skills (0-1)	1. Use of online sources to find information on the types of learning styles (1)	Excellent evidence of using online sources to find information on the types of learning styles (1)	Good evidence of using online sources to find information on the types of learning styles (0.5)	Little or no evidence of using online sources to find information on the types of learning styles (0)		

Figure 1: Example Rubric for Blog 2 Theme.

Embedding Scaffolds

The students were required to engage independently in regular online blogging activities outside the scheduled class times. To make 'learning through blogging' possible within this learning space, we took into consideration the aforementioned past research findings on educational blogging in our design and implementation of blogging activities (e.g. Krause, 2004; Brownstein & Klein, 2006; Kerawalla, *et al.*, 2008). Table 3 shows where and how we systematically embedded scaffolds throughout the 12-week semester.

Week	Scaffolds
1	Blog Assignment Orientation: Teacher
	+ gives Practical Session (1) on how to post blogs and comments, using MyUni LMS, and also provides MyUni blog instruction sheet.
	+ hands out Blogging in Japanese assignment notice and explains rationale, objectives, expectations and marking criteria with emphasis on both language and reflection skills criteria.
	+ explains the system of 'blog buddies' with its rationale.
	+ highlights the importance of adhering to the set due dates for posting blogs and comments.
	+ emails later this same assignment notice inviting questions about expectations and marking criteria, etc.
2	Release of Blog 1 theme: Teacher
	+ explains the content requirement of Blog 1 theme and emphasises its reflective nature as part of the requirement, presenting Blog 1 marking rubric.
	+ gives Practical Session (2):
	- Students given useful Japanese vocabulary and sentence structures for blog writing.
	- Students given hands-on practise of using online language tools.
	- Students read and comment on teacher's blog that contains YouTube video clip "What is a blog?": <http://www.youtube.com/watch?v=NN2I1pWXjXI>
	- Each class discusses "what constitutes a good blog?"
	- Each class discusses effective use of emoticons, pictures, video clips, etc. to enhance blog content.
	+ Follows up and reminds students of marking criteria, emphasising the reflection skills criteria via email.

3	Blog 1 entry due
	Teacher emails advice on the mindful use of online 'translation' tools.
	Teacher emails effective use of Kanji characters for controlling blog length.
4	Blog 1 commenting due
5	Blog 1 Feedback
	◆ Students receive their Blog 1 scores on a marking rubric with teacher feedback comments.
	◆ Teacher gives class feedback targeting common issues both orally in class and in writing via email.
	◆ Consultations offered for individual students or as a group on a set date.
	Release of Blog 2 theme: Teacher
	◆ explains the content requirement of Blog 2 theme with its marking rubric and starter questions to prompt reflection.
	◆ makes explicit and reinforces expectation, objectives and rationale for the blog assignment both orally and via email at the time of blog 2 theme release.
	◆ provides a list of useful Japanese vocabulary and sentence structures specifically for writing Blog 2 in her blog space.
	◆ shows a list of excerpts from several students' Blog 1 writing as useful reflective writing examples, which can be utilised in Blog 2 writing.
	◆ presents teacher's exemplar blog on her learning style for students to read and comment on.
6	Blog 2 entry due
Break	Blog 2 commenting due
7	Blog 2 Feedback
	◆ Students receive their Blog 2 scores on a marking rubric with teacher feedback comments.
	◆ Teacher posts a video blog, containing her video feedback on Blog 2.
	◆ Consultations offered for individual students or as a group on a set date.
	Release of Blog 3 theme: Teacher
	◆ explains the content requirement of Blog 3 theme with its marking rubric and starter questions to prompt reflection.
	◆ provides a list of useful Japanese vocabulary and sentences structures specifically for writing Blog 3 in her blog space.

8	Release of Video Blog theme
	Students view teacher's Video Blog as an example.
	Students discuss what hardware/devices they could use to record their video and teach each other how they can upload and link their video blog on MyUni.
9	Blog 3 entry due
10	Blog 3 commenting due
11	Video Blog due
12	Video Blog commenting due

Table 3: Provision of Scaffolds (note form) for Blogging Activities Embedded in the 3rd year Japanese curriculum.

Quantitative Data Collection and Analyses

Quantitative data were obtained from the 49 students' Blogs 1-3 in two skills areas: language skills area (scores ranging from 0 to 5) and reflection skills area (scores ranging from 0 to 4). Each student's blog (49 students x 3 blogs) were double marked using a marking rubric (Figure 1), which was also subsequently utilised for giving each student feedback. Where two markers could not agree on a score, a third marker was involved for moderation. Table 4 summarises overall mean scores of language and reflection skills scores that the students obtained in Blogs 1-3. Blog 3 showed the highest scores in both language and reflection skills areas, while Blog 1 showed the lowest in both areas.

Skills Areas		Blog 1 (n=49)	Blog 2 (n=49)	Blog 3 (n=49)
Language Skills Scores (0-5)	Mean	3.418	3.714	3.990
	(SD)	(0.888)	(0.969)	(0.923)
Reflection Skills Scores (0-4)	Mean	2.490	3.224	3.255
	(SD)	(0.759)	(0.756)	(0.763)

Table 4: Overall Mean Language Skills and Reflection Skills Scores.

The results from a one-way repeated measures ANOVA revealed the highly significant main effect of Blog Number in language skills scores (p< .001) and also in reflection scores (p< .001). Following these highly significant ANOVA results, *post hoc* multiple comparisons were conducted on the Blog Number effect, using Ryan's method. This was done in order to pinpoint further which two sets of blog scores differed significantly.

Firstly, in the language skills area, the results revealed that Blog 3 scores were significantly higher than those of both Blog 1 (p< .001) and Blog 2 (p< .05), whilst Blog 2 scores were also significantly higher than Blog 1 scores (p< .05). This suggests that the students' language skills scores increased significantly from Blog 1 to Blog 2 and then from Blog 2 to Blog 3. Secondly, in the reflection skills area, the results revealed that both Blog 2 and Blog 3 scores were significantly higher than Blog 1 scores (p< .001), whilst showing no significant difference (p=0.798) between Blog 2 and Blog 3 scores. This indicates that the students' reflections skills scores increased significantly from Blog 1 to Blog 2, but not from Blog 2 to Blog 3. These results were not surprising, given the mean scores of Blog 2 and Blog 3 were similar and equally high (Table 4).

This can be further interpreted as suggesting that the students' reflection skills scores improved significantly in Blogs 2 and 3, because they were able to understand and use the rubric-guided, reflection skills feedback they received on their Blog 1, in their Blogs 2 and 3 writing. As seen in Table 3, it is important to note that we provided an additional hard scaffold for Blogs 2 and 3 themes that we did not provide for the Blog 1 theme. This was done because of the more complex nature of these two themes than that of Blog 1. For the Blog 2 theme, we posted more scaffolds: a list of useful vocabulary and phrases pertinent to learning styles, various reflective excerpts from several students' Blog 1 writing as student examples, and the teacher's own reflective blog on learning styles as an exemplar. For the Blog 3 theme, we also provided a list of relevant vocabulary and phrases relating to the theme. So, it is possible that these additional hard scaffolds helped the students see and understand what a reflective blog involves.

Qualitative Data Collection and Analyses

Qualitative data were collected from the students' reflective Video Blog. The theme of the Video Blog posted in Week 12, was: 'Blogging in Japanese: Any benefits I have gained and any challenges I have faced?'. On this topic, the students were asked to reflect upon their own learning to produce a video blog in Japanese (duration of 2-3 minutes). They then posted it on the class blog site, in order for their blog buddies and any other classmates to comment upon.

We transcribed and analysed the students' reflective commentaries extracted from their Video Blogs, adopting a phenomenographic approach to analyse such qualitative data. This approach focuses on the categories of description, emerging from a collective analysis of the breadth of understandings, experiences and perceptions (Åkerlind, 2005) held by this student group. We searched for the major themes expressed by the students, from which four qualitatively discrete description categories emerged to inform our design considerations for skills development, which we further discuss in the next section. In addition, we also utilised peer (written) comments posted upon these video blogs by other students, to further support the findings under these emergent categories. As all the video blog commentaries were originally made in Japanese by the students, all the excerpts we quote hereafter are translated into English by the first author.

In terms of language skills development, 37 out of 49 students commented that their Japanese language skills, particularly grammar and vocabulary, had developed through their blogging activities themselves and also through vicarious learning. A particular focus was on 'using the language' as opposed to studying or memorising it: *"I was able to use Japanese to find my weaknesses in Japanese"* (S8), *"I tried to use the kanji characters and vocabulary I have not learned [in the textbook] before"* (S40). Moreover, five of them further commented that they experienced using the Japanese language to gain new knowledge, rather than learning Japanese *per se*.

In relation to reflection skills development, evidence emerged from 34 out of 49 students' comments: *"Blogging made me think about myself"* (S23), *"Reflecting became easier as I wrote"* (S30), *"Blogging made me think of reasons for learning"* (S7). The following peer comments posted upon such video blogs also support this: *"I was anxious about reflection [at first], because I had never practised it before. But after writing the three blogs, my reflection skills have definitely improved"* (S5), *"For me, blogging was hard, but it helped me learn how to actually write meaningful sentences, using my reflections"* (S16), *"It was difficult to write reflective blogs at first. After writing Blog 1, I felt I learned a lot"* (S44).

To conclude, these qualitative findings on the students' skills development positively correlate with the aforementioned findings from our quantitative analyses that this blog learning space effectively developed both language skills and reflection skills, thus fulfilling our first study objective:

i)   to examine learning outcomes in terms of skills development – whether language skills scores or reflection skills scores or both can be improved within this blog learning space;

In addition to the evidence for such (language and reflection) skills development, a total of 20 students also remarked on their 'other' skills development through the blogging activities, such as IT skills, independent learning skills, communication skills and research skills. One student stated that they had gained *"independent learning using online tools"* (S15), whilst another student said that they were now able to *"read unknown kanji characters using new online tools"* (S41), which could enable them to read online Japanese sources pertinent to their own disciplines in the future. Another student alluded to his communication skills development, saying *"using reflection skills, I became good at expressing myself"* (S27). Finally, we also found ample evidence from 27 students, relating to their discovery of the transferability of the reflection skills that they gained through the blogging activities. Typical comments were *"reflection skills are useful for future jobs"* (S46) and *"I see the usefulness [of reflection skills] for my future studies"* (S2). As one student interestingly commented: *"I couldn't reflect [even] in English before, but now I can!"* (S32).

Design Considerations for Skills Development

Based on our phenomenographic analyses, four qualitatively discrete categories of comments emerged, with each category informing an important design consideration for realising both discipline-specific skills and reflection skills development in blog learning spaces (Figure 2).

Figure 2: Design considerations for skills development in blog learning spaces.

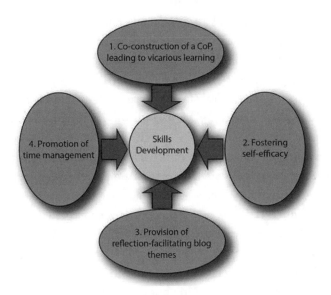

Design Consideration 1: Co-construction of a CoP, Leading to Vicarious Learning

The first design consideration that emerged from the vast majority of students' comments relates to the construction of a CoP. We found that 32 out of 49 students alluded to the connectedness made possible by the blog learning space: *"I found new friends with the same ideas and interests via blogging in Japanese"* (S40), *"Commenting was fun and made me think about others"* (S35), *"I understood the bloggers' personalities and felt connected through reading their blogs"* (S3). Such comments demonstrate that through these blogging activities, students developed a sense of connectedness and belonging, which is a requisite for the creation of a CoP. Indeed, that the students felt a sense of CoP is also demonstrated as evidenced by the following peer comments, posted upon these video blog commentaries: *"You gave me good and useful [feedback] comments on my blogs"* (S11), *"I have never commented on your blog, but I have to comment on your video blog, because it is so interesting"* (S10), *"I was so happy to find someone leaving a comment under my blog, particularly when they commented upon the content of my blog"* (S24).

Similarly, we also found evidence for vicarious learning. We found that 35 out of 49 students commented that reading others' blogs helped them learn new vocabulary, kanji characters and grammar: *"I was taught by others. I can't [just] write comments without reading [the blog]"* (S18), *"By reading others' [blogs], I understood grammar does not have to be perfect"* (S14), indicating 'lurking' behaviour was, indeed, taking place within the blog learning space, as several 'lurking' students said, *"reading different ideas under the same topic is fun"* (S40), *"I realised other students also have difficulties with kanji characters"* (S37). Thus, these students' comments strongly support the positive effect of vicarious learning within a CoP. Furthermore, these posted peer comments upon such video blogs confirm such vicarious learning: *"I also learned lots of grammar and vocabulary usages from you"* (S4), *"This semester, reading your blogs, I learned lots of new words and grammar points! Thank you!"* (S2).

We put the system of 'blog buddies' into place, in order to ensure that all students would receive peer input and feedback on their reflective blogs. It appears that this blog buddy system enabled the students to feel supported by each other, knowing that their buddies will definitely be reading their blogs and commenting upon them. As one student announced in his comment, *"We are the blog buddies!"* (S26), this facilitated a sense of connectedness in a CoP, resulting in vicarious learning.

Design Consideration 2: Fostering Self-efficacy

A second design consideration also emerged from the vast majority of comments. In relation to the blogging activities some 40 students expressed a sense of increased self-efficacy: *"I was not confident at first, but now I am"* (S25), *"I feel like I can write natural Japanese in the future"* (S15), *"I feel like a Japanese person"* (S20), *"My Japanese improved much more than expected!"* (S22). This is of particular importance, as those students with a greater sense of self-efficacy are more confident in their own abilities, thus being more predisposed to push themselves further with more complex tasks (Bandura, 1977).

Many students confided in their video blogs that, at the beginning, they were in fact very scared and also felt embarrassed to write a blog in Japanese to upload it to be read by others: *"At first, I didn't like it, but love it now!"* (S11), *"It was difficult and I was also afraid of making mistakes"* (S17).

Of particular interest within this category, was that some 25 students said they liked writing a reflective blog and felt that they actually 'learnt', whilst they were having fun. And, as a result of learning through enjoyment, they were now more motivated to learn than before experiencing blogging: "*Commenting in Japanese was fun*" (S24), "*Blogging was fun and good practice, better than other assignments, because it was motivating*" (S49), "*I want to challenge myself*" (S38). Similarly, the following peer comments made upon these video blogs support the increasing sense of self-efficacy: "*Now that I can write a blog in Japanese, I feel I could write an essay!*" (S20), "*When I started to write a blog, I felt so embarrassed. But I have now built up my confidence to use Japanese*" (S19).

Design Consideration 3: Provision of Reflection-facilitating Blog Themes

We found a somewhat unexpected category of commentaries in the students' video blogs as a third design consideration. Eight students specifically commented that the 3rd blog theme was the most interesting for them to reflect upon, and five students remarked that the 2nd blog theme on learning style was very useful for them to reflect upon. Furthermore, one student succinctly expressed, "*if the topics were not hard, it would be boring*" (S8), whilst another student said, "*the topics motivated me to think more*" (S49). Given that the 3rd blog theme demanded the most complex reflectivity on the part of the students, our choice of the three blog themes played an important role in facilitating student reflection in the blog learning space. Thus, the increasing complexity of the given themes seems crucial for developing reflection skills. However, there were also three students who only commented that the topics were too hard and serious in nature, instead of reflecting on their own learning.

Design Consideration 4: Promotion of Time Management

An interesting category of comments emerged, as a fourth design consideration, in relation to time management issues. Nine students' comments specifically referred to their poor time management, whilst another 11 students reported that their time management skills actually improved through the blogging activities: "*I used to run out of time, but as I wrote more blogs, I got better"* (S46), *"With the first blog, it took me one day, my last blog took me 2-3 hours"* (S20). Likewise, the following peer comments on the video blogs are congruent with these views: *"My biggest challenge was time management. I have to improve my time management"* (Student 6), *"My biggest problem was also time management. I could not usually post my blogs until the very last day"* (S13). It seems from these comments, that the students' learning experience within the blog learning space helped them become more aware of the significance of improving their time management skills in their studies.

To sum up, these findings from our study indicate that the above-mentioned four design considerations are important issues for the students, thus fulfilling our second objective:

ii) to examine learning processes in order to inform design considerations for (language and reflection) skills development – what kind of categories of description emerge from the students' comments?

Therefore, these considerations should be addressed in the design of a blog-based learning space, in order to bring about students' discipline-specific and reflection skills development.

Summary and Discussion

In this study, we examined a blog as a learning space for developing discipline-specific language skills and generic reflection skills in an HE context. We conducted two specific investigations into the effectiveness of our design and implementation of the blogging activities.

Firstly, our findings revealed that both language skills and reflection skills scores were significantly improved overall. These findings also point to the significant role played by the provided hard scaffolds, particularly, teacher exemplar and rubric based-feedback within this blog-based learning space. Secondly, our findings also revealed that our design and implementation of the blogging activities succeeded in creating a CoP, whereby the students' senses of connectedness and belonging were facilitated. This, in turn, increased the effectiveness of the blog as a learning space, leading to vicarious learning. Such vicarious learning provides a plausible explanation as to why a blog can offer an effective learning space where the students can learn from each other's language use (e.g.

grammar, vocabulary and communication conventions) and through the reflective content they write in a such a blog-based learning space.

In summary, this study shows that, when designed successfully, a blog can create a CoP that provides not only a learning space for developing reflection skills, but also opportunities for the students to benefit from vicarious learning, through observing and modelling other students' reflective practices. Moreover, these findings demonstrate the significance of systematically embedding sufficient and appropriate scaffolding measures for creating successful reflective learning spaces in higher education.

Conclusions

This chapter has explored the specific scaffolding measures required to exploit effectively blogging as a virtual learning space for developing reflection skills in a 3rd-year language course. Our approach to design and implementation was framed within the theory of situated learning (Lave & Wenger, 1991). We utilised students' existing skill bases and realities as Net Gen students, and therefore, their situated cognition to create a CoP. To do so, we embedded sufficient and appropriate scaffolds as the course developed.

In today's higher education, we face challenges in getting students to reflect in their learning process. This chapter has revisited educational blogging and demonstrated one effective way of designing and using a blog as a learning space for facilitating reflection. Our findings lead to the following key recommendations for designing and implementing a blog-based learning space for developing reflection skills:

+ make explicit the rationale, objectives, expectations and marking criteria for each blogging activity, to begin with and during the process of blogging activities;

+ construct a reflection-facilitating theme for each blog so that given themes demand an increasing degree of reflective complexity from the first blog to the last;

+ provide opportunities for students to read relevant and concrete examples of reflective blogs and 'starter questions' to prompt reflection;

+ design a marking rubric containing all marking criteria to support student writing processes and also use it to give feedback;

+ consider the amount, appropriateness and timeliness of hard scaffolds and be responsive in providing soft scaffolds as the course develops;

+ form a group of 'blog buddies' to comment on each other's blogs to ensure that all students receive peer input and feedback on their reflective blogs; and

+ set clear due time/date for each blog post and comments in advance.

The focus of this chapter is centred upon a blog as a virtual learning space for developing both second language and reflection skills with Net Gen students. However, these recommendations, we believe, are transferable and can be applied to other disciplines and courses to engage and enhance the learning experiences of similar digital natives.

Acknowledgements

This research project was supported by a University of Adelaide e-learning development grant. The authors wish to thank Dr Julia Miller and Dr Mariko Sakamoto for their insightful input, and Craig Penny, Miwako Takasawa, Maki Sugimoto and Kazuko Glass for their invaluable support in the implementation of blogging activities.

About the Authors

Kayoko Enomoto is a Senior Lecturer at the Centre for Asian Studies in the School of Social Sciences at the University of Adelaide, Australia. She can be contacted at this e-mail: kayoko.enomoto@adelaide.edu.au

Richard Warner is a Lecturer in the School of Education at the University of Adelaide, Australia. He can be contacted at this e-mail: richard.warner@adelaide.edu.au

Chapter Nine

The Perfect Storm; Education's Immediate Challenges

Lennie Scott-Webber

Introduction

This chapter contributes to the anthology on learning space design in higher education by focusing on the impact of the learning space on student success. I define the learning space as the formal learning environment, the classroom and the general spatial design. Dealing with the impact of learning space on student success, I also look at the historical, technological, and economic influences on learning space design, and draw on research insights from learning research and brain scientific theories, which enables me to connect the learner, the learning, and the learning space. In the chapter, I share a guiding framework, the Active Learning Ecosystem framework, which helps educators make qualified decisions about learning space design. Reading this chapter you will:

1. gain an awareness of the trends, influences and outdated business model gripping the ability to make changes in higher education relative to teaching and learning;

2. recognise the need to move from a teacher-centric setting to one of a learner-centric setting as articulated by research; and

3. become familiar with a framework proposed to guide holistic thinking for designing active learning environments and student success.

My reason for writing this chapter is that I sense a perfect storm is brewing. We are in a pivotal time. Historical influences (Scott-Webber, 2004), the rate of technological changes, economic reports, and evidence from multiple scientific fields, are converging at a rapid pace. This convergence is headed for the academic arenas (pre-school through post-secondary, or higher education) and these arenas do not appear to be prepared for the massive change that is currently and rapidly accelerating towards them. Alarms are sounding but falling on deaf ears. The epistemological view includes:

1. an unwillingness to recognise the need for change relative to teaching and learning methods supporting today's student;

2. a business model of one-to-many, supporting a wrongly conceived efficiency-based belief that knowledge can be transferred through presentation; while perhaps the reality is that when teachers distribute information, knowledge is transformed only when individuals engage in the process of their own learning;

3. a need for spaces to be holistically designed, supporting the student and the educator in learner-centric teaching methods; and

4. a need for a framework to guide holistic design/planning practices as a practical application supporting new identified functional requirements.

The formal learning environment, the classroom, is used as an example to explain and articulate the need for new educational experiences.

As with all emergency situations early planning is essential (see Daniel & Fleishman; Boys & Hazlett, in this volume); yet frameworks to guide a planning process are not readily available; particularly in deficit are those that intentionally link interdisciplinary teams responsible for pedagogy, technology and space. This chapter will attempt to create an awareness of the elements within the storm (historical, technological, and economic issues), and share evidence and theories from sciences (learning and brain) connecting us to the learner, the learning, and the learning place. This background information sets the context for the need to provide a robust planning tool, or guiding framework that works at both micro and macro levels helping abate the oncoming surge of change – the Active Learning Ecosystem (ALES) framework is offered as one such tool. By way of making a start to exploring the storm and its causes, we might ask ourselves the following questions:

+ why are we in the situation in the first place?

+ what are the historical, technological, and economic influences affecting the current state of affairs?

+ what are the theories and research evidence relative to learning we have ignored to a large degree?

+ where do we go from here?

+ what tools/frameworks can be used to move us from here (present state) to there (future state)?

Trends influencing learning space design

If we look at the way in which learning space design has been carried out in higher education, it seems to me that it has been influenced by at least three major trends: historical trends, technological trends, and economic trends. I shall look at these in the first part of the chapter.

Historical trends

Arguments made suggest we are in this situation (a passive learning one) in the first place due to education institutions' historical influences. Educational entities, particularly ones of higher education have enjoyed a time-honoured belief that the presentation of information by an esteemed faculty member means he/she is 'transmitting knowledge' in that formal learning environment – the classroom. Evidence of successful learning would suggest otherwise. Yet this formal learning environment or the classroom is the physical place where educators attempt to plan, control, and orchestrate their students' experiences. But let us think about this notion. Have you ever gone to see a highly rated movie in a cinema and left with the impression that it wasn't as good as you had expected? Filmmakers cannot plan, control or orchestrate your experience. Only the individual can do that. So why continue the ruse in the educational sector?

The classroom as a design has evolved from early buildings constructed for worship where an authoritative figure was physically placed on a raised dais, or stage, to transmit the teachings of the day. Row-by-column seating was arranged for parishioners, the early 'learners,' to sit and listen in a rectangular building structure (Scott-Webber, 2004). The hierarchy is recognised in these ways: (1) the physically raised platform, (2) the space allotted to one versus the space allotted to the masses, and (3) the recognised role of where the knowledge resided – the person of authority. A sketch of an early painting in the Medieval era depicts this scenario (see Figure 1). Maybe our development of these situations started here.

Figure 1: Sketch of early teaching and learning method.

From these early models and with the schooling of the masses a behavioural conditioning to stand and deliver, or sit and listen depending on one's role was promoted. In this 21st century it is sad to report that not much has changed; we teach as we were taught and in places depicting earlier centuries' solutions. For example:

+ the building shape, a rectangle – the same;

+ the dais or stage – the same (even in a flat floor at least 1/4 to 1/3 of space is devoted to one person);

+ the method of delivery – essentially the same;

+ the hierarchy, or recognised role of where the knowledge resides – the same;

* the row-by-column seating – the same;

* the static visual representations (e.g., tapestries and/or paintings) – almost the same (e.g., PowerPoint presentations);

* the one-to-many ratio – the same; and

* the passive learning scenario – the same.

My argument is that the role of presenting information has remained unchanged across these many eras with the misaligned assumption that knowledge is gained by the recipient. A person from an earlier century could walk into any one of our classrooms today and be able to conduct a session as if they were in their own time. Evidence indicates that only 5% of knowledge is retained in a lecture and 85% when we begin to teach others (Greenfield, 2013); so, why this type of space? Architecture further embeds this model, at least in North America, and leads to designs of rectangular buildings, multiple rectangular classrooms within and between which is the circulation corridor – thus providing a 'double-loaded' corridor effect. This design supports a factory model organised to push students by the bell along a conveyor belt of knowledge delivery, and pour knowledge into these young heads for 50 minutes at a time. *"The factory line was simply the most efficient way to scale production in general, and the analog [sic] factory-model classroom was the most sensible way to rapidly scale a system of schools. Factories weren't designed to support personalisation. Neither were schools."* (Rose, 2012:np).

In this factory education model, only one person is the content expert (the teacher) and gets up for a few minutes and shares that content (to students); this one-to-many is an entrenched business model. Why are traditional education systems so stuck in time? Programmes or disciplines with small number of students (e.g., 15-24) in studios or writing courses are deemed expensive while other disciplines that practice only the lecture model are the 'cash cows.' What other discipline has not changed – medicine, architecture, you name it? Maybe the answer is simple. It's easier to do what we know how to do and have been taught how to do than to change, even though we know the change is probably for the better. What of the other indicators contributing to this perfect storm?

Technology trends

Several authors provide the following arguments identifying issues relative to the rate of technological change.

"The pace of change has been blinding. The nature of technology itself has undergone a transformation – it is no longer just a 'device', leaving us all as consumers with a sense of breathlessness and expectation – what next?" (Sinha et al., 2013:np).

"Technology will change our experience of education. It will ensure that learning is distributed and freed of the confines of a classroom and an age. No longer will education be the privilege of those who can afford it. We will learn more things from more people and sources; learning curves will be shortened and deepened. Our new learning experience will transform us as human beings...In the last decade, we have only witnessed a small part of what is possible. It was so because technology was the preserve of the few who could afford it. As the technological possibility envelops all in society, it will imbue us with a sense of belief, a sense of faith that has traditionally been only associated with religion" (Sinha et al., 2013:np).

"Every technology has changed our lives, some of them in manner more aggressive than other. It's hard to point out to a specific technology and makes it responsible for the major changes in a life of person, because every one of us may be influenced by other things." (Softpedia, 2013:np).

The list of quotables goes on; but we don't need others to tell us how our lives have changed due to technology. As our personal lives have changed so too has the integration of technology into the classroom from blackboards and chalk, to interactive white boards, to personal devices; the way we communicate in these places should be different. If it isn't, then students of today and tomorrow probably won't stay in the traditional educational system. It will be important to start the conversation around technology as a tool to enhance the learning process and not just think about these as a fad. Although the adjustment of adding technology is one of the compounding issues relative to the technological changes for education, economic factors contribute to this storm as well.

Economic trends

We are in a time of unprecedented expense for education. Students and parents alike are questioning the value of post-secondary education due to the lack of apparent balance between debt load and education's value.

> "Outstanding student debt in America has hit $1 trillion, students are on the streets of Quebec, demanding no rises in tuition fees, and French professors are bemoaning the rising costs and 'Harvardisation' of higher education. But how much do students actually pay around the world?" (Taylor, 2012:np).

The data presented in Table 1 is from a 2010 report (Huffington Post, 2012):

WHERE	AVG.TOTAL
USA	$13,865
Japan	$11,865
Australia	$6,792
Canada	$5,974
UK	$5,288
Mexico	$5,077
Latvia	$3,299
New Zealand	$3,118
Germany	$933

Table 1: College degree average costs per annum.

More recently, figures have shown a trebling of costs in England and Wales to about $13K per academic year (theguardian, 2012:np).

> "According to Bloomberg, college tuition and fees have increased 1,120 percent since records began in 1978. Earlier this year, the Associated Press reported the average tuition at four-year public universities had increased by 15 percent between 2008 and 2010. Private universities were also found to have had significant price increases" (Huffington Post, 2012:np).

Clearly, the cost of being educated is a global concern. In summary then, we see that historical influences, the speed of technological change, and economic pressures have a profound effect on the design of learning spaces. Educational practice is at the centre of this perfect storm and we must recognise how to listen, learn, change, and plan for this change by incorporating lessons from brain science, learning science, environment behaviour as well as information from the US National Survey of Student Engagement (NSSE). This evidence is discussed below.

Research evidence

Multiple scientific fields have built a body of evidence that should no longer be ignored. Sciences such as brain science, learning research, environment behaviour theories as well as data from NSSE impact one of the primary responsibilities of the academe – helping others become educated. What does this body of work have to teach education? Lots! The obvious one is that research evidence is an important contributing factor and that knowledge should be embedded into methodologies and practices supporting learning. How can we, as educators, continue to blithely ignore what the sciences about learning are telling us? How can our institutions continue on this path as well? Each scientific field's contribution to the learner, to learning, and to learning spaces is discussed briefly below.

The learner

What do we know about the learner and what are the developmental differences across time? The learner referred to here is both the student as learner and the educator as life-long learner. This question is not about demographics or generations, but more about how individuals are wired for the job of learning. Wolfe (2010) in her text *Brain matters: Translating research into classroom practice (2nd edition)* shares information about the brain development and some brief descriptive points are provided next just to give context. They include:

+ *"Brain development from birth through adolescence – the brain is not only shaped by its inherited genetic code, but is heavily influenced and shaped by its environment;*

* *neuroplasticity exists from cradle to grave;*

* *babies are born with cells that allow them to hear and pronounce the sounds of every language in the world;*

* *activity is critical; children do not like to learn through passive input... (this approach – this author's input) deprives children of the natural interaction with the world that is essential to their development. What children need and enjoy is rich, varied input in natural settings.*

* *the brain is primed for learning...(Wolfe, 2010:71-79).*

Is this evidence of a need to blend the ideals of andragogy and pedagogy? The answer is yes in the form of self-determined learning – heutagogy. Why should we care about how the brain works from early childhood through to adult learners? Because, depravation in anyone of these time-frames could jeopardise a person's ability to learn. That deficit impacts those in higher education. Brain science also tells us that all of our information comes to us through sensory input (Erlauer 2003; Wolfe 2010; Lengel & Kuczala, 2010); meaning all of our senses are engaged. Stimulus comes from our immediate environment. However, all sensory input is just noise until the brain figures out how to make sense of all of the stimuli it receives (Wolfe, 2010). Lengel & Kuczala (2010:17) suggest there is a powerful brain-body connection and stress that coming to understand and utilise the connection between the two represents some of the most exciting advancements of scientific inquiry in this area for the 21st century. However, it would appear this information about the human experience is not incorporated into the teaching and learning processes, yet it would certainly enhance both. A consensus is held within the brain science community that memory is the key to learning. How then do we learn?

The learning

It's complicated. As mentioned, humans take in information through sensory input received from one's environment. The brain then processes this information. "...100 billion brain cells" (neurons) (Lengel & Kuczala 2010:17) are in the brain. A chemical is released for these neurons to talk to one another and thus a network of neurons is formed. When these neurons connect we learn. We…"*…process information, and form memory traces. If the memory trace is not lost through inactivity and if rehearsal of new information takes place, more neurons are called on and a stronger alliance (neural network) is formed. When strong networks are formed, information from these neural communities is more easily retrieved*" (Lengel & Kuczala 2010:17).

There are long-held teaching practices supporting different types of learning. Anderson (1990), a student of Bloom, revised his 1956 taxonomy (Overbaugh & Schultz, 2013). This taxonomy was one of the early efforts to understand the learning process and intellectual behaviours. Gagne (2013) furthered Bloom's work by providing the theory of the conditions of learning. This theory postulates that there are different levels of learning (an agreement with Bloom) and then Gagne argued that for each level a different teaching practice is required. Components regarded as a holistic approach as suggested by Hall and Johnson (1994) include: (1) cognitive (Cognitive domain defining knowledge classification), (2) psychomotor (defining physical skills or tasks classification), and (3) affective (defining behaviours that correspond to attitudes and values). What can perhaps be agreed upon is learning is a complex behaviour. Packer and Goicoechea (2000) help us put all of these learning theories together in their work that shared the constructivist theory. This theory indicates that each learner is an individual and as individuals we construct knowledge one 'floor' at a time. It makes sense. We all come from different backgrounds with different experiences and cultures. Why then do we continue to deliver education in a 'batch mode?' A batch mode requires that the student advance due to his/her age not because of the evidence of learning. Constructivist theory then asks the educator to pay attention to these differences and prepare teaching strategies to support them. Many scientists have, and continue to, help us understand the issues relative to how we learn. This scientific history is rich yet rarely applied. As educators in the K-12 arena are actually taught the work of learning research, or the scholarship of learning, and certified to teach our children, many higher education educators are not taught how to teach nor expected to learn about learning as these individuals are 'content' experts and typically teach as they (or we) were taught. Obviously a large gap exists here. Although this gap analysis is for another chapter, what can be addressed is how place makes a difference in supporting an active learning structure

(Scott-Webber, 2004). Although learning can happen anywhere, and active learning is important, the 'learning place' remains important and deserves consideration.

The learning place

Brain science (Erlauer 2003; Wolfe, 2010) asks us to…*"Build a brain compatible classroom…Brain compatible learning is understanding what the brain needs for optimal learning potential and then creating a teaching environment to accommodate those needs"* (Furman, 2013:np). As technological tools have become more precise, scientists are able to track what the brain does and where in the brain certain functions reside; as a result this work teaches us more and more about how we learn. The research is conducted from controlled experiments and not yet tested in the classroom. However, we do know that *"the brain learns through the processing of sensory information from its surrounding environment"* (Lengel & Kuczala, 2010:17). The physical place then makes an important contribution to how the brain gathers information. In the text *The Kinesthetic Classroom: Teaching and Learning Through Movement* (Lengel & Kuczala, 2010:23-29), the authors argue there are 10 clear identifiers why the "brain-body connection" and movement is important to facilitate and enhance the learning process. Namely that *"movement:*

+ *provides a break from learning and refocuses attention;*

+ *allows for implicit learning;*

+ *improves brain function;*

+ *meets basic needs;*

+ *improves the learning state;*

+ *engages the senses;*

+ *reduces stress;*

+ *increases circulation; and*

+ *enhances episodic learning and memory."* (Lengel & Kuczala, 2010:23-29).

How can we provide for movement in highly dense, row-by-column seating arrangements that reflect the factory model? In fact, evidence indicates that only 5% of knowledge is retained in a lecture and 85% when we begin to teach others. (Greenfield, 2013). These relics of design (i.e., lecture halls) and the current business model are impeding real learning. It could be stated that education has not really been about education, but rather the transmission of knowledge from one to many. Efforts to change from a teacher-centric to a learner-centric (not just in name) model are emerging. This change is fundamental if true education reform is to be realised. How can space make a difference? Environment behaviour theorists suggest it already does (Sommer, 1959, 1969; Altman, 1970, 1975; Scott-Webber, 2004). If space is so important, why is that fact relatively unknown? Why do we insist on generating the same types of designs that have permeated the landscapes for centuries? Perhaps we don't learn enough about how space impacts behaviours (Scott-Webber *et al.*, 2000), or at the very least how to think about the issue. The next section of this chapter provides a framework for thinking through the three main components impacting space – pedagogy, technology, and space itself. The framework is the Active Learning Ecosystem (Steelcase Education Solutions, 2011) framework and is offered as a tool to build consensus across disciplines responsible for developing new solutions for learning environments.

Active Learning Ecosystem (ALES) framework

The Active Learning Ecosystem framework is used to illustrate how pedagogy (teaching and learning strategies), technology, and space are integrally linked. The Venn diagram (see Figure 2) has three interconnecting circles. Purposefully, the circle for pedagogy (teaching and learning strategies) is placed at the top. It is considered that both technology and space are 'tools' supporting the pedagogy, or 'scaffolds.' Each of these supporting tools is intentionally developed in conjunction with the plans for pedagogy and pedagogical change. When working together, these components act as a holistic ecosystem delivering the 'engagement factor,' or active learning result. The compendium of pedagogical change referred to here is from a passive (i.e., teacher-centric) model to an active (i.e., learner-centric) one. It is believed it takes an active educator for active learning to occur.

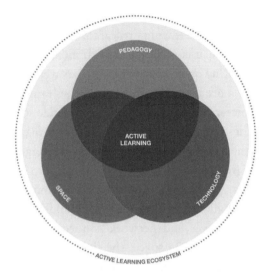

Figure 2: Active Learning Ecosystem framework (used with permission from Steelcase Education Solutions).

Each component of the framework is self-explanatory. However, a few factoids may add clarity. Again, pedagogy here is the generic name for teaching and learning strategies. Technically, "ped·a·go·gy (n) is used in K-12 education and refers to:

1. *The art or profession of teaching.*

2. *Preparatory training or instruction"* (*Wikipedia:np*).

A definition of Andragogy is the process of teaching adults how to learn.

> *"While pedagogy refers to the teaching of children, where the teacher is the focal point, andragogy shifts the focus from the teacher to the learner. Adults learn best when they have control over their learning."* (*Wikipedia:np*).

A term that refers more to self-determined learning is heutagogy. "Heutagogy places specific emphasis on *learning how to learn...*" (Wikipedia:np). Perhaps active learning is the acknowledgement that it helps all learners to be in control over their own learning. This definition certainly reflects the overall movement from passive to active learning, or teacher-centric to learner-centric strategies. Technology, the circle on the lower right in the Venn diagram, often refers to digital tools. However, as we have heard from brain science and learning research, the brain needs multiple sensory inputs. Therefore, it is encouraged to think about how to support the 'analogue' (i.e., writing on boards, paper, etc.) as well as digital means. Active learning asks more from the learner and the learning place has to deliver multiple choices, and all choices should coincide with the defined pedagogical strategies. Again, technology is a supportive tool only if it works to enhance the curriculum and pedagogical strategies.

How can space (the lower left circle in the diagram) support? The 'envelope' of space is another important 'tool' and must recognise the purpose, need, and challenge of both pedagogy and technology. Infrastructure to conduct power and network connectivity is critical. The shape of space, the walls of the space, the lighting, furniture, fixtures, finishes, and equipment are all parts of this envelope. It is additionally important to recognise that it takes more square feet/square meters per person to move freely. This fact is in direct tension with the current business model of one to many in tight quarters. It is complex. Yet each, when developed in concert with one another, allow for a harmony between the three resulting in a teaching and learning 'work' place that is intentionally and holistically designed for the users' behaviours. Therefore, this ALES framework informs the conversation between the educator, instructional designer, information technology expert, as well as the architect/designer/facility planner on a micro level. Sometimes the mere fact that these different disciplines are having a conversation is a big start to support the evolution of education change at one facility. However, the framework can also be used at the macro level. Some examples might include:

+ the development of a campus master plan; and/or

+ the development of learning place standards.

A caution should be mentioned here. The history of space design for formal learning places is the ubiquitous rectangle with row-by-column seating (Scott-Webber, 2004) all facing forward. Basically, this amounts to a 'one size fits all' design solution. The last thing we need to replicate in future plans is a single type of solution. Just as in many areas of life, choice is important; as the place where the educator and students go to do the work of learning, a variety of formal learning places should be conceived (see Figure 3) and all should rely on evidence-based design.

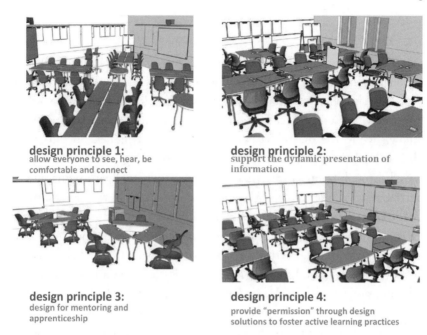

design principle 1:
allow everyone to see, hear, be
comfortable and connect

design principle 2:
support the dynamic presentation of
information

design principle 3:
design for mentoring and
apprenticeship

design principle 4:
provide "permission" through design
solutions to foster active learning practices

Figure 3: Examples of research insights / design principles / application ideas (with permission from Steelcase Inc.).

Architects and designers (A/D) will need to go beyond the initial questions, "How many classrooms do you need?" and "What is the capacity for each?" Usually, these two questions finish the interview for classroom design as the A/D community has built multiple AutoCAD (i.e., computer generated drawings) templates for them. This quick and easy fix should be made to go away. A new conversation should emerge; one that asks, "How do you envision learning occurring in these places?" "What pedagogies will be employed and what is the variety?" "Are the academics on your campus prepared to make pedagogical changes?" The ALES framework acts as the facilitator to ensure these vital questions get asked, identified, and prioritised. Why? Because different disciplines who often do not connect on projects are asked to work together from the very beginning and throughout the process of renovating or building new learning places. That connection and interconnection is critical to the overall success of a project that moves toward active learning.

Conclusion

A rectangular space design is still present since early centuries focused on sharing information with the misaligned assumption that knowledge is gained through this effort. The earliest examples are places of worship where one person is placed on a stage high above all others to transmit knowledge to the masses; was and is an efficient model. So too is the double-loaded corridor design of academic buildings. Today we understand through brain science that our brains are actually changing due to technology (Wolfe, 2010). Why do we continue to lecture as the main mode in higher educational settings? Our research and others suggests that active learning/engagement/interaction (whatever action verb you choose) is the more effective way to learn (NSSE, 2013). This Learning in Higher Education (LiHE) call communication for proposals summed the situation up well. *"Pedagogy (or its Latin equivalent education) has traditionally focused on the operations of teaching and learning. But the context of teaching and learning — the places in which learning occurs — is equally important. Indeed, these 'learning spaces' can limit the types of activities which can be used by the teacher. They can influence the social interactions between teachers and students, and between students themselves. They can impact the affective and cognitive, the behavioural, and even the physiological responses of students. In summary, they can help or they can hinder learning"* (Learning in Higher Education, 2013:np).

Alarms will continue to sound as this perfect storm brews about us. Will those in higher education listen? Historical, technological and economic forces are pushing together enlarging this storm's power. Scientific evidence and theories from brain and learning sciences can no longer be ignored. There is recognition that education reform is necessary from kindergarten through higher education. The Active Learning Ecosystem is offered as a framework to bring together disciplines from pedagogy, technology, and space in one place to develop intended design solutions supporting the learner, the learning, and the learning place for the learner of this 21st century.

Thus, if active learning is the "north arrow" the goal, then we must listen and attend to all of the forces pushing higher education into this perfect storm and develop planning guidelines for change and the strategies to support them. The focus on changing educational practices and connecting the dots using the Active Learning Ecosystem's framework offers a practical guide for the development of a holistic learning place that is functionally different as it supports new (intended) behaviours. At both the micro and macro levels the framework facilitates an organised and intentionally planned approach to support this revolution in education across the higher education arenas.

About the Author

Lennie Scott-Webber is Director Education Environments of Steelcase Education Solutions at Steelcase Inc. in Grand Rapids, U.S.A. She can be contacted at this e-mail: lascottwe@steelcase.com

Chapter Ten

Faculty Development: Precursor to Effective Student Engagement in the Higher Education Learning Space

Gary M. Pavlechko and Kathleen L. Jacobi

Introduction

Assuming that furnishings and technology are present, what else needs to occur before students enter an active learning space in higher education? A learning space can include the most elaborate and up-to-date components but will that assure a successful and engaged learning experience? The additional critical factor to address prior to the first day of class is instructor preparation. An effective faculty development programme influences an instructor's rethinking of the teaching and learning relationship that leads to engaging and active interaction between the various elements of the class – students, instructor, technology, furnishings, and space.

This chapter contributes to the anthology on learning space design in higher education by addressing how a faculty development programme can best prepare instructors to teach in learning spaces, encouraging active versus passive learning. In this chapter, we define learning space as the physical location where teaching and learning takes place. Furthermore, we discuss the learning space in terms as either *traditional* – lecture hall or chairs in rows with the instructor at the 'front' of the room – or *interactive*

– without a designated instructor space, flexible seating arrangements, and supporting learner collaboration. Reading this chapter you will:

1. be able to reflect on your current faculty development programme;

2. identify the needs of your faculty members; and

3. determine how the proposed faculty development model might be adapted for your institution.

Interactive Learning Space Initiative

Ball State University, a mid-sized institution located in the Midwestern United States, established the Interactive Learning Space (ILS) Initiative with the purpose of strengthening learning in higher education through effective pedagogy, learning space, and technology. This initiative addresses the issues of teaching the 21st century learner and how exploratory teaching and learning environments encourage instructors to think differently as they prepare learners to be active in the learning space. A key issue is to create learning space that encourages the curiosity of learners and teachers in the face-to-face learning environment. This opportunity is the responsibility of those on campuses responsible for the design and creation of learning space. Universities have seen an increase in interest to adapt traditional classrooms into learning spaces that invite innovation and exploratory teaching (Radcliffe, 2009).

Traditionally, classroom renovations are the product of various units – architects and interior designers addressing the physical space to accommodate enrolment expectations, and, more recently, instructional technology departments addressing technology, connectivity, and projection. Since the responsibility for teaching is that of academics, it is important for learning space design to include representation from this community. *"Community catalyzes deep learning and should be a critical consideration when planing physical and virtual learning spaces. In higher education, however, specialization has a long and comfortable history – in the way our institutions are partitioned and also in the way our institutions are organized. Tradition encouraged specialists to attend to their individual areas: faculty developed pedagogy and curriculum; information technologists made decisions about technology; and facilities managers designed and developed classrooms and other spaces."* (Bickford & Wright, 2006:4.1)

With this cooperation among university agencies or units, the emphasis moves from focusing on the newest technology and furnishings, to then deciding what to do with them and how they will best support the pedagogy implemented in the learning space. The Learning Spaces Project at Dennison University, in the United States, offers the following considerations for learning space design: *"learning spaces should:*

+ *support various styles of learning;*

+ *offer versatility;*

+ *be comfortable and attractive to many;*

+ *consist of relevant information and consistently reliable technology;*

+ *be maintained appropriately and is accessible."*

(Radcliffe, 2009:13).

With this focus on pedagogy, and for the initiative to be successful, those teaching in newly designed learning spaces need to be prepared to address the elements that will impact student learning – pedagogy, learning space, and technology. *"Learning environments aren't revolutionized by installing a few cool gadgets here and there. Far more important is the educator's role in employing today's technologies to make material accessible and engaging – in other words, encouraging students to create, communicate, and collaborate in ways never before possible."* (Stevens, 2011:1).

The redesign of a learning space, as well as taking into account the pedagogical approach to the teaching and learning expected to occur in the renovated space, requires a programme that addresses challenges that arise as a result of the space and pedagogy redesign. First, ages of instructors in higher education can span numerous generations, leading to a wide spectrum of comfort with the technological advances of the late 20th and early 21st centuries. Second, a vast majority of higher education faculty members were trained in their discipline but not in the art of teaching. This absence of teacher preparation often results in faculty members teaching the way they were taught which, in many instances, was lecture-based with passive learners, rather than through student-centred pedagogies requiring engaged learner behaviours.

Our university's effort to provide innovative space and technology led to the addressing of faculty development necessary for a successful transition to learning spaces designed specifically for active learning. Since our campus faculty development programme is divided into two support units – one for face-to-face instruction and the other for online instruction – the Office of Educational Excellence, responsible for the former, was charged with overseeing the redesign of the classrooms and creation of a faculty development programme to support instruction in the newly designed learning spaces.

Emerging from this context, our chapter describes a faculty development model designed to assist ILS faculty members in addressing instruction enhanced by space and technology to actively engage students with course content, inside and outside of formal learning spaces. The faculty development programme, implemented by the Ball State University's Office of Educational Excellence, begins with an application process and concludes with dissemination of research findings regarding faculty members' Interactive Learning Space Initiative experiences.

Creation of the Interactive Learning Space Initiative

Except for minor adaptations to traditional higher education classrooms through the past decade, our institution's two interactive learning spaces provide faculty members an opportunity to teach in spaces that are quite different from traditional classrooms. Learning spaces, large and small, created in previous years had data projection systems installed, but this still encouraged a teacher in the front of the room addressing her/his students in rows looking directly ahead. This passive learning style has been part of the higher education system for many years. What was not enforced was an active learning model that moved students to become participatory in multiple ways. Interest in higher education has increased regarding the cultivation of existing, physical space into learning spaces that embrace the characteristics of 21st Century learners (Savin-Baden, 2008) and allowing for today's students to participate in environments that allow for social and cultural engagement into a space of situated cognition (Enomoto and Warner, this volume) a conceptual subset to faculty members considering teaching to students through a community of practice model.

It is overly stated that technology should not drive pedagogy, as it could be contended that this is understood by most; nonetheless, it is still a relevant proposition given ongoing advancements in instructional technology. A third component to this consideration has come to be learning space, which includes furniture. Many of us remember yesterday's college classrooms being four walls of painted cinder block, single desks facing the front of the room, a chalkboard, and projection screen. Today, we have the pleasure of experiencing teaching and learning in spaces that go as far as to not even have a front of the room. This new concept is designed to promote teaching and learning activity that is all about engagement with a community of learners *"Although learning involves individual behavioral changes, the context in which those changes occur is a social environment involving many people. All aspects of education-including the planning of space design should acknowledge community."* (Bickford & Wright, 2006:4.2)

When it was determined that our building was to be renovated, our faculty development office was asked to research 'next generation' classrooms and to begin to redesign two classrooms for which our unit, the Office of Educational Excellence, was responsible for maintaining. In the past, these two rooms had been tagged as exploratory teaching spaces and were unique to the rest of campus. As with the advancement of instructional technologies, the rooms had become somewhat commonplace on campus, with the exception of content capture technology. This new opportunity allowed us to examine other universities and their efforts to create learning spaces that allow for interactive and collaborative learning. Our search took us to the commonly known success stories (in the United States) – University of Minnesota, University of Iowa, and North Carolina State University.

As well, we were led to *Steelcase* – a large classroom and business furniture company whose research group had become a leader in studying the ecosystem of pedagogy, space, and technology (Scott-Webber, in this volume). This relationship proved to be an effective means to the design and development of our space and technology, and it also led us to emphasise an active learning curriculum for ILS courses.

In autumn/fall 2011, we were informed that as part of a building renovation, and specifically the first wave of the renovation, we had additional funding to create 'next generation' classrooms (a term used to describe classrooms befitting current technology, at the time) so we began exploring learning spaces in higher education. Educating external and internal architects and others in facilities management about impending changes was an interesting task; those persons were not familiar with this type of classroom design. As well, we had to educate ourselves about designing such learning spaces, being mindful that *"the ways in which a space is designed shape the learning that happens in that space"*(Chism, 2006:2.2). Researching what other universities had done was a start, as was initiating communication with *Steelcase* – Ball State's supplier of classroom furniture, whose research team, *Steelcase* Education Solutions, conducted numerous studies to arrive at conclusions about effective furniture and classroom design. Extensive discussions took place with our furniture supplier and others who would assist in helping us make informed decisions.

Johnson and Lomas (2005:20) address the importance of dialogue among the various units and constituents to *"ensure that the new space is designed around learning needs instead of space requirements."* Radcliffe (2009) states that the process needs to be organic and should be built by considering institutional context, its values, strengths and limitations, and the learning principles that are to be promoted. A charrette – an activity commonly used by architects to determine the design needs of a client by including all stakeholders – was conducted with external and internal personnel, autumn/fall semester 2012. Included in this session were interested faculty members, students, university architects, interior designers, and research personnel as well as reprentatives from the supplier of furniture for Ball State. Interactive learning space was not a common discussion topic on our campus at the time, and opening up discussion to diverse constituents was a positive move; it not only brought multiple perspectives, it demonstrated our office's effort to build an interactive learning system from the ground up, not top down.

In order to gain insight from faculty members and academic administrators, the Knowledge Group for Interactive Learning Space, a nineteen-member group representing all seven academic colleges, was formed for interested university personnel to advise us in preparing the application as well as to develop a research agenda for the ILS Initiative. After these initial steps, a few Knowledge Group members continued with the initiative as instructors and/or researchers, but the majority of the teaching and research responsibility was inherited by the inaugural cohort of faculty members to be accepted into the ILS programme.

ILS Classrooms/Interactive Learning Spaces — Space Redesign

Classroom redesign resulted in both spaces accommodating twenty-four students and fostering learner engagement via the use of interactive whiteboards, smaller portable whiteboards placed through the spaces to be used for notation of ideas, as well as projection from various sources for viewing by the entire class. The type and arrangement of furnishings support student collaboration. Encouraging students to reach out to each other to solve problems, share knowledge, co-author written artefacts, and receive peer review not only builds collaborative learning skills, it leads to deeper learning and understanding (Barkley, Cross, and Major, 2005). Replacing the traditional rows of desks with a variety of configuration possibilities allows students to see each other, thus augmenting peer-to-peer interaction. Furnished by *Steelcase*, one Interactive Learning Space is a *Media:Scape™ LearnLab™* configuration seating six students around a table with a display attached at one end for viewing the laptop/mobile device content of those seated at the table.

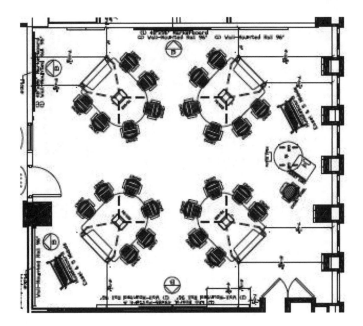

Figure 1: *Media:Scape™/LearnLab™ classroom floorplan.*

The other learning space has *Node*™ chairs allowing multiple classroom arrangements to better facilitate small and large group interaction. The traditional instructor desk/podium was replaced by a mobile stand and placed within the space to support a facilitator, rather than lecturer, role.

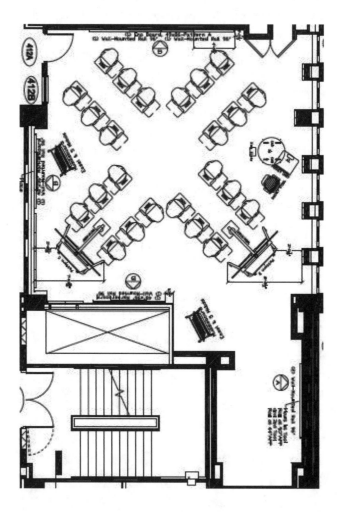

Figure 2: Node™ classroom floorplan arranged in LearnLab™ configuration.

The Interactive Learning Space (ILS) Faculty Development Programme

The Interactive Learning Space Initiative Faculty Development Programme is a six semester sequence based on a cohort system modeling an authentic class experience promoting skill development over time; individual, small-, large-group experiences; and exploratory and collaborative learning. This approach addresses current trends in pedagogy for 21st century teaching and is relevant to the needs of today's active learning classrooms. Therefore, the ILS Faculty Development Programme is designed to increase faculty members' time to perfect new skills associated with ILS, reflect on their teaching practice, collaborate with peers, improve upon their scholarship of teaching and learning, and strengthen their professional networks for mentoring throughout the year. This approach produces collaborative advancements in teaching and scholarship; it is about professional learning.

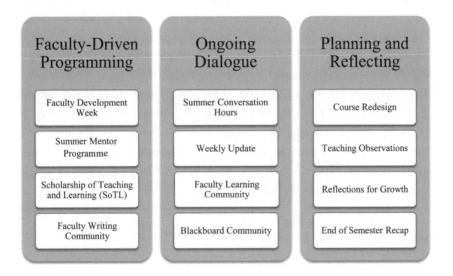

Figure 3©: Tenets of the Interactive Learning Space Initiative Faculty Development Programme.

The foundation of the ILS Faculty Development Programme is built upon three tenets 1) Programming is most effective when it is designed and implemented by the faculty; 2) Ongoing dialogue continues the momentum of the initiative throughout the teaching and research cycle; 3) Reflection and planning allows for analysis of what is occurring in the classroom and what improvements might be implemented to address active learning. Whenever possible, all ILS related activities are held in the ILS classrooms. This provides participants the opportunity to continually engage with the space, furnishings, and technology on an ongoing basis.

Tenet 1: Faculty-Driven Programming

The goal of the Interactive Learning Space Initiative Faculty Development Programme is to create a longitudinal process that allows faculty members in ILS to enhance their teaching abilities and research/scholarship productivity in active learning space. A sound rule of practice for a successful faculty development programme is that it is faculty-driven (Malnarich, 2008). This is why the ILS faculty development experience is designed, facilitated, and evaluated by the members of the current cohort. As it is repeated for future cohort members, the ILS faculty development experience is based on research data gathered by ILS faculty and used to design upcoming processes. A 'pedagogy first, then technology' philosophy (Moore, Fowler, & Watson, 2007) focuses on active learning and the design of learning experiences that are immersive and pertinent to everyday living. This multi-phase programme allows for the transformation of higher education faculty to become more cognisant of feedback, motivation, and environmental tools (Park & Ertmer, 2008) in spaces that promote authentic learning.

Tenet 2: Ongoing Dialogue

Interactive Learning Space faculty members improve teaching practice through ongoing dialogue with peers. There are numerous opportunities to communicate with fellow teachers in this programme. Since the ILS Initiative is built upon collaboration between members, it is necessary to facilitate a continuous conversation allowing members to share their experiences, inquire about others', and establish partnerships in research and scholarship.

Tenet 3: Planning and Reflecting

It is imperative that time is allotted for ILS participants to share what they are doing and how they would like to construct future learning experiences. This reflective practice philosophy is essential to effective teaching. Time is afforded faculty at the end of summer term to meet with OEE personnel to discuss both course redesign efforts (Cohort 2) and progress on research agendas (Cohort 1).

ILS faculty members experience the three tenets throughout the six semester participation process based on a Jerome Bruner's (1977) spiral curriculum concept commencing with the application process and concluding with a scholarly product based on their experiences teaching in the Interactive Learning Space Initiative.

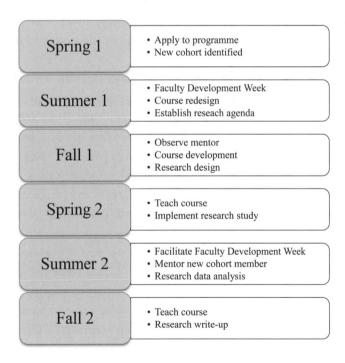

Figure 4©: Interactive Learning Space Initiative – Participation Process.

ILS Teaching and Research Grant Application (Spring 1)

Faculty members interested in teaching in an Interactive Learning Space are required to complete a brief application. In addition to basic questions regarding the course title, typical enrolment, and schedule information, applicants are asked to address why the course lends itself to the ILS Initiative. They are encouraged to visit the renovated learning spaces as they prepare their application to further inform their initial ideas for course redesign as well as consider which Interactive Learning Space is best suited to their course content, objectives, and outcomes. Signatures from the department chair and college dean are required, so appropriate academic administrators are aware of the intentions of the applicants. Often, department chairs provide consideration to increase class size for another section(s) taught by the applicant in order to meet the twenty-four seat capacity of both ILS rooms. This not only assists with promoting the initiative to administration, but it enhances the support for the ILS faculty member.

A second, and equally important, component of this initiative is the pursuit to study how innovative pedagogy, learning spaces, and technology intersect to impact student learning. ILS faculty members are expected to participate in scholarly work. This can be accomplished individually, with another ILS faculty member, and/or as part of a larger research study conducted by the University's faculty development unit.

The initiative includes a modest monetary award (in the form of a stipend or travel funding) provided to those selected to participate – $1000 for course redesign and $1000 for research/scholarship activity.

Applications are due mid-spring semester and are reviewed by a committee consisting staff from the Office of Educational Excellence and faculty from the current ILS cohort. Applicants are informed in April and become a member of the incoming ILS cohort upon acceptance into the programme. At this time, they are given a survey to identify their comfort level with active learning strategies as well as a needs assessment regarding the topics to be addressed during a week-long workshop: Faculty Development Week – the first in a series of preparatory events for the Interactive Learning Space experience.

As of this writing, two cycles of Calls for Applications have occurred – the first in the spring of 2012 and the second in the spring of 2013 – with both cohorts currently participating in the ILS Initiative. The forty-nine faculty members participating come from sixteen disciplines, or departments, representing all colleges at Ball State (College of Applied Sciences and Technology; College of Architecture and Planning; Miller College of Business; College of Communication, Information, and Media; College of Fine Arts; College of Sciences and Humanities; Teachers College; and Honors College), and all ranks (Graduate Assistant, Instructor, Assistant Professor, Associate Professor, and Full Professor). In addition, the faculty members' years of higher education teaching experience range from two to fifty years!

Faculty Development Week (Tenet 1, Summer 1 and Summer 2)

Faculty Development Week is held the week between spring semester and summer session when no classes are held. While this week is typically sacred time for faculty to be away from campus, attendance averages 95%. It consists of five, four-hour days and includes immersive learning activities that engage the participants. Faculty are expected to become active learners in the ILS classrooms, best preparing them for what to think about as they redesign their ILS class during the summer semester.

This week of sessions is to represent what learning in ILS is supposed to be; therefore, information transfer is limited and participatory activity is the focus. Current cohort members plan the week of interactive activities based on what they think the next cohort members need to succeed in ILS. The information sessions are comprised of small amounts of information being presented and have included numerous opportunities for the faculty to become interactive with technology and classroom elements. With current cohort members leading next year's ILS teachers, we institute a professional development community that assures us of a cultural shift in on-campus teaching. Faculty members in ILS know they have a collective support group that will be there for them as they embark on this new teaching experience. Faculty Development Week provides the incoming cohort with a 'hands-on' experience with the space and the elements within the space, which of course includes the technology. The technology may be new to the teachers, so it is important to take time to orient the faculty to this component during Faculty Development Week.

As the week progresses, each teacher has ample opportunity to experience the technology tools.

To further replicate an active learning experience, Faculty Development Week is designed with learning outcomes to provide the participants an opportunity to engage, as their own students will, in small-group, collaborative learning experiences. At the week's end, each small group presents information about a type of active learning, such as problem-based learning. This gives them an opportunity to practise implementing active learning pedagogies, while in the space, and with the technology.

The planning of Faculty Development Week 2013 resulted in the following schedule:

MONDAY, MAY 6th
1:00 – 1:30   Introductions
1:30 – 2:15   21st C Learners
2:15 – 2:30   Break
2:30 – 3:15   Scholarship of Teaching and Learning
3:15 – 4:00   Active Learning Group Project

TUESDAY, MAY 7th
1:00 – 1:45   Learner-Centred Teaching
1:45 – 2:15   Overview of Rooms
2:15 – 2:30   Break
2:30 – 3:00   AMX Panels
3:00 – 4:00   Technology Toolbox

WEDNESDAY, MAY 8th
1:00 – 1:45   The Flipped Classroom
1:45 – 2:30   Movement in the ILS
2:30 – 2:45   Break
2:45 – 3:30   Re-working Course Activities
3:30 – 4:00   Active Learning Group Project

THURSDAY, MAY 9th
1:00 – 1:45   Online Activities & Experiences
1:45 – 2:45   Breakout Sessions (20 min segments)
               Research

Teaching Strategies
Course Redesign
2:45 – 3:00   Break
3:00 – 4:00   Active Learning Group Presentation Prep

FRIDAY, MAY 10th
1:00 – 2:20   Active Learning Group Presentations
2:20 – 2: 40   Breakout Sessions (20 min segments)
Motivating Students
Instructor Vulnerability
Active Learning
Scholarship within the Cohort
Research Agenda
2:40 – 2:50   Break
2:50 – 3:30   Breakout Sessions, cont.
3:30 – 4:00   Looking forward to Summer
Mentor programme
Course Redesign
Conversation Hours

Summer Mentor Programme (Tenet 1, Summer 1 as a mentee, Summer 2 as a mentor)

As Faculty Development Week progresses, members from both cohorts begin to establish working relationships. Members from both cohorts are in attendance during Faculty Development Week. This provides an opportunity to form Summer Mentor partnerships between members from both cohorts. The mentorship programme allows next year's faculty to interact extensively over the summer term with a member of the current cohort. New ILS faculty benefit from current cohort members' expertise. The Mentoring programme enhances summer course redesign for ILS. It provides new ILS faculty with an opportunity to share ideas about teaching in ILS with a seasoned faculty member, who has been an instructor in ILS for a semester. Course redesign considerations are more relevant, creative, and exploratory based on the dialogue between the faculty members. This interaction was observed during the summer of 2013 when four Department of Mathematics faculty members (Cohort

2) preparing to teach in our learning spaces spring semester 2014, were mentored by a colleague in Cohort 1 who had taught Math 125 for the initiative the previous academic year. This special collaboration helped the Cohort 2 members to rethink their instruction and practice during the summer in anticipation of the Cohort 1 member actually teaching redesigned lessons in autumn/fall 2013 prior to their teaching it in spring 2014. In addition to the faculty mentor, instructional support personnel are available to provide assistance with course redesign.

Course Redesign (Tenet 3, Summer I and Fall I)

Immediately following Faculty Development Week, members of the incoming cohort begin redesigning their ILS courses during the summer months. Each incoming faculty member is assigned a mentor from the current cohort. The mentor provides primary assistance for course redesign with additional support coming from the faculty development unit. Prior to the start of the fall semester, each faculty member in the course redesign phase meets with the faculty development unit to discuss their progress and identify areas of concern.

Conversation Hours (Tenet 2, Summer I, Summer 2)

Since summer is primarily a semester for research by members of the current cohort and course redesign by members of the incoming cohort Summer Conversation Hours are established. These informal gatherings are opportunities for members from both cohorts to come together and converse about their summer efforts. It also allows the faculty development office to introduce new elements of ILS to the faculty. These elements may include updates on research and teaching items, facilities upgrades, and general information about ILS. This also allows members from both cohorts to begin to form a community of learners – a relationship that will develop through the Faculty Learning Community during the coming academic year. This is another way to emphasise the importance of communication between the members of ILS.

Blackboard Community (Tenet 2, Summer 1 – Fall 2)

Blackboard, Ball State University's learning management system, serves as a repository for a variety of materials pertaining to the Interactive Learning Space Initiative. Faculty members have continuous access to information such as:

+ list of cohorts;

+ semester room schedules;

+ Faculty Development Week;

+ manuals and guides;

+ learning space floor plans;

+ information on learning;

+ books and articles of interest.

Faculty Learning Community (Tenet 2, Fall 1, Spring 2, Fall 2)

A Faculty Learning Community (FLC) is conducted during autumn/fall and spring semesters. Meeting every three weeks in the classroom space, FLCs provide members from both cohorts time to discuss active learning, issues related to their teaching, and research progress. It also allows for demonstrations related to the classroom space and technology. Benefits of the FLC participation include building multi-disciplinary relationships and the outgrowth of smaller cohorts focusing on collaborative research and writing. This mirrors findings by Glowaki-Dudka and Brown (2007) in reasons given for participating in and benefiting from Faculty Learning Communities.

Scholarship of Teaching and Learning (Tenet 1, Fall 1 – Fall 2)

ILS faculty participants are expected to engage in scholarly research regarding their experience in the initiative. This provides a natural introduction into the Scholarship of Teaching and Learning (SoTL). With some faculty members unfamiliar with this type of research, success is achieved through guidance from ILS faculty members with extensive SoTL experience. From the beginning of the ILS experience, assistance from the Office of Research and Academic Effectiveness and the Office of Academic Integrity is available to ILS faculty members. Research design is a critical element in understanding a research agenda. New cohort members are exposed to research ideas presented by the current cohort during Faculty Development Week, reinforced during summer mentorship, and enhanced during autumn/fall semester Faculty Learning Community presentations about scholarship.

While there are no specific requirements for the type of scholarship produced, all ILS participants are encouraged to work toward publication submissions. It is most gratifying to see joint efforts coming from faculty members from different disciplines This cross-departmental collaboration is a healthy aspect of ILS. Faculty express pleasure in having this opportunity presented to them through our programme. The ongoing dialogue of ILS faculty development is not only essential for professional learning, but it enhances community on our campus.

Faculty Writing Community (Tenet 1, Spring 2 – Fall 2)

It became apparent that ILS faculty needed additional support to work on their research. Providing a place to write seemed to be a logical and natural step. The faculty members were encouraged to come to the ILS classrooms during open times to engage in a common writing time. One result of this writing opportunity was the creation of a small group, multi-disciplinary faculty collaborative research project. Faculty members from four different departments embraced the opportunity to meet outside their departments and share common interests in teaching and learning. This is a positive example for other ILS members to consider.

Weekly Update (Tenet 2, Fall 1, Spring 2, Fall 2)

Electronic messaging remains a strong component of ILS. During both fall and spring semesters, Weekly ILS Updates are sent to ILS members via e-mail. These updates are a means to provide information, request information, and highlight issues regarding teaching and learning. Faculty members claim these updates to be a necessary component of their work in the initiative. This element may be the most important feature of ILS. In addition to keeping participants informed, it serves as a thread for the programme – reinforcing the concept of a community of practice. Faculty come to not only expect the weekly issues, they use the content shared in each message as a means to stay in touch with ILS thinking from Office of Educational Excellence personnel and ILS colleagues. In addition, it is a strategic means to share what others are doing in learning space design and research, nationally and internationally. A suggestion that is being considered is the formation of a monthly learning space research update.

Teaching Observations (Tenet 3, Fall 1)

Each ILS classroom was built with a transparent window allowing for observations from outside of the learning space. ILS faculty members come to understand that they may be observed at any time, and many invite observers into the space so they can hear, as well as see, the class interaction. During the autumn/fall semester, the incoming cohort is encouraged to come into the learning spaces and observe their mentor as well as other ILS instructors. This provides an opportunity for them to observe the pedagogy, space, and technology in action as they make final preparations for teaching during the upcoming spring semester.

Reflections for Growth (Tenet 3, Spring 2)

These sessions are healthy for mid-semester feedback. ILS teachers have an opportunity to share ideas that are working well. In addition, ILS faculty can communicate to faculty development personnel their needs to make instruction more effective. During these one-on-one sessions, faculty development personnel can flush out course instructional needs and can also work to create new mentoring partnerships that could further enhance their teaching. Equally so, support personnel can identify teaching techniques and ideas that can be shared with other ILS faculty through Weekly Updates and FLCs.

End of Semester Recap (Tenet 3, Fall 1, Spring 2, Fall 2)

This culminating event is a gathering of ILS faculty at the conclusion of autumn/fall semester to share what has been learnt. This time is a coming-together of faculty members who have taught in both active learning classrooms. ILS faculty members enjoy the chance to communicate their successes with their peers. Time in each of the two learning spaces allows for sharing of ideas, strategies, best practices, and lessons learned.

ILS Research and Scholarship

A primary purpose of the Interactive Learning Space initiative is to cultivate a new perception of teaching 21st Century learners in higher education. In addition, involvement in the initiative provides each faculty participant an opportunity to develop a research agenda based on their ILS experience whether it addresses issues specific to one's discipline or broader issues regarding teaching and learning in higher education (SoTL).

As of this writing, the ILS initiative is in its second full semester of implementation; Cohort 1 is completing their teaching assignment and progressing with data gathering and analysis. Each faculty member determines their research topic. A few are able to compare their ILS class to a traditional class that they teach concurrently. Others are taking this opportunity to address active learning issues across disciplines. Fifty percent of Cohort 1 members have presented at various conferences around the United States, sharing their experiences teaching in the ILS Initiative. We anticipate additional presentations and publications at the conclusion of their ILS teaching and research experience.

Conclusion

Having a history as a teaching institution and, more recently, emphasising an innovative and entrepreneurial attitude toward learning in higher education, the Interactive Learning Space Initiative brings the importance of active learning to the forefront of teaching and scholarship at our university. For active learning to be successful in the higher education classroom, several elements must be present – active learning pedagogy, a learning space, and technologies that support active learning. Equally, this faculty development framework invites all that are involved in ILS to reflect on what has been accomplished as new space is designed and developed. However, a critical element that might be overlooked is that of faculty development. The professional development required to prepare faculty members must go beyond the 'one and done' single workshop model where information is presented in a short timeframe and easily forgotten if not used consistently afterward. We propose a model that incorporates:

+ frequent and continuous interactions over the course of several semesters, if not years;

+ programming developed and facilitated by the faculty directly involved in the initiative;

+ emphasis on reflective planning and teaching; and

+ the inclusion of the study of best practices in higher education active learning spaces and the dissemination of findings.

We, as educational developers, serve our faculty by affording opportunities to rethink teaching for the best reason – the enhancement of learning. We search for ways to advance the culture of teaching and learning. It is common to observe instruction that is merely a replication of how teachers were taught. This is evident in higher education, where most faculty members have not had education in teaching and learning strategies. Therefore, it is obvious that in order to generate a rethinking of teaching for active learning, faculty most definitely need a programme of learning that allows them to explore and develop teaching and learning strategies. Coupled with different learning spaces and accompanying 21st Century instructional technology assets found in active learning classrooms, such a faculty development programme is essential.

In our experience, those faculty members coming to the ILS with a lecture-style instructional behaviour not only rethink teaching in the ILS but in the traditional space as well. A fundamental pedagogical change is occurring with these instructors. Members of Cohort 1 are reporting changes to their teaching when they are in traditional learning space for their other classes, which they attribute to participating in the ILS Initiative. Some changes are strictly pedagogical while others are making attempts at incremental changes in the physical learning space to promote and support active learning. We have yet to document teaching behaviours of Cohort 1 – but we will, once they leave the Interactive Learning Spaces and return to traditional learning spaces full time in spring 2014. While we hope the ILS Initiative results in the renovation of additional learning spaces across campus and we are confident that this initiative has prompted a cultural shift in teaching and learning at Ball State University.

About the Authors

Gary M. Pavlechko is Director of Teaching Technology in the Office of Educational Excellence at Ball State University. He can be contacted at this e-mail: gpavlech@bsu.edu

Kathleen L. Jacobi is Assistant Director of Faculty Development in the Office of Educational Excellence at Ball State University. She can be contacted at this e-mail: kjacobi@bsu.edu

Chapter Eleven

Designing a Learning Space for Creativity and Collaboration: from Studio to Computer Lab in Design Education

Ryan Daniel and Katja Fleischmann

This chapter contributes to the anthology on learning space design in higher education by exploring the extent to which the computer lab and other formal and informal learning spaces offer a viable alternative to the traditional design studio in supporting students to learn collaboratively and be creative. We define learning space as the various places where teaching and learning occur, including formal and informal locations as well as those in both physical and virtual environments. Reading this chapter, you will:

1. get a deeper understanding of the key features of learning spaces that support successful cross-disciplinary and creative collaboration;

2. gain insights into how students view a range of typical formal and informal learning spaces in higher education; and

3. be inspired to reflect on how the best features of traditional learning spaces might be replicated in new forms of physical learning spaces.

Introduction

The education of undergraduate design students typically aims to reflect industry practice and methods of working. While for many years the principal learning space for designers – regardless of the specific sub-discipline e.g. industrial design, graphic design, urban design – was the traditional 'studio', recent developments in technology and changes in design practice have seen the computer lab become increasingly prevalent. This is particularly the case in the area of media design and visual communication, also referred to as digital design, multimedia design, interaction design, graphic design or communication design (Design Council, 2005; Design Institute of Australia, 2009). Media design students typically learn to create print designs (e.g. logos, brochures, posters) and a variety of interactive online and offline media (e.g. websites, animations, games and video).

Alongside this change in physical learning spaces is a shift in working style from individual to multi- or trans-disciplinary teams, with designers now expected to be able to work across various domains in response to complex problems. Hence, contemporary learning spaces for designers need to support not only individual practice but also interaction. Despite the prevalence of design in industry as well as the number of programmes and students studying this discipline worldwide, there is little recent research that explores the functionality and impact of the shift from studio spaces to computer labs. Hence, this chapter sets out to explore this shift and consider the extent to which the computer lab offers a viable alternative to the traditional design studio, in this case at James Cook University, an Australian higher education institution.

Signature pedagogies in design education

In order to prepare students for a successful transition from the classroom to the workplace, most design programmes worldwide employ project-based learning as part of the curriculum (McCarthy & Almeida, 2002; Duggan & Dermody, 2005; Ellmers, 2006; Shreeve et al., 2008; Poggen-pohl, 2012). These projects are often applied in nature and simulate or imitate professional practice (Shreeve, 2011), hence they are scenarios with authenticity as an intent (Drew, 2007; Fleischmann & Daniel, 2010).

Students usually work on projects in a studio. Studio-based teaching is a central pedagogy of design (Sara, 2006; Shreeve *et al*, 2008), or, as Shreeve (2011) describes it, a signature pedagogy, which *"frequently relies on a reconstruction or simulation of the circumstances of practice"* in order *"to equip the student as a professional"* (Öztürk & Türkkan, 2006:97). Studio-based teaching or the 'studio', as a central pedagogy, is utilised in art, design and architecture education and was, until recently, typically found across all design disciplines (e.g. fashion design, communication design, product design).

The studio is anchored in the 'atelier' method, based on the 'Ecole Des Beaux Arts' model (1819-1914) and later the Bauhaus (1919-1932) model, which is considered ideal for contemporary design education. In the studio, students learn according to the traditional master-apprenticeship model (Broadfoot & Bennett, 2003; Lee, 2006; STP, 2009; Hart *et al.*, 2011; Souleles, 2011), which is centred around the pedagogical concept of *"learning-by-doing"* (Schön, 1983) and grounded in Kolb's (1984) experiential learning model. The key focus of the studio is on learning through creativity and creative practice where students go through a cycle of action and reflection (Schön, 1987) on their learning of creativity through design. In other words, students typically work on projects that require them to learn new creative skills and/or practices.

The studio is seen as both a physical space and a teaching approach (Broadfoot & Bennett, 2003). It is a learning environment that has been shaped by pedagogy (Hunt *et al.*, 2011). Although studios might differ across creative disciplines in the types of space required to support specialisation, there are some common characteristics in the design of the physical space as well as in the pedagogy used (STP, 2009). A traditional art, design or architecture studio usually comprises a larger space in which each student has a desk or area as a dedicated workplace (Sara, 2006). Studio spaces often have flexible elements reflecting *"the interactive nature of studio learning... including the opportunity for impromptu group activities and demonstrations"* (STP, 2009:19). Modes of learning in an undergraduate design programme usually include one-to-one, group work, seminars, formal lectures, computer lab sessions, and workshops (Walliss & Greig, 2009). The formal learning component is at times also provided outside the studio environment in traditional lecture or seminar rooms (Boys, 2011).

Most studios have wall space available for students to personalise their area or to pin 'work-in-progress'. This work-in-progress is shown to and discussed with peers, design educators and tutors. Some studio environments also provide space for exhibitions or events to showcase work to the wider design community (Hart et al., 2011). Reasonable group sizes for a studio are considered to be between 12 and 20 depending on the kind of activity (STP, 2009). Access to the studio space is often flexible; next to scheduled academic time some studios are available 24 hours, seven days a week, while others offer extended access after hours in the evening for example (STP, 2009; Lee, 2006).

Key to connecting physical space and pedagogy is the studio's attempt to avoid the teacher-focused pedagogy of the late 20th century (Martin et al., 2009), which resulted in the design of *"one-way facing and presentational"* learning spaces (Jisc (formerly the JISC), 2006:10). The current focus on student-centred approaches to learning and subsequent design of physical learning spaces (Temple, 2007; Jamieson, 2009) has been inherent to studio-based teaching since its beginnings (STP, 2009). Studio-based learning is built around *"dialogical learning and teaching"* (Danvers, 2003:51). Learning is structured by ongoing dialogue between students and educators, tutors (who are often design practitioners) and support staff (Danvers, 2003; Shreeve, 2011). Critiques or 'crits' of student work, another signature pedagogy of design education (Klebsedel & Kornetsky, 2009; Shreeve, 2011), occur frequently in formal and informal ways from educators, tutors, peers or visiting professionals (Kuhn, 2001; Wands, 2001). It is this dialogue and ongoing conversation in the studio that *"can be extremely restricted or nonexistent"* in a traditional lecture classroom (Kolb & Kolb, 2005).

When considering the range of activities and learning modes the studio supports, on the basis of Scott-Webber's (2004) archetypal environments for knowledge sharing, it can be seen as an environment that facilitates the pedagogical activity of delivering, applying, creating and communicating knowledge, as well as an environment where knowledge is used for decision-making (Scott-Webber, 2004). The studio space therefore provides an environment that is very different to standard higher education learning spaces, given it allows for *"simultaneous engagement in several learning modes supported by a natural flux between unstructured and structured learning"* (STP, 2009:18).

Studio spaces, like workshops and laboratories, have an important social dimension that is widely recognised (Temple 2007). The design studio in particular is described as *"both a work and a social environment, [and] ...vital to facilitating the type of camaraderie required for creative learning"* (Hart et al., 2011:4). Shreeve (2011) supports the notion of the studio as a social space that is central to support creativity (Peterson et al., 2012). Successful studios *"rely on the establishment of communities of learners and teachers"* (Hart et al., 2011:13). The encouragement of peer communication, collaborative learning and sharing of information and ideas in the studio (Shih et al., 2006; Hart et al., 2011) is key to the development of a community of practice (Wenger, 1998), which has been acknowledged as a driver for more effective learning (Temple, 2007). Overall, the studio in design education has *"distinguishing characteristics, ... to be understood in four essential dimensions: a studio culture/community of people; a mode of teaching and learning; a program [sic] of projects and activities; and a physical space or constructed environment"* (STP, 2009:vi).

The rise of the computer lab

The emergence of digital technology has introduced computer labs as a new central learning space for design students. Since this change, higher education institutions have struggled to sustain a vibrant studio culture in the traditional sense (Ellmers, 2005). This is particularly the case in media design education where in recent years the creation and production process has shifted from analogue to digital. The creation of magazine layouts, 3-D animations, videos, websites and interactive media applications require a variety of specialised hardware and software, usually provided by the institution in a computer lab (Sara, 2006). Rapid technological developments require frequent updates or renewal of hardware and software making them expensive to maintain. As a consequence, computer labs are usually shared between design students and other disciplines. The notion of providing each design student with a dedicated workspace, equipped with necessary hardware and software, is unsustainable in many situations. This is particularly the case today where tertiary institutions are moving towards greater rationalisation and efficiency (Jisc (formerly the JISC), 2006; Hart et al., 2011; STP, 2009). Increasing student numbers are also contributing to the decline of the traditional studio (STP, 2009), despite the fact that characteristics of the studio have been identified as supporting interaction, active learning and social engagement (Carbone *et al.*, 2000; Sara, 2006; Shreeve, 2011) and which have recently been highlighted as significant for the future education of students, regardless of their discipline (Brown & Long, 2006; Milne, 2007; Felix, 2011).

In relation to the design of contemporary computer labs, Bemer *et al.* (2009) refer to the significant body of literature that exists in terms of how they are laid out and the relationships that occur within these types of learning spaces. In the typical or traditional scenario, computer labs have been configured to support teaching and learning by providing rows of computers in a lecture style classroom (Blink, 2009). This reflects a teacher-centred approach (Handa, 1993 in Bemer *et al.*, 2009), the design of which remains common in some tertiary institutions, including design degree programmes. More recent texts focus on computer labs as "*technologically rich spaces accessible to students to use as workplaces as well as to build friendships and collaborations that help them achieve their goal*" (Selfe, 2005 in Bemer *et al.*, 2009:140). This new focus reflects the intent of the traditional design studio where the design of learning spaces is driven by pedagogy (Jisc (formerly the JISC), 2006). Recent computer lab designs with flexible seating and computers arranged in pods are reflective of a student-centred approach (Blink, 2009; Bemer *et al.*, 2009). Computer labs are therefore transformed into a combination of lab and learning space (Blink, 2009).

From individual designer to working in multi- or trans-disciplinary teams

The design industry has undergone significant change since the introduction of the computer and the emergence of interactive digital media. Designers work and need to be educated in a multitude of new areas such as web, e-commerce applications and mobile devices; interface design and interactive content creation; digital video and animation production; 3D modelling and game design. An enormous shift in the way design is practised has therefore occurred including a move away from the tradition of designers working as individuals (Wild, 1998). Today, designers often work as part of multi- or trans-disciplinary teams to facilitate the production of complex interactive multimedia projects (e.g. Kerlow, 2001;

Sommese, 2007; Whyte & Bessant, 2007; Icograda, 2011). Therefore, collaboration and interaction with other disciplines is increasingly articulated as a key skill to be fostered in design graduates (Heller & Talarico, 2011; Hunt, 2011).

Although research relevant to the effectiveness of learning spaces in design education has only recently started to emerge, some key characteristics that support successful cross-disciplinary and creative collaboration can be identified. *"Collaboration and creation aren't bound to designated areas; they evolve throughout a space, absorbing different people, places, and perspectives"* (Kelly, 2012:5). Therefore, key learning spaces need to be flexible to facilitate various phases of the collaborative team process (e.g. brainstorming, prototyping, reflection). For example, Rogers (2012:144) suggests the use of *"adjustable walls or flexible seating alternatives to enable a shift into focus"*. Flexibility can also be achieved by building an *"instant studio"* through using rolling dry erase boards and foam cubes to be used to sit on or to create walls (Doorley & Witthoft, 2012). Movable sliding whiteboards as dividers and hanging screens with dual-surface projection can be added which facilitate a 360-degree engagement (McGrew & Northrup, 2012). Numerous writable surfaces facilitate instantaneous idea generation and creative collaboration (Ford, 2012). In addition a *"comfortable pause zone"* needs to be created, *"a spot at which to linger and chat before or after gathering"* in order that *"conversation can transpire that might otherwise have been lost"* (McGrew & Northrup, 2012:98).

New spaces for media design education: an Australian case study

During the years 2006-7, we were directly involved in the design phase of a purpose-built specialist School of Creative Arts (SoCA) facility to accommodate a number of disciplines including media design. This facility was a new space for James Cook University (JCU) in Australia. Given the limits of available funding and the fact that multiple disciplines required access to hardware/software, numerous decisions had to be made to best recreate the distinguishing features of the studio for the 250-300 media design students who were typically enrolled across a three-year undergraduate New Media Arts degree. In reality, there was insufficient funding to provide each student with a specialist studio space (desk and computer). This was especially the case given media design classes at first year typically involve 120-150 students, 80-100 in second year, and 60-80 in the third and final year, and this pattern of enrolment is becoming increasingly common in the Australian higher education sector. The standard pattern of instruction involves a 1-hour lecture followed by a 2-hour workshop/tutorial with 25 students per session.

While there was general literature to give guidance about the ways in which the facility might be designed to support learning and student engagement, in relation to media design education there was minimal direction. There was certainly an intention to recreate the distinguishing features of the traditional design studio, the latter well documented in the literature for its signature features (e.g. Kuhn, 2001; Broadfoot & Bennett, 2003). There were also references in the literature to the need for formal and informal learning spaces (a move also considered by Dobozy (in this volume) and Enomoto & Warner (also in this volume)) which would enable self-directed learning, construction of knowledge, interactions between students, increased students' motivation to learn and a sense of belonging (e.g. Kuh et al., 2005; Jisc (formerly the JISC), 2006; Temple, 2007).

The learning spaces that were ultimately designed included a flexibly constructed specialist computer lab (SoCA Computer lab) which replaced the traditional studio space. The SoCA Computer lab features 'collaborative' small learning pods and opportunities for large group interaction, multiple white boards for idea generation and brainstorming, as well as three high-end data projectors that can operate individually or in unison. In addition to the specialist computer lab, a high-end specialist computer studio (SoCA Fish bowl) for advanced project work was designed, as well as a multi-purpose space designed for flexible usage by staff and students (SoCA Multipurpose room). The building also included pre- and post-production print facilities, two galleries as well as open and covered outdoor areas designed as pause zones to encourage informal learning, collaboration and reflection (SoCA Courtyard, Grass area).

The facility was initially opened in 2008 and has now seen three cohorts of new students graduate. While anecdotally these learning spaces seemed to be working in terms of providing an alternative to the traditional studio model, it was deemed necessary to gather empirical evaluative research evidence to provide a fuller picture relevant to this approach. After giving consideration to various paradigms or philosophical approaches, an interpretivist methodology was adopted (Punch, 2009). This approach was chosen in order to develop a deep understanding of the students' experiences and perceptions of how different learning spaces support and enable them to be creative learners. As an initial step, the following four research questions were identified.

1. Is the computer lab as a specialist creative learning space a viable alternative to the traditional design studio?

2. What other learning spaces do students believe are valuable in terms of supporting and enhancing their capacity to be creative?

3. What are the particular aspects of specialist formal and informal learning spaces that students identify as most important in terms of supporting and enhancing their capacity to be creative?

4. Given the shift in design practice and industry from individual practitioner to trans- or multi-disciplinary teams, in what locations do students in fact collaborate?

Methods

Given the size of the student cohort (over 200 students) we decided to work with online surveys in order to gather a wide range of views and reflections. In terms of the first three research questions, a number of specifically designed learning spaces in the School's specialist facility and which the students were using were photographed, including the computer lab, high-end workstations, external courtyard, tutorial room etc. In addition, other learning spaces on campus which students used were photographed, including the library, coffee shop and a large lecture theatre, the latter another example of change where previously, resourcing had enabled course sizes to be kept to 20-30 students. That is, given the significant increase in enrolments (e.g. 120 students in first-year design courses), large lecture theatres and relevant pedagogies were now required. Figure 1 presents the ten learning spaces captured via photography:

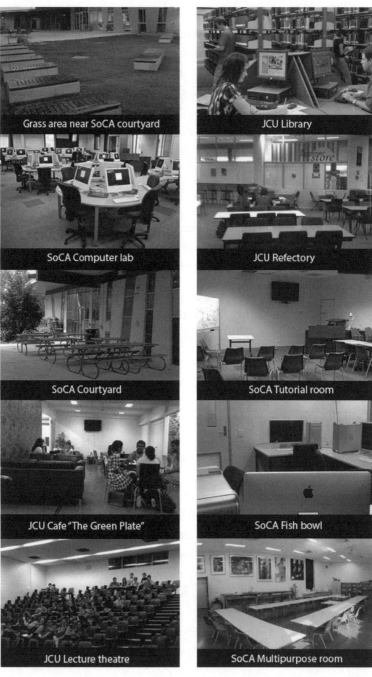

Figure 1: Ten learning spaces presented to students for reflection, ranking and written response.

These ten images were collated into an online survey (via *Surveymonkey.com*) and students invited to rank them, with the highest ranking assigned to the learning space where they feel they are able to generate the most creative design ideas. They were then asked to provide the three main reasons for choosing their top-ranked learning space – in order to add richness to the data.

The researchers then invited each year level's cohort of media design students enrolled in first semester 2013 to complete the survey. This included 121 students in the first year introduction to graphic design course, 81 in second year introduction to web design, as well as 42 in the third year interactive media design course. In terms of fully completed surveys for analysis, 95 were obtained, resulting in an overall response rate of 39% (57 students at first year level, 14 at second year and 24 at third year). Finally, in order to develop a response to the fourth research question, an additional short survey was sent to the 42 third years, who were all working in teams with 3rd year information technology students. We asked them to reflect on the balance of their time spent working collaboratively in the specialist computer labs, in other on-campus learning spaces, and virtually. Of these 42 students, who were working across ten different teams, 20 individuals responded (47.6% response rate) with all ten teams represented.

The resulting data from both surveys was both quantitative (via rankings, percentages of time) and qualitative (written explanations) in nature. In terms of analysis, the first survey data was downloaded as an Excel file, with pivot tables applied in order to group rankings by learning space, and linked to the reasons students gave for both their rankings as well as enhancements for their top-ranked learning space. The qualitative reasons were then analysed inductively with themes quickly emerging (Saldana, 2009), after which these were quantified in terms of the number of times they were referred to by students. The overall data set offered numerous insights into students' reflections and thoughts, these findings presented below.

Findings: learning spaces data analysis

In terms of students' ranking of the ten photographed learning spaces, Table 1 below presents the average scores by year level and across the three years, with the latter sorted in descending order.

Learning space	Average across three years	1st year (n = 57)	2nd year (n=14)	3rd year (n=24)
SoCA Computer lab	7.8	7.8	7.6	7.9
Grass area near SoCA courtyard	6.4	6.1	6.5	6.5
JCU Library	5.9	6.9	4.9	5.8
SoCA Courtyard	5.8	5.8	5.1	6.5
SoCA Fish bowl	5.7	5.0	5.6	6.5
SoCA Multipurpose room	5.6	5.5	6.2	5.0
JCU Café "The Green Plate"	5.0	4.7	5.6	4.6
SoCA Tutorial room	4.7	4.9	5.1	4.1
JCU Lecture theatre	4.2	4.4	3.6	4.4
JCU Refectory	4.1	3.9	4.8	3.6
(Scale 1 = least creative learning space, 10 = most creative learning space)				

Table 1: Average ranking of learning spaces overall and by year level.

The data in Table 1 above reveals that:

+ the SoCA Computer lab is rated the highest by all three year level groups in terms of the learning space that best supports their capacity to work as creative learners;

+ several traditional and formal learning spaces (e.g. Lecture theatre, Tutorial room) tend not to rate highly, although first year students did rate the JCU Library as second most valuable learning space for them. This is most likely due to the fact that the library has recently been re-designed to include a new learning centre, at the same time when these first year students commenced their studies;

+ informal learning spaces in the SoCA building, including the grass area and courtyard, rate reasonably highly; and

+ the value of the specialist and student-dedicated SoCA Fish bowl also increases across the three years, largely due to the fact that students have an increasing requirement for high-end project work by the third year and that this space is designed to support it.

Interestingly, across the three years there are no significant variations in the rankings of which learning spaces best support students' capacities to work as creative learners, however slight differences exist. Future research could therefore explore the relationship between the nature of the curriculum and particular learning activities in each year to the popularity of learning spaces.

To understand the situation at hand, students were invited to identify their three top reasons for choosing their most highly ranked space. These are summarised below in Table 2, in descending overall order, with the main reasons presented and quantified as themes, as well as an exemplar quote provided to reveal the student voice.

Learning space	1st yr (57)	2nd yr (14)	3rd yr (24)	Total
SoCA Computer lab	23	6	10	39
Equipment (23), Comfortable (15), Quiet (12), Creative (11), Collaborative (10), Concentrated environment (10), Software access (9), Peaceful (6), Spacious (6), Access to information (5), Accessible (4), Versatile (3) *"A great collaborative environment"* (3rd year)				
Grass area near SoCA courtyard	11	3	2	16
Open space (11), Being outside (10), Quiet (9), Inspiring (7), Green (4), Fresh air (4), Relaxing (3), The environment (2) *"Outside amongst fresh air and views of nature helps me breathe and focus and unclutter my mind"* (1st year)				
JCU Library	7	-	4	11
Quiet (8), Inspiring (7), Relaxing (4), Access to information (3), Atmosphere (2), Equipment (2), Spacious (2), Cool, Friendly *"It is a quiet place where you can concentrate and focus"* (1st year)				
SoCA Fish bowl	3	1	3	7
Concentrated environment (7), Computers/software (4), Comfortable (3), Quiet (2), Peaceful, Social, Cool, Collaborative " *Isolated area – minimal distractions allowing for easy flow of ideas"* (1st year)				
JCU Refectory	3	2	1	6
Confined (3), Relaxed (3), Quiet (2), Collaborative (2), Fun, Friendly, Food, Access, Spacious, Inspiring, Alive, Couches, Access to information " *The place is loud and feels 'alive'"* (2nd year)				

SoCA Courtyard	3	1	2	6
Quiet (5), Work on my own (4), Space (3), Outdoors (2), Fresh air (2), Inspiring "*Lots of inspiration*" (2nd year)				
SoCA Multipurpose room	2	1	-	3
Quiet (3), Inspiring (2), Equipment (2), Relaxing "*It's a quiet area I can relax and just do stuff if I want to*" (3rd year)				
SoCA Tutorial room	2	-	1	3
Learning (3), Inspiring (2), Equipment (2) "*I get to know more about the [course] matter when I am in here*" (1st year)				
JCU Lecture theatre	1	-	1	2
Creative ideas (2), Accessible, Spacious, Quiet, Collaborative "*The creative ideas that you get from the lecture*" (1st year)				
JCU Café 'The green plate'	2	-	-	2
Internet access, Food helps creativity, Collaborative, Ambient, Cultural "*Food always helps me with creativity*" (1st year)				

Table 2: Students' first choice learning space, summary of top three reasons in support, and exemplar quote of relevance.

Table 2 above provides clear evidence that students see most value in the computer lab for supporting their capacity to be creative design learners, although the value of the 'green' space within 20 meters of the computer labs is also identified. In relation to the lab specifically, students reflect not only on the equipment and layout, but the attributes that support their chance to be creative learners, such as the atmosphere and how it supports concentrated activity including collaboration. When looking at the qualitative comments about the computer lab (top-ranked space) again by first, second and third reasons presented, the following emerged as the key aspects or features:

- 1st reason: 'access to technology' (19), a finding which is arguably logical given the space features the most current *iMac* computers with the latest software relevant to creative media design practice (e.g. *Adobe Creative Suite*);

- 2nd reason: 'being in the vicinity of creativity/people/ collaboration' (18), reflecting a community of collaborative practice and which was part of the rationale for the design of the lab in pods and with flexible arrangements including 24/7 access; and

+ 3rd reason: 'a positive atmosphere/environment' (13), which largely emerges as an outcome of the 2nd reason but which also reflects students' sense of contribution to and ownership of the learning space.

Findings: where and how do students collaborate?

In terms of third-year design students indicating where and how they collaborate as project teams, a percentage breakdown over the course of a semester is presented in Table 3. The table shows the averages for each team with the second column from the left ranked highest to lowest in relation to time spent in the computer lab.

Team	Face to face in computer lab	Face to face elsewhere	Using digital technology
Team H	100	0	0
Team E	80	5	15
Team C	60	20	20
Team D	50	0	50
Team F	50	5	45
Team J	40	10	50
Team B	30	0	70
Team G	30	0	70
Team A	30	10	60
Team I	10	10	80

Table 3: Student self-analyses of time spent collaborating in both physical and virtual spaces (as %).

As can be seen in Table 3 above, there is a notable difference in the way that the ten teams report on how and where they collaborate. In terms of this particular group, five of the teams preferred to spend at least half or more of their time in the school's computer lab, while others work virtually for a considerable percentage of time. Furthermore, for several teams there is a mix of times spent across locations, a trend which Lange and Smith call *"moving between spaces"* (this volume). Thus, while the computer lab is ranked most highly by students for its capacity to support access to technology, for collaboration and creative ideas generation, it appears to no longer be enough in terms of catering for the different and potentially competing ways in which students work and collaborate.

Summary of key findings

The SoCA Computer lab has to a large extent offered a viable alternative to the traditional design studio environment. It is ranked highly by the majority of students in terms of the space that best supports their capacity to be creative learners, which is possibly influenced by the fact that they are used to working in computer-based environments. Pragmatic reasons such as *"up-to-date equipment and software"* and to *"have access to tools which I can use in my creativity"* evidence the centrality of the computer lab in the contemporary workflow in design education. Student feedback also references a variety of characteristic features of the traditional design studio. For example, the interactive nature of the design studio as a foundation for building a community of learners is highlighted by comments such as *"You can exchange ideas with people next to you"* and *"Other people in there help me generate ideas."*

Contemporary learning spaces benefit from being flexible, as can be seen in the feedback on the design of the computer lab which enables students to work individually as well as collaboratively. The student-centred design of the computer lab supports interaction and also solitude if needed, as expressed by a student: *"I can still have other people's input whilst alone"*. Flexibility, however, goes beyond the physical design of the computer lab and is also encapsulated in the access provided and through offering a combination of formal and informal spaces. Students can use the computer lab 24 hours, 7 days a week – a feature taken from the design studio and which drew positive comments such as *"I like working here at night time free from home distractions"*. Arguably, one of the most challenging but crucial features to recreate in a computer lab is the social aspect of the design studio. Students in this study agreed that this was achieved, referring to *"other friendly students who help each other think and create"* and a space with a *"social atmosphere"*.

Other spaces are also important and seem to add value to or

complement the functionality of the computer lab. Creativity is not confined to one space and some students find informal and outdoor spaces as important for them in pursuing their learning of creativity and creative design practice. References to 'outside', 'wide space', 'sound of nature', 'green' and *"being outside gives me more of an open mind"* suggests that students find it important to be able to work beyond formal learning spaces only. Therefore, the cycle of action and reflection as core to design learning appears to include a flexible combination of learning spaces that support both individual and collaborative practice.

When considering the extent to which the specifically designed learning spaces support the capacity for design students to learn, one significant form of evidence in support of learning are the pass rates across the three most recent years and at all levels of the media design major: first year (91.5%), second year (93.5%), third year (95%). While this is a positive outcome at this time, ongoing work is required to keep our learning spaces current and aligned to the changing ways in which students appear to be working. This became particularly clear in the way students collaborate in different ways, be this face to face on campus in computer labs and other spaces, as well as virtually through the various interaction tools and methods now available in web 2.0 environments (e.g. Skype, Facebook).

Conclusions

Media design education has changed considerably over the past two decades due to the shift from analogue to digital production and the emergence of digital media. As a result, the computer lab has emerged as a central learning space in media design education. While the traditional studio is often referred to as the ideal paradigm for new types of learning (Boys, 2011), in many cases it is disappearing (Ellmers, 2005; STP, 2009). At James Cook University, a purpose-built facility was designed to support interaction, communication, sharing of ideas and co-designing in teams. The flexibly constructed computer lab, which featured small collaborative learning pods and room for large group interactions, replaced the traditional studio and was designed to replicate its characteristics. The evidence obtained suggests it is largely successful, given media design students at all year-levels identified the computer lab as key to supporting and enabling them to be creative learners, as well as enabling them to be in the vicinity of creative peers. Flexibility emerged as key quality in physical design, combination of learning spaces and access to the computer lab.

There are clearly numerous opportunities for further enquiry and research that emerge from this study. For example, further investigation of activity in learning spaces could occur via observational or video analysis of the forms of interaction and behaviour that design students engage in within learning spaces. A deeper understanding of the prior experiences students have in different learning spaces would also enable educators to potentially create an easier transition to higher education. In relation to collaborative learning, it would be useful to explore the nature of how students interact and what influence this has on their decisions to work either in a face to face mode or virtually. Other research opportunities could include inviting a sample of students to diarise their time and learning spent within and across different learning spaces during a typical week or month. In addition, as this study indicates, the concept of learning is changing; communication, creation and collaboration are taking place in virtual environments. This shift is a reflection of new ways of working and collaborating in the design industry where virtual studios are beginning to emerge, thus representing the next challenge for higher education providers of design education in terms of how they cater for this and other forms of learning that will emerge in the future.

About the authors

Ryan Daniel is a Professor of Creative Arts and Creative Industries at James Cook University. He can be contacted at this e-mail: ryan.daniel@jcu.edu.au

Katja Fleischmann is a Senior Lecturer in Media Design and Design Researcher at the School of Creative Arts at James Cook University. She can be contacted at this e-mail: katja.fleischmann@jcu.edu.au

Chapter Twelve
The Active Agency of Learning Spaces

Aileen Strickland

Introduction

This chapter contributes to the anthology on learning space design in higher education by heightening an awareness of how the active agency of higher education learning spaces shapes the development of citizens and society. To heighten this awareness, I review the social theory of structuration, establish the concept of spatial agency in context, and discuss this relevance to higher education and its application to learning spaces. Finally, I discuss the implications for theory and practice within higher education learning spaces. For the purpose of this chapter I define a learning space – with reference to structuration theory – as active locales that influence and are influenced by the interaction of human agents (Warf, 2011). I shall come back to a thorough discussion of the implications of this definition of learning space. Reading this chapter, you will:

1. be familiar with the key arguments of structuration theory and its implications for learning space design;

2. be aware that learning spaces have active agency in the development of citizens and society; and

3. become empowered to see, act and impart the values needed in the 21st century.

One of the roles of higher education institutions is to prepare students to build, shape and function within local and global economic and social systems (Cortese, 2003). It is acknowledged by many institutions of higher education that current traditional models of student preparation are no longer adequate for the quickly changing economies and the myriad of challenges these changes present for current and future generations. There is a recognised shift from an industrial-based society to a globalising knowledge society (Kefela, 2010; Levy *et al.*, 2011). In order to support these shifting systems, the ways students are taught must shift as well. In order to address this shift, the embrace of active learning pedagogies is becoming more prevalent in higher education (Nygaard *et al.*, 2013). What is considered less often is the role that learning spaces play in supporting emerging pedagogies. Physical space is typically viewed as the backdrop to which activity, agency, structure, and social systems unfold rather than being considered an active agent in the process. While critical geographers and theorists have long argued that space plays an active role in shaping the ways we operate within the world and the resulting social systems that emerge, the matter has not been adequately explored within the realm of physical higher educational learning spaces.

Structuration theory

The reasoning behind employing the sociological theory of structuration as a framework to think about the active agency of learning spaces is three-fold. First, the theory applies systems thinking, understanding how systems influence one another as a whole. Employing a framework that takes into account the multi-faceted eco-system is imperative to understanding the complexity of variables in studying the impact and influence of space. Second, by using a sociological theory over an architectural-based one, the origin of exploration remains human-centred, looking beyond the physical dimension to place emphasis on the more holistic and conceptual ways these spaces affect our lives. Third, higher education profoundly shapes our social systems, thus by embedding the active agency within learning spaces, the bridge between the importances of its agency and resulting society can be more easily built.

Structuration theory is an influential sociological theory proposed by Giddens (1984) that promotes the creation and reproduction of a social system based on the interrelations of structure and agency, unfolding across space and time. In his writings, Giddens defines agency as human action and structure as rules and regulations instantiated in social systems. Each enabling and constraining one another to produce and reproduce the social systems in which we are embedded. Instead of building on sociological macro theories, which maintain individuals are shaped by society *or* micro theories, which uphold that interactions between individuals shape society, structuration theory proposes that the macro and micro dimensions of life must be seen as mutually complementary, effectively two sides of the same coin. The microstructures of our everyday life are interwoven with the macrostructures of our larger society by the individual drawing on rules and resources, which in turn structure the individual's actions, establishing a cycle that is *"simultaneously determinant and mutually recursive"* (Warf, 2011:179).

In relation to space, structuration theory asserts that routinised patterns of an individual's behaviour unfold temporally and spatially, thus attesting that place matters (Warf, 2011). In effect, structuration theory enables the view that places are *"contingently produced entities continually in a state of becoming via the actions of the human subjects in every day life"* (Warf, 2011:182). Or in other words, spaces are active locales that influence and are influenced by the interaction of human agents (Warf, 2011). While geographers exploring this application have primarily developed these spatial contributions of structuration theory on a larger environmental scale, the concept can be applied at a smaller scale. Spatial agency is an exceptionally provoking application when considered in the context of higher education learning spaces. This is because, if educational settings have active agency to influence interaction and behaviour, which in turn enable and constrain our social systems, it is increasingly imperative that consideration is given to the social systems institutions enable and constrain through their current learning spaces. What types of social systems does higher education want to enable in the future, and how can their learning spaces support these types of systems?

Establishing spatial agency

Before attempting to answer that question, a basic understanding of spatial agency must be established, first at an individual level then at a societal level. The assertion that space has active agency on our experiences is not novel. The understanding of ourselves in relation to space has been conceptualised and written about for centuries, from Eastern religious ideology (Hagen, 1997) to Western economic theory (Locke, 1995), to 20th century philosophy (Heidegger, 1962; LeFebvre, 1974; Merleau-Ponty, 1962) to modern-day humanist geography (Massey, 1994; Tuan, 1977). While a deep dive into the conceptualisations of our relationship with space is outside the scope of this chapter, a brief establishment of historical and current perceptions of spatial experience is necessary to contextualise an understanding of spatial agency and its alignment with structuration theory and higher education. This is done by illustrating how influential philosophers have separated, and subsequently rejoined, conceptualisations of the mind, body and space.

The perception of space being abstracted from experience is a fairly recent construct. In the latter half of the 17th century, Locke (1690/1995) articulated a theory on space, stemming from his desire to set up control for a larger system of trade and economy within Western civilization. In setting the groundwork for his political agenda, Locke had to divorce space from the self to illustrate that space was an abstract, possessable, blank slate that individuals could commodify. Furthermore, Descartes (1641/1993) and other thinkers at that time philosophised that the mind was governed solely by logic and reason. The body and emotion were rendered imperfect and disconsidered as a dimension of human experience. These ideas spread quickly from doctrine to practice through art, architecture, economy, trade, land use, politics, and culture. In a short amount of time, a new conceptualisation of space and way of operating within the world was established (Bordo, 1987). While this dominant manner of being in the world has been enculturated for centuries, many 20th century critics have challenged this foundation of thought and sought to re-establish our experiences within a spatial context.

In studying and discussing our connection with space, whether it is through the lens of culture, sensation, psychology, sociology, neuroscience or geography, for many scholars, the point of reconnection begins with our perception, one of the building blocks of experience. In examining the shift in visually represented perspective in painting between medieval and post-Lockean Renaissance art, Bordo (1987), a cultural scholar, stressed the ways that we are acculturated into a way of seeing the world. The phenomenologist Merleau-Ponty espoused that the body is the medium for what he called 'primodial openness to the life world'; it is first through what we corporeally sense and perceive that we begin an experience in the world (Merleau-Ponty, 1962). Tuan, a renowned human geographer, takes these phenomena of sensing and perception and enfolds it even deeper with the individual mind. Tuan (1977:16) states that, *"Human spaces reflect the quality of the human senses and mentality"*, contending that the mind often infers beyond sensory evidence and quickly begins to build a connection to the space around us through interpretation and meaning making. These processes then shape our actions, reactions and behaviours with and within those spaces. It is in these multi-dimensional interactions that space begins to have agency on the human agent.

By building from this established fluidity of connection between self and space, social theorists have explored what this may mean on a collective, societal scale. These explorations connect directly back to the point in structuration theory that it is through these patterns of individual action that structure emerges, and in turn social systems. Henri Lefebvre, a prominent French sociologist, asserts this idea when he states, *"there is an immediate relationship between the body and space...each living body* **is** *space and* **has** *its space: it produces itself in space and also produces that space"* (Lefebvre, 1974:170, emphasis [bold] is his). Whether intentional or unintentional, by engagement of the mind/body in the production of space, the individual becomes an involved agent of change and renders a space that is dynamic and engaging (Lefebvre, 1974). If one remains unaware to this spatial agency, they may continue to unintentionally produce a mirror of what exists. This speaks to the question posed earlier in the chapter, what types of social systems does higher education want to enable? Educational scholar David Gruenwald explains that by not recognising that place is an articulation of human decision, we become complicit in the processes that bring these places into being (2003). Changing society means nothing without the production of an *"appropriate"* space (Lefebvre, 1974:59). In considering this all in the context of higher education learning spaces, these spaces are not simply a container in which learning experiences unfold, rather learning experiences are inherently spatial.

From these philosophical pontifications on the foundations of our spatial experiences, academics have begun to study experiences within specific environments with a more practice-based focus. Within the realm of education, 20th century early educational theorists focused on student-centred, constructivist learning. Dewey, Montassorri and Malaguzzi (of the Reggio Emilia approach), have all promoted the idea that the learning space makes a difference in the students' learning and development (Hall *et al.*, 2010; Strong-Wilson & Ellis, 2007). In schools that are developed under these approaches to early education, the learning spaces are intentionally designed to provide a multi-sensory experience, engaging the child's whole self in their learning process and supporting the school's philosophy and pedagogies (Hall *et al.*, 2010). Both Montessori and Reggio educators believed that children are transformed by everything that they see, hear, touch, or encounter within their environment and purposefully designed spaces are vital to the child's development (Hall *et al.*, 2010). Children are able to learn and construct meaning within environments that support *"complex, varied, sustained, and changing relationships between people, the world of experience, ideas and the many ways of expressing ideas"* (Cadwell, 1997:93). Furthermore, the definition of 'learning spaces' not only encompasses these classrooms and school spaces but extends to envelop the surrounding community, as the education of the student is considered a collective responsibility of the community. Because the learning spaces are considered 'third teachers' (Stonehouse, 2011), there is great concern for what the environment is teaching. The design of the schools reflects the structure of the community (Designshare, 2001). This practice within early education environments is an illustration how learning spaces have active agency within the system illustrated by structuration theory.

More recently, architects and designers have begun to address the agency of other learning spaces from an intentional and practical design perspective (Bergsagel *et al.*, 2007; Doorely & Witthoft, 2012; Lippeman, 2010; Nair, Fielding, & Lackney, 2009; OWP/P, VS Furniture & Bruce Mau Design, 2010). While these explorations have mushroomed in the last decade, the majority of this examination centres on primary or secondary educational spaces. Many insights gleaned from these examinations may be generalisable, applicable and relevant to higher education, however the unique considerations, context and purpose of higher education should shape more pointed questions and explorations into the agency of these particular learning spaces.

Relevance to higher education

Those working in higher education institutions across the globe would agree that one of its main objectives is to prepare students to build, shape, and function within the local and global economic and social systems (Cortese, 2003). In many cases across the globe, the education system is synonymous with a state- or national-provided system in which the government sets educational policy as to what should be taught, to whom and how (Broadfoot, 2002). These policies, which are realised within institutions and their classroom environments, function as a structure that engages human action, simultaneously restricting and facilitating it. From this dialogue between learner and practised structure, a societal system is systematically created. This idea is reflected in the quote: *"Universities are multi-faceted amalgamations of economic, political, judicial and epistemological relations of power, which still reflect the exclusionary and inclusionary binaries of their origins...they multiply and reinforce the power-effects of an expanding stratum of intellectuals and, not least, as a result of new global demands for active, multi-skilled and self-regulated citizens"* (Deacon, 2006:184)

Within higher education, comparative education studies have challenged the existing assumptions and methodologies within traditional education, both in purpose and delivery (Broadfoot, 2002). Within the last decade or so, there has been an urgent recognition that these axioms are no longer adequate in preparing students for the future that will exist. While a deep introspection into this issue is beyond the purposes of this chapter, it calls to light the importance of challenging and questioning current models and practices in place within higher education, and in doing so impugn the associated current learning spaces.

There is no shortage of recognition that students need to be educated and prepared to function within a 21st century economy (Applegate, 2011; Johnson, 2009; Smith & Hu, 2013; Steven, 2012). A foundational transition of global economy is underway, shifting from an industrial model more reliant on the production of goods to a model more dependent on the production of knowledge. As economies evolve to become more global and knowledge-based, it cannot be expected that the old way of doing things will work (McKibben, 2004). We know that in order to support what may be needed in 21st systems, the manner future generations are taught has to shift with the knowledge, skills and talents required. In preparing students for the 21st century, much of the discussion centres around the emerging pedagogies like collaborative, team-based or problem-based learning (Cortese, 2003; Nygaard et al., 2013) and in developing citizens that can engage in critical thinking, passionate inquiry, social collaboration, productive co-creation and dynamic modes of sustainability (Cortese, 2003; Stevens, 2012). Expanding beyond content and siloed study, focus is needed on the transference of values and critical skills through interdisciplinary insight, action, ethics and opportunity to develop students prepared for a systemic, dynamic and global society (Perkins, 2013). To cultivate new ways of thinking, new ways of structuring, new ways of producing and new ways of being involves a paradigmatic shift towards a systemic approach (Cortese, 2003).

This restructuring comes as a result of a multitude of driving variables, including the emergence of more advanced technology, greater global connectivity and sustainability. In her book, *The Nature of the Future* (2013), Marina Gorbis, a renowned futurist and Silicon Valley thought leader, mirrors this call to action by reflecting on the ways that technology has empowered individuals to change the structures of the ways we work, solve issues and create value. In speaking to how technology impacts the human agent, Gorbis (2013) calls on us to rethink our social structures by upholding that technologies facilitating innovation produce new economic models that will increasingly replace the institutional production we have come to rely on in so many areas of our lives. Just as Gorbis argues the agency of technology impacts the system, I argue as does space.

This consideration of what has agency should shake institutions of higher education into deeply thinking upon the environments in which the students' education is taking place. With so much intentionality put into the purpose of higher education, and building off the previous discussion of spatial agency, intentionality must also be carefully considered in the conceptualisation of these learning spaces. For it is not only what is taught that is learnt but also that which is perceived in the environments that surround us.

Application to learning spaces

From campus plans to the interior of a classroom, all spaces express a set of values actively acting upon the students and educators occupying and operating at that institution. At the same time, the students and educators are acting upon these spaces. Through the preceding sections of this chapter the theory of structuration and the active agency of space have been established, along with a discussion on its relevance to current issues within higher education. In the next section, I will weave these concepts together by discussing how the agency of the learning space, learner and rules interact to produce certain social systems (see Figure 1). To concretely illustrate this, two types of learning space will be compared and discussed, one 'traditional' designed learning space, and one designed to support active learning. The conceptual framework applied in the following section can be widely applied to a myriad of different learning spaces, as well as the space in general. For the sake of this chapter, and to illustrate the point most clearly, the example will be limited to the formal classroom.

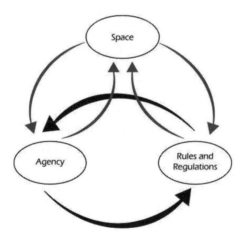

Figure 1: Sub-process of spatial agency within structuration theory.

Traditional learning spaces

In a 'traditional' learning space, the physical design of the learning space is some version of the following: static, unmovable desks or tables in neat rows that all face forward towards a board or screen and a larger open space near one end of the room. Usually there is one point of control for the technology within the space and a very limited number of tools, such as markers or chalk for the board. This learning space affords specific pedagogies, behaviours and rules.

When a learner enters this type of learning space, sees rows of chairs facing forward, it indicates to the learner that they are to enter the space and passively learn. The spatial design affords the behaviour of sitting and listening, confined to the chair in which they choose. With only one point of visual focus, a fixed, front-facing orientation, inability to move the furniture (unless given permission to 'break' that rule), no control of the tools within the space and lack of collective areas; collaboration, discussion, and creation with peers is discouraged – all activities that lead to the support of desired 21st century skills. In addition to affording the learner to assume certain behaviours and roles within the room, the space affords the educator to create and own the 'front' of the room, thus signalling that they are the holders of the knowledge. Not only is the space designed to afford this behaviour, the rules and regulations of the classroom have long enforced, and been reinforced, by this behaviour. The students follow the rules and roles of the listener while the teacher follows the rules and roles of the sage on the stage. It is a cyclical system, creating and recreating itself through the interactions of space, human agency and rules.

In their book *The Language of School Design*, the authoring architects and scholars express that the classroom is the most visible symbol of an educational philosophy (Nair *et al.*, 2009). If one unpacks and applies this thought, the traditional design of a learning space developed in parallel with the societal need for mass schooling; with rows of desks facing forward focused on a stage for the educator becomes quite telling. The introduction of this design layout immediately projected specific ideas of power, production, behaviour and rules on how one should operate – directly aligning with the industrial economy those students would be expected to work within. It is the educator that holds the power and knowledge and tells the students what to know and how to know it, just as a foreman on a floor may tell his/her employees what to produce and how to produce it. It is a factory-line model that compartmentalises the tasks and knowledge into specific silos; a model that still exists at many higher education institutes throughout the world. These spatial designs begin to call attention to the subtle ways that students may be internalising larger societal messages on power, knowledge acquisition, and modes of operation. This industrial-era, factory-line design for educational spaces stands in sharp opposition to the shift towards cross-disciplinary, integrated, active models for teaching and learning. To shape students who are able to build and function in social systems based in dynamism, diversity, sustainability and production of knowledge, education must create new epistemic learning spaces structured around the values higher education institutions seek to embrace and impart.

Active learning spaces

Twenty-first century learning spaces are envisioned as places where the learner is engaged in self-directed and co-operative learning activities, and the physical environment affords routine re-organisation to mediate this learning (Partnership for 21st Century Skills, 2002). They are places where the students' learning, rather than the delivery of the educators' content, is placed centre-stage. The student engages in learning activities that stimulate all ways in which they learn; visually, aurally, kinesthetically, emotionally, and socially. Rather than relying on the educator to 'tell them what they need to know', the students are charged with assuming ownership over their own learning. They are asked to grow beyond the silos of study and instead to connect concepts in a cross-disciplinarily way. They are not simply memorising facts for a test but expected to apply, analyse, evaluate and create together. Given such aims, what do these new learning spaces look like? I argue these spaces can be characterised by:

+ flexible furniture that remains adaptable to the dictation of the students to design and support the learning activity;

+ the lack of an owned front of the room thus democratising the classroom and distributing the power and ownership to the students;

- seating arrangements that allow students to face one another – allowing eye contact and community building;

- the presence of analogue and digital tools throughout the learning space, allowing students to use, take ownership and co-create with one another; and

- facilities for visual display and sharing of information, so all students can see, use and incorporate, as well as allow educators to give immediate feedback.

This list is certainly not exhaustive yet begins to suggest ways to spatially support the principles 21st century education seeks to uphold. These characteristics must remain dynamic and adaptable as we, and our educational systems, evolve. In summary, spaces that allow for all of these things, and more, to take place and so conveying an entirely different mode of being; one that is immediately more symbolic of dispersed, democratic control, and embracing various modes, methods, and manners of learning, giving students and educators permission to act differently within that environment.

By designing a learning space that permits them to act differently, the space has agency. It allows the students, as Lefebvre (1974) would say, to produce a new space. It is this production of new space by the learner that the rules and regulations (structure) are either enabled or constrained. Just as Gorbis (2013) highlighted technology's agency to empower individuals to change the structures of the ways we work, solve issues and create value, so learning spaces, while perhaps more subtly, possess active agency as well.

The growing interest and study in this area indicates that there is a budding recognition and awareness of the agency that learning spaces have in the education process. As argued in this chapter, the effects of a newly designed learning space extend far beyond just new furniture and tools, the learning space has active agency within the entire system. It is a sub-process existing within the meta-process of structuration (see figure 1). There is momentum in this sub-process of spatial agency. The rules, affordances and signifiers actively present in 'traditional' learning spaces keep the momentum of the existing system. In order to shift the direction of a system, if even slightly, there needs to be a recognition of all the variables present in the system and an added effort to create that momentum in the direction we want that system to move. Because the students, educators, and others are entrenched in the rules and behaviours of the 'industrial' model, they will continue to operate that way unless that cycle is interrupted. This must be done at every point in the process. The learning space is affording a new way of teaching and learning, affording new behaviours, but just because a space is designed to afford certain behaviours, it is not automatic that these will be adopted within the space. These desired, new learning behaviours will be enabled and constrained not exclusively by the space, but also by the rules in place and the behaviour of others. The administration of the institution, has to put these new rules in place, so that the educators and students know they can start to behave differently, and then by educators and students seeing that others are behaving differently it signals that they can as well – resulting in the desired shift to the system. All three variables are part of this cyclical process to shift a system, and must be considered in the successful adoption, integration and implementation of these new learning spaces. As Lefebvre (1974:54) states: *"A revolution that does not produce a new space has not realized its full potential... A social transformation, to be truly revolutionary in character, must manifest a creative capacity in its effects on daily life, on language and on space"*.

Implications

The implications of heightening awareness about the agency of spaces in shaping our social structures to elevate the importance of thinking critically about the design and effects of our environments, specifically within higher education, are both theoretical and practical.

The theoretical implications of expanding upon the understanding of structuration theory to include a more intentional consideration of the active agency of spaces evolves the framework of understanding about the systems around us to become more holistic, connected and spatially embedded. Specifically within higher education, in figuring out how to prepare students to build, shape, and function within society, the agency of all dimensions that affect the outcome must be considered. Further research into complex issues within, and outside, higher education should consider the role that the learning spaces may play in the particular phenomenon under study.

Beyond the primary intention of bringing a conscience awareness to the active agency of space, there are practical implications for concerned parties within higher education; administration, educators, students, and designers.

At the level of administration, it is the agency of an institution's administration that creates its governing structure, or rules and regulations. If it is understood that from this dialogue social systems emerge, and that learning spaces have agency in this equation, the importance of carefully considering what, how and where learning is unfolding is critical. In order for higher education institutions to successfully evolve, the vision needs to be seen and supported by its leaders. If the learning space is conceptualised as an articulation of their values and the type of social system they seek to contribute to and be a part of, an institution's administration must give deep and careful thought to the physical designs of these learning places. Because the new learning spaces are a part of an entire systemic shift, it is imperative that great consideration is given to the ways in which these new learning spaces are implemented and supported. The learning space is a process, not simply a product.

For educators, gaining this awareness is perhaps most important. Because they are the orchestrators of the learning experience on a daily basis, understanding that the learning space has agency on them and their students, they can begin to use and leverage the learning space to support their pedagogical strategies. Most often, educators are unaware that the learning space is a designed tool that they can employ, manipulate and use to help them accomplish their educational goals. As mentioned earlier, simply redesigning a learning space that affords new behaviour will not automatically elicit that new behaviour. Educators must be taught *how* to think about, use and integrate the learning space into their curriculum. They have been operating on the rules set up by the old model, and in order to change their behaviour and create new rules, they must become aware of why and how to do that.

For architects and designers, the concept of the agency of space is most likely already established, whether explicitly articulated or not. The practical implication for this group extends beyond awareness, as in gaining a greater understanding of the particular ways in which the learning environment plays into the creation of social systems. By parsing out how each architectural and design element may contribute to the learning spaces' agency through affordances, human behaviour and creation or re-creation of rules, intentional spatial articulations of the envisioned pedagogies and learning can be supported by design decisions at each stage of the design process. In order to ensure the success of the design, it is also the responsibility of the designer and architect to educate the end-user on the agency that the space has in the system.

For students, understanding that the learning space can be employed to support their learning experiences can empower them as active agents over their own learning. The students are the most important part of this structuration equation, as it is from their agency that the structure that creates our social systems are enabled and constrained. While this may not be at a consciously aware level for each learner, by designing learning spaces that afford students to act differently and produce a new space, it leads to the creation of a new structure to which our social systems are produced.

Conclusion

Only through the realisation of the ways in which learning space is connected to the production of our social systems, can we begin to under-stand the implicit language that our learning spaces speak in shaping our future. In exploring the relationship between agency and structure within our learning spaces, this chapter seeks to elevate the awareness of the presence of this relationship so as to deepen our understanding of the concept and impact of learning spaces within higher education. By conceiving and understanding that the importance of learning spaces in higher education extends beyond just the physical ability to support emerging active pedagogies, we are empowered to see, act and impart the values that are needed in the 21st century.

About the author

Aileen Strickland is Lead Design Researcher at Steelcase Education Solutions in Grand Rapids, Michigan. She can be contacted at this e-mail: astrick2@steelcase.com

Chapter Thirteen

Collective Learning Spaces: Constraints on Pedagogic Excellence

Clive Holtham and Annemarie Cancienne

Introduction

This chapter contributes to the anthology on learning space design in higher education by offering a case study drawn from City University London, which sees improvement in its 'collective' learning spaces as an integral dimension of its search for academic excellence. The chapter highlights key factors that have impacted on the design process for learning spaces, including problematic areas. It also outlines methods that have been developed within the University that aimed to address these problems. For the purpose of this chapter we define a learning space as the physical, virtual or imaginative spaces within which learning takes place. Reading this chapter, you will:

1. get an appreciation of how a technical/rational approach to the building commissioning process is unlikely to take account of problematic dissonances, which are almost inevitable in learning space improvement projects that involve multiple participants with differing goals and perspectives;

2. be introduced to Lefebvre's (1991) theories on the production of space in order to understand such dissonances; and

3. understand how these theories can lead to some potential approaches to reducing these dissonances.

This chapter is therefore concerned with the search for excellence in the design and implementation of physical learning spaces in higher education, specifically the formal spaces that form part of the physical estate of the campus.

Collective learning spaces

In over a decade of researching and implementing learning spaces in higher education, we have steadily observed that the design and implementation of buildings and facilities which are dedicated to a single faculty, department or unit seem to be less problematic than what we have named 'collective' learning spaces, that is those which have no single academic discipline with a dedicated involvement. This chapter examines why this might be the case, and although caution needs to be exercised around drawing wider conclusions from a single experience, it opens up an avenue for further research.

Once there is a conglomerate aggregation of users as opposed to a single client, the scope for misunderstanding grows significantly. Of course almost any building, even a small family home, is built for an agglomeration of users with conflicting needs not just at a given point in time, but also over successive periods of time. In a primary school, where a single teacher keeps a single classroom with a single pupil group for a year, there is very considerable scope to customise and adapt that learning space. In a university, with rooms being booked for 3, 2 or even 1 hour 'sessions' multiple times through the course of a day, every general space 'belongs to nobody'. There are a variety of methods to address this diversity of needs. One possibility is to produce a wide diversity of rooms to meet different teaching styles and different cohort sizes. Another is to enable rooms to be quickly reconfigured. Of course, these options come at a variety of costs, with flexibility being more expensive – both in construction and in operation.

Even when a room seems to meet the required needs, a space can fail for practical reasons. Room shape (a long rather than wide orientation) can prevent students from seeing or engaging with the lecturer; poor acoustics and no microphone (or being located adjacent to a noisy social space) can lead to problems in hearing the lecture; the heating/ventilation, the lack of windows or indeed too many windows on a sunny can also contribute to a poor learning (and teaching) experience.

At the University that is the focus for this chapter, two specific rooms tend to be unpopular with staff and students. One is nicknamed the 'school gymnasium' due to the use of retractable sport-centre style seating. Another, deep underground, is known as 'the bunker'. Of course, there could be someone for whom these two rooms are just perfect (the bunker would suit a situation where absolute darkness is a prerequisite), but these examples go to show the complexity of creating 'collective' learning spaces that meet the needs of a diverse teaching and learning community. In-the-know lecturers will aim to select a specific room that best fits their needs, but the University has to juggle the collectivity of diverse spaces and diverse learning and teaching needs.

Participant action research

This chapter is based on a longitudinal case study based around learning spaces in a single inner-city university. In this anthology it shares a number of features with Boys and Hazlett (in this volume). The co-authors have not been independent researchers over the evolution of this case study. They have played dual roles in many of the situations described. On the one hand they have been actively and directly involved in the unfolding events. On the other hand they have documented those events, and developed hypotheses and personal insights separate from their academic and administrative roles. Clearly, the existence of these dual roles raises concerns about bias and other potential weaknesses in the design and execution of the research. Hammersley (2004:176) takes a strict perspective and calls for recognition of *"the distinctiveness of the two kinds of inquiry which result: inquiry-subordinated-to-another-activity and research as a specialised occupation."* We would categorise this work as "inquiry-subordinated-to-another-activity". More positively Winter and Munn-Giddings (2001:21) argue that: *"... although an action research project is always focused on practice, it always has a theoretical scope – a specific but shifting horizon of general ideas and general possibilities and implications, arising both from the outcomes of the work (as they emerge) and from the process itself. This means that action research can also 'generate' theory, not by establishing links between variables or by supporting a hypothesis but by portraying a specific sequence of events in such a way (in such complexity of detail, in such 'depth') that others can perceive its implications for other situations"*

The university context

City University London was founded in 1894, with a Victorian-era heritage central building dating from that time. University status was gained in the 1960s and a modernist high-rise building was built along-side the original campus. The surrounding area is high-density largely high-rise residential property, with the large number of small enterprise workshops and offices steadily being replaced by further residential developments. The Social Sciences School is in an adjacent custom-built property that is 10 years old. The Business School is in the historic financial district; some 20 minutes walk away, and is also a custom-built property that is 11 years old. Overall the university estate is highly constrained by its already intensively occupied locations, and by the costs and dis-benefits of upgrading the types of buildings it occupies: the physical design of both the Victorian and 1960's campus buildings has made both expansion and reconfiguration difficult.

A new university strategy was approved in 2011, involving a move to 'academic excellence' and large investments in new faculty and in improved learning spaces. As we, the co-authors, argued in a 'manifesto' (Learning Spaces Development Group, 2012:2) adopted by the academic advisory committee: "*While other Universities would like to make lecture rooms more dynamic and flexible, what they are often lacking is funds. City's strategic investment in estates places us at a privileged point by giving a strategic framework for this desire for dynamic spaces, as well as the means to bring about world-class spaces that are at the forefront of what Universities, world-wide, would like to do.*"

Wider higher education context

Planning and implementing excellent learning spaces in higher education is far from easy at the current time. There is uncertainty over, for example, demography and regulation. There is a general climate of cost restraint and reduction. There is increased and some entirely new competition. Some previously traditional universities are re-thinking their approaches to teaching and learning, though they may do so through very different means, for example as illustrated by comparing Melbourne and Adelaide. There are rising expectations of students (and faculty) stoked by consumerist tendencies and government publicity. New undergraduates are millennial learners with diverse digital and face-to-face literacies. New technology is highly publicised but often academically problematic.

Our local focus on academic excellence relates in part to an institutional strategy, which is based on reaching an internationally excellent position in teaching and research. There is no doubt that excellence, however defined, poses disproportionate problems for those working on traditionally developed campuses. The combination of rising student expectations, changing student learning styles and preferences, cost constraints and the challenges from new learning technologies make for difficult planning decisions. On an urban campus, such as the one we are examining, this problem is further exacerbated: the physical footprint of the campus is difficult (or very costly) to change, and it is harder to create a coherent campus-based student body, with students drawn between commuting and taking part in any of the many activities on offer in the wider urban environment.

In marrying together the notions of academic excellence and learning spaces, the university is beginning to embrace two notions: that a lecture does not just occur, but that the physical dynamics of the lecture space affect the lecture itself; and that students will feel more a part of their university if they feel their campus is a home. For a long time, this university's spaces have pushed students away, into coffee shops, pubs, and their own homes, in order to study individually or as a group. Giving students inviting, exciting, and multi-purpose spaces to learn and study in is vital to keeping them on campus and making them feel like they belong to a university rather than just attend it.

Wider higher education learning spaces context

The learning spaces movement is growing, nationally and internationally, with the dawning awareness that the dominant form of teaching spaces (rows of desks facing a single person speaking) hasn't changed dramatically since the 19th century. This form endures because it is very good at addressing a certain function – of an instructor sharing knowledge with students – but it is less good at facilitating other, less didactic forms of instruction. While primary and secondary schools have created spaces that move away from this one model of room design, university education has not made as many strides. We have identified several drivers at work in the learning spaces movement, including shifting pedagogies, institutional investment in space, and greater proliferation of student-owned technology in the lecture room. In a report commission for the UK Higher Education Space Management Group, Barnett and Temple (2006:19) acknowledge the complexities of space management but also of the parallel need to consider institutional drivers when constructing spaces, so that new spaces support (rather than contradict) a university's strategic direction. They also note the sector-wide demands for *"more flexible and highly-serviced spaces, and the blurring of the boundary between academic and social areas"*, and predict that: *"HEIs of all sorts will need to remodel their existing space, or to redevelop parts of their estates completely, to provide for new teaching and learning methods, new research approaches, new technologies, and new social expectations. The extent to which they can do this will obviously be constrained by the capital funds available to them and institutional choices of various kinds."*

Learning spaces dedicated to a single academic entity

There are many examples of successful learning spaces relating to a single faculty/college, department or academic unit; and the Business School in this case study provided such an example. It is possible to identify a variety of reasons why involvement of a single academic entity might lead to more successful learning spaces. Firstly, the academic entity perceives a direct connection between the physical space and their own goals. They have a strong emotional commitment to that physical space, not least in intimately reflecting their values and brand. They are likely to put in sufficient resources of time and energy to ensure their entity goals are met as closely as possible.

Secondly, a single entity may well have one signature pedagogy (Schulman, 2005), so that the physical learning spaces are explicitly geared to that pedagogy. This is also partly relating to being part of a common academic "tribe" (Becher, 1989). Thirdly, there are as likely to be tensions and disagreements within any given faculty as between faculties. But within a faculty there is essentially a pyramid system for resolving tensions, ultimately relying on a Dean or a collective faculty group to take resolving decisions. Internal dissent within the school will be addressed by a combination of participative and coercive approaches, but however it is done it will typically lead to a clear and unambiguous academic view. So when it comes to the academic interests being represented in negotiations with architects and property managers, it is possible to achieve a single and unambiguous representation of the academic viewpoint.

These areas can be contrasted with a situation where there are collective learning spaces as opposed to a single academic entity. Firstly, where multiple academic entities are involved, it is very difficult to achieve a high degree of emotional interest in the building project and its outcome. It may not be possible to harness sufficient resources to pursue key goals, not least relating to the time and energy commitment necessary. Secondly, not only may there not be a single signature pedagogy across the university as a whole, there may in fact be pedagogies which are perceived as conflicting.

Thirdly, compared to an individual school there may be no mechanism for synchronising the academic interests of different entities when they are in conflict. Such mechanisms may physically exist in the form of committees and Senate, but they are not generally inclined to create a mediation process for conflict. There are multiple voices, so in the absence of a clear patron willing and able to mediate, some central body who may or may not have relevant learning expertise will by default lead the final decision making, which could lead to a compromise or indeed a simple selection of just a minority of the signature pedagogies.

If the central body is also responsible for project management of the building improvements, they will typically be faced with a conflict between cost, time to completion and learning space quality. In the absence of an effective client, it is most likely to be learning space quality (broadly defined), with no explicit champion, which is reduced when these three are in tension.

Academic excellence – a pedagogic framework

Our starting point for reviewing the connection between academic excellence and learning space design came from Goodyear's (2001) framework, originally developed for the design of distance learning. We use a slightly adapted version (Holtham & Courtney, 2004) as presented in Figure 1.

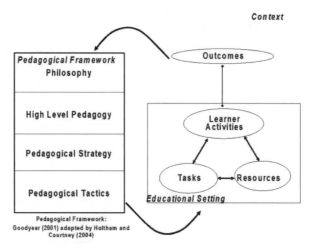

Figure 1: A Framework for locating physical space in a pedagogic context.

In this framework, learning spaces are just one of the resources, albeit very important ones, contributing to the educational setting. Two crucial issues to consider are: just how the "pedagogical framework" is explicitly and coherently expressed, and how the framework is made manifest through the building design process. Of course, sometimes the student learning opportunities that are offerable are significantly narrowed by inappropriate learning spaces.

We have reviewed several frameworks that have been developed to inform learning space design. Jamieson *et al.* (2000) proposed seven principles:

1: design space for multiple uses concurrently and consecutively;

2: design to maximise the inherent flexibility within each space;

3: design to make use of the vertical dimension in facilities;

4: design to integrate previously discrete campus functions;

5: design features and functions to maximise teacher and student control;

6: design to maximise alignment of different curricula activities; and

7: design to maximise student access to, and use and ownership of, the learning environment.

A body concerned with effective use of technology, Jisc (2006:3) identified that: *"the design of its individual spaces needs to be:*

+ *Flexible – to accommodate both current and evolving pedagogies;*

+ *Future-proofed – to enable space to be re-allocated and reconfigured;*

+ *Bold – to look beyond tried and tested technologies and pedagogies;*

+ *Creative – to energise and inspire learners and tutors;*

+ *Supportive – to develop the potential of all learners; and*

+ *Enterprising – to make each space capable of supporting different purposes."*

We would agree with these lists but they are somewhat too generic to be anything more than a starting point. A much more focussed and distinctive list comes from SKG in Australia (2013), which has:*"…seven principles of learning space design which support a constructivist approach to learning: that is, principles which support a learning environment which is student-centred, collaborative, and experiential."*

Comfort	a space which creates a physical and mental sense of ease and well-being
Aesthetics	pleasure which includes the recognition of symmetry, harmony, simplicity and fitness for purpose
Flow	the state of mind felt by the learner when totally involved in the learning experience
Equity	consideration of the needs of cultural and physical differences
Blending	a mixture of technological and face-to-face pedagogical resources
Affordances	the "action possibilities" the learning environment provides the users, including such things as kitchens, natural light, wifi, private spaces, writing surfaces, sofas, and so on.
Repurposing	the potential for multiple usage of a space

Table 1: SKG Framework; Seven principles of learning space design.

Chism (2006:2.6) argued that Intentionally Created Spaces are *"harmonious with learning theory and the needs of current students"*. In City University London, the 'light bulb moment' between the facilities department and academic representations came when learning and education were expressed using Chickering and Gamson's (1991) seven principles for undergraduate education. Room design activities were mapped to each principle. For example, *"develops reciprocity and co-operation among students"* is manifested in seating that allows students to easily see one another when speaking, and furniture that can be quickly and easily reconfigured to allow group work, a room-design template was created that helped guide the facilities department in their decision making in creating new collective learning spaces.

Does space design matter?

A recent study (Beery, 2013) found there was no significant difference between collaborative and transmissive teaching whether used in appropriately-designed teaching rooms or not. This could be used to argue that space design is not actually that important, but they go on to conclude: *"While it was disappointing to find that there was no significant increase in the use of active learning pedagogies in the collaborative classroom, it was not entirely surprising to the research team. Informal observations and discussions with colleagues led us to believe that teachers will choose the pedagogy they use according to their preference and teaching style. Teachers who use collaborative/ cooperative learning will do that no matter how prohibitive the classroom design. In our experience, students are flexible and will find creative ways to arrange themselves for group interactions. That said, using active learning is certainly facilitated by having furniture that is conducive to group work and having technology that enables groups to function efficiently."* (Beery 2013: 386)

We would go further than Beery and contend that there are many circumstances where even if group work is possible in a raked lecture theatre, that is significantly sub-optimal for a number of reasons – for example, the faculty cannot easily visit each group at work and there is no large flat space for each group's shared workspace. At the margin, inappropriate physical space may actually deter some faculty from innovating or taking risks. And symbolically, the maintenance of traditional transmissive facilities at the expense of more collaborative spaces could ultimately harm the recruitment of students and both the recruitment and retention of faculty.

What is actually happening?

As we continued to analyse the problem of the design process for collective learning spaces, we decided to move outside the extensive but often technically oriented literature on higher-education learning spaces, to examine the wider social science literature. A practising architect (Pouler, cited in Scheer & Preiser, 1994:175) remarks that architecture "*is a social practice and as such cannot avoid being part of a complex network of power relationships. The fact that it impacts upon the production of one quarter of the built environment clearly indicates the political implications of aesthetic control. Space is neither innocent nor neutral: it is an instrument of the political; it has a performative aspect for whoever inhabits it; it works on its occupants. At the micro level, space prohibits, decides what may occur, lays down the law, implies a certain order, commands and locates bodies.*"

We were particularly struck by the work of Lefebvre (1991), who was concerned with space in all of the geographical, physical, social and emotional senses. Lefebvre was an academic at Nanterre, a greenfield and modernist Parisian university of the 1960s, with whose physical buildings he was deeply unimpressed. According to Elden (2004:180), Lefebvre "*considered Nanterre a gathering of the contradictions of the late Gaullist era. Similarly to the Haussmannian reorganization of Paris, he considered Nanterre to be an expression and tool of the dominant social order... he saw the campus as a projection into space of an industrial rationality producing "mediocre intellectuals" and "junior executives." According to Lefebvre, the late modernist architecture of the campus reflects the intended project: the attempt to reproduce the social relations of production.*"

Elden (2004:186-187) summarises Lefebvre's conceptual triad of spatial practice:"*Space is viewed in three ways, as perceived, conceived and lived: l'espace perçu, conçu and vécu .... This Lefebvrian schema sees a unity (a Marxist totality) between physical, mental and social space. The first of these takes space as physical form, real space, space that is generated and used. The second is the space of savoir (knowledge) and logic, of maps, mathematics, of space as the instrumental space of social engineers and urban planners, of navigators and explorers. Space as a mental construct, imagined space. The third sees space as produced and modified over time and through its use, spaces invested with symbolism and meaning, the space of connaissance (less formal or more local forms of knowledge), space as real-and-imagined.*"

We have found this triad invaluable in coming to terms with the tensions surrounding collective learning spaces. Lefebvre is highly critical of specialists and experts who plan and design with little or no reference to the wide range of stakeholders. So he would see much higher education planning today, including that of learning spaces, in very much the same way as he saw French universities being run in the 1960s. The designed (and actually built) learning spaces are in effect theories or mental constructs (*conçu*). He does not count the walls and floors as *real* space. Reality (*perçu*) is what happens when users come into contact with the space, in his terms the space becomes generated and used. The third lived (*vécu*) dimension takes place over time, again as users consistently modify the space and invest it with their own symbolism and meaning.

Jessop and Smith's (2008) review of the University of Winchester found many of the same themes as identified in this paper, and included "power" in their title to emphasise this dimension. They highlighted three main themes: "*The first related to the emphasis on public image, iconic buildings above more routine teaching spaces. The second was the tendency of most teaching room layouts to support traditional transmission model pedagogy, in contrast to student-centred and social-constructivist approaches to learning. Our third and final theme reflects on some of the less visible dimensions of space on campus – the distribution, cohesion and dispersal of spaces, and their relationship to academic hierarchies (Becher, 1989)*" (Jessop & Smith. 2008:1).

Building commissioning is project management

Reconciling diverse user needs is a problem that exists in most complex projects (Lippincott, 2009). They particularly exist in information technology projects, not least in universities, but there have been some improvements in the commissioning of IT projects both generically and in universities in recent years. Buildings have even-longer term costs and benefits than IT. There is a need to avoid wrong decisions even if it is difficult to make the right decisions. A decision on the overall size and indeed nature of a space (flat versus raked) is likely to last for decades. Even if furniture and fittings could be replaced or renewed every 5-10 years, it does not mean that the institution will actually be able to afford to do that, and indeed high quality furniture and fittings will certainly have a minimum life of at least 10 years.

As part of our learning space review we interviewed other universities and inquired how much influence pedagogic strategy has had on the planning of centrally shared facilities. One frequently recurring response was that often it was short-term timetabling issues came first when it came to difficult decisions on priorities. In the case of one leading American university, their own study into this question has led to the conclusion that 'janitorial arrangements' had in fact been the primary factor in determining learning space design. Several interviewees reported that where informal learning spaces were developed with moveable tables and chairs, the cleaners routinely rearrange these into straight rows facing the front of the room.

There are layered roles even internal to the building commissioning process. There may be a strategic lead (internal), a project manager (who could be internal or external) and the usually external architects. Consultation processes may take place under time pressures. Grummon (2009) highlighted the paradox that *"Engaging those who will use a learning space in its planning yields the greatest benefits"*, yet *"the people who manage a space usually determine its design."*

Jamieson *et al.* (2000:6) argue that: *"Less than optimal spatial outcomes... are largely the result of two factors. First, teaching is a contested practice and it is difficult for a university to convey a unified view of the approach to teaching that may be undertaken in any specific area of a building. This is exacerbated when facilities are being designed to support emergent (as distinct from traditional) pedagogical practices. The authors' experiences suggest that the assumptions about intended pedagogies that underpin project design briefs tend to be unstated, or unknown to, or unshared by, those who use the facilities... a participatory or social form of design process is all but a dream in most cases."*

If our pessimistic hypothesis is correct, the more that decisions on learning space design are centralised or collective, as opposed to based on the explicit needs of specific academic units, the less likely it is that such spaces will reflect in particular emerging space needs. There are several possible and overlapping options to address this problem:

1. a change in the governance arrangements for learning space;

2. the explicit creation of an unambiguous client role, which is added to the building commissioning process. This needs to represent the

wide range of faculties or schools who will collectively be using the space either now or in the future; and

3. the use of mediation devices to reconcile different needs.

Learning space dialogue – transitional objects

Winnicott (1953) developed the concept of a transitional object to help infants to progress from a known to an unknown state. These can be relevant to adults too, and one method used in the case study was jointly to develop a "Manifesto" agreed across all the academic units, that would help the institution to progress, at the margin, from traditional learning spaces to more progressive ones. There was a consultation process leading to a pedagogically oriented artefact in credit card format, the Manifesto, which is exemplified in Figures 2 and 3.

> Our learning spaces will be bright, inviting, flexible spaces, able to accommodate the full breadth of teaching (and learning) approaches. Students and lecturers will be able to communicate with one another easily, and share and develop ideas between themselves in these spaces. Our spaces will communicate the pride we have in our learning, and help engage students in the City University London academic community through being world-class spaces that meet their learning needs.

Figure 2: The overall text of the manifesto.

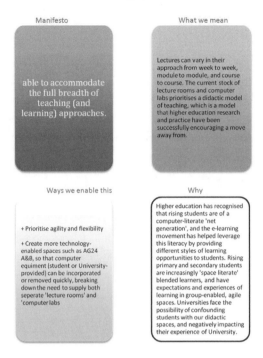

Figure 3: The presentation of one detailed section of the manifesto.

Conclusion

At the time of writing it remains to be seen how far a specific device such as a transitional object can impact on a large complex programme of building works for higher education learning spaces. However given the costs and risks involved in such as large programme of works, it is to be hoped that this approach may add another dimension to closing the gap between aspirations for teaching and learning excellence, and the concrete reality (or in Lefebvre's terms the concrete but imagined reality) of physical building plans.

About the authors

Clive Holtham is Professor at City University London in London, England. He can be contacted at this e-mail: c.w.holtham@city.ac.uk

Annemarie Cancienne is Head of Educational Technology at City University London in London, England. She can be contacted at this e-mail: annemarie@city.ac.uk

Chapter Fourteen

The Doctoral Student-Supervisor Relationship as a Negotiated Learning Space

B. Liezel Frick, Eva M. Brodin and Ruth M. Albertyn

Introduction

This chapter contributes to the anthology on learning space design in higher education by conceptualising the doctoral student-supervisor relationship as a negotiated learning space and further theorising about the implications of this conceptualisation for doctoral students' identity (competence, personal growth, and creativity). We have chosen to focus on doctoral education as it constitutes the most advanced educational level in the higher education spectrum. We define the negotiated learning space as a *relational* learning space, rather than a physical or virtual space; we contend that the pedagogic relationship between the doctoral student and research supervisor(s), forms an important *relational* learning space, which exists regardless of the doctoral programme format.

After reading this chapter, you will:

1. know of a new framework that conceptualises the doctoral learning space as a negotiated learning space which is affected by identity positions and relationship dynamics;

2. have insights into the effect of different supervisor and student identity positions for the doctoral student learning space;

3. be able to reflect on the major differences for the doctoral student learning space that appears from seeing the doctoral

student-supervisor relationship as a negotiated learning space or as a non-negotiated learning space.

In the chapter, we develop a new framework for conceptualisation of the doctoral learning space characterised by key elements in the doctoral student-supervisor relationship. Our framework provides a point of departure for understanding how a negotiated learning space affects such a relationship. McCombs and Whisler (1997, in Temple 2004:197) argue: "*Education involves relationships. The more positive and effective these are in educational contexts, the more likely it is that all members of the learning group will thrive both as individuals and lifelong learners.*" In our view, it is important to focus on the negotiated learning space, because it helps understand its complexity. Supervisors are often assumed to know what makes this pedagogic relationship in this learning space productive and ultimately successful, including which supervision styles are appropriate throughout doctoral candidature (Gatfield, 2005). However, other authors have alluded to the relationships within this learning space as: "*complex and unstable ... filled with pleasures and risks*" (Grant, 2003: 175); "*unpredictable and demanding*" (Grant, 2011:247); "*private*" (Manathunga, 2005:17); "*conducted behind closed doors in spaces remote from undergraduate teaching ... presumed but uninterrogated*" (MacWilliam & Palmer, 1995:32); the "*most genuinely complex*" and one of the "*least discussed aspects*" in higher education (Connell, 1985:38); and under-theorised (Green & Lee, 1995). Evidently the learning space created in the relationship between doctoral students and their research supervisors is problematic, which may be attributed to its "*peculiarly intense and negotiated character*", as well as its "*requirement for a blend of pedagogical and personal relationship skills*" (Grant, 2003:175).

To begin, we first explore the unique nature and challenges of the relationship in the context of the doctoral learning space, as characterised by the above quotations. Transactional analysis theory (TA) is used as a point of departure from which theory regarding supervisory styles can be developed. Functions of supervisors, and responses in the student, influence the dynamics evident in the power and identity of each of the relational partners and underscore the need for creating a *negotiated* learning space in doctoral education. We furthermore argue that a negotiated learning space provides room for relationship convergence and ultimately relationship enhancement. A conceptual framework reflecting this negotiated learning space concludes the chapter.

We argue that both doctoral supervisors and students take part in negotiating their relationship, but that supervisors often take the lead in establishing this relationship – and thus lead the formation of the foundation of the learning space so created.

Doctoral student-supervisor relationships: demystifying a private learning space

There seems to be concern about the high dropout rate amongst postgraduate students (Golde, 2005; Lovitts, 2005), which is commonly attributed to non-functioning interpersonal relationships between students and their supervisors (McAlpine & Norton, 2006; McCormack & Pamphilon, 2004). The importance of the positive constructive role of the supervisor in the postgraduate education process has been noted (Maxwell & Smyth, 2011; Lee, 2008). At each phase in the process the supervisor has a crucial role to play, which calls for a *"symbiotic orientation towards the maintenance of a cooperative relationship"* (Li & Searle, 2007:522). However, the private nature of the supervisory relationship is at times problematic (see Manathunga, 2005, 2007; Pearson & Kayrooz, 2004), which adds to the difficulty in accessing and studying these relationships (Manathunga, 2005). Such private pedagogical spaces are fraught with underlying issues of identity and power (Grant, 2003). Conceptualising the interpersonal supervision relationship could facilitate what Manathunga (2005:24) calls compassionate rigour: *"a delicate pedagogical balancing of ... providing students with support, encouragement, and empathy, while at the same time giving them rigorous feedback on their performance"*. Delamont et al. (1998) indicate that supervisors sometimes find it difficult to balance the need for students to work independently and manage the student's work towards completion, which Eley and Murray (2009) refer to as finding the balance between freedom and neglect. Gardner (2008) refers to the paradoxical quality in the interpersonal relationship regarding guidance and support needed by students and their increasing feelings of competence and independence. These challenges highlight the need for a clearer conceptualisation of the dynamics of the student-supervisor relationship within a doctoral pedagogy.

Creating learning spaces through negotiated relationships

In sharing our ideas we draw on the work of Lusted (1986) and Green and Lee (1995) who conceptualise pedagogy in terms of relations amongst learners (in this case doctoral students), teachers (doctoral supervisors) and the knowledge generated through these relations (which, at the doctoral level, results in an original contribution in the form of a thesis or a collection of published or publishable papers). This conceptualisation of pedagogy implies both *"how we come to know"* (Lusted, 1986:2-3), and *"how we come to be"* (Green & Lee, 1995:41) – taking into account the complex interplay between student, supervisor(s) and knowledge at the doctoral level. Our conceptualisation of the relationship between doctoral students and research supervisors as a key element of doctoral pedagogy and as a negotiated learning space is based on Garfinkel's (1967) notion of pedagogy as a social activity that occurs within social, cultural and institutional structures, relationships and actions. Inman *et al.* (2011) highlight the centrality of the relationship in the doctoral process illustrating the sphere of influence emanating from the quality of these interactions. Social (inter-) actions therefore govern processes, contexts, interactions and relationships with/between stakeholders, decisions, and eventual outcomes – including those of doctoral students and their research supervisors.

We also take note of Tudor's (2009) view that traditional pedagogic learning spaces are built on a hierarchical model of training characterised by parent/child-like relationships between a teacher and pupil. The apprenticeship approach to doctoral education may contain elements of this model, which has inherent dangers for the development of independent researchers and original work (Mackinnon, 2004). Tudor (2009) argues in favour of a more andragogic approach, which builds on the learner's existing knowledge and develops self-directedness (based on the work of Knowles & Associates, 1985). Rogers (1969) argues that interpersonal relationships lie central to the facilitation of learning in learning spaces based on andragogic principles. Such relationships are characterised by open communication, clear contracts, as well as mutual authenticity, acceptance, empathy, and trust. This conceptualisation of learning spaces is reminiscent of Freire's (1972) notion of education as dialogue, where education transcends the divide between teachers and students. Of course such a view may threaten the notion of the teacher (supervisor) as expert and gatekeeper to legitimate disciplinary knowledge, but we agree with Tudor (2009) that education is meant to encourage curiosity, creativity, critique and reflexivity; and therefore learning spaces need to be negotiated between doctoral supervisors and students. This view of pedagogy also aligns to Dobozy's work (this volume), which emphasises the role of power and agency in making pedagogical decisions.

The supervisor needs to adapt to facilitate the student learning process and support progress throughout (Maxwell & Smyth, 2011). A pedagogy of supervision therefore demands that supervisors are aware of, and are sensitive to, students' identity development, conceptual capacities, learning styles, and modes of intellectual processing beyond epistemological and methodological concerns (see Fataar, forthcoming, and Frick, 2010). Furthermore, Cree (2012) describes doctoral supervision as both a moral and an educational activity that needs to go beyond the current individualistic and competitive focus on throughput and completion to a more holistic pedagogy of care and support. However, supervisors often focus on roles and responsibilities instead of seeing the situation and various elements as a whole with the relationship at the centre (Emilsson & Johnson, 2007). This is unfortunate as supervision is, we contend, a dynamic process embodied in the interaction between the supervisor and the student. Accordingly, it is important to understand supervision as a learning space of negotiated relationships.

Identity positions as a basis for negotiating learning spaces

Various theories of interpersonal relationships have been reported across disciplines in the literature and provide possibilities for application in doctoral education. In this chapter we use transaction analysis theory of Berne (1961) as a point of departure to explore identity-power-relationships in negotiated learning spaces in the context of doctoral education. The theory has been adapted over the years (see for example Newton, 2012; Sills, 2006; Sills & Fowlie, 2011; Temple, 2004), which will be taken into account in our conceptualisation. Although we acknowledge the clinical psychology origins and nature of the theory, we will argue that it has value beyond pure psychological application, as Newton (2011) also suggests. Oates (2010) describes transaction analysis as a theory that is both robust and versatile. Cree (2012) applied transaction analysis autobiographically to PhD supervision in the context of Social Work, while Fataar (2005) reflexively focused on negotiating student identity in the doctoral proposal development process. Both these authors (Cree, 2012 and Fataar, 2005) influenced our conceptualisation of the doctoral student-supervisor relationship as a negotiated learning space.

The theory of transaction analysis (Berne, 1961) proposes that how we establish and maintain relationships depends largely on the identities of the individuals involved (based partly on our ego states) and the power we exert in these relationships when we communicate with each other. transaction analysis theory claims that all human interactions take place by means of transactions – the way in which people communicate with each other. Underlying these transactions are the communicators' ego states. Our ego states form the basis of how we interact with each other (and thus how we negotiate our relationships). Berne (1961) proposes that people's personalities consist of Parent, Child, and Adult ego states, each of which consists of positive or negative possible dimensions that could facilitate or hinder communication and personal growth. Ego states determine people's worldviews. Worldviews also influence behaviour and actions (Mezirow, 1991).

The Parent ego state relates specifically to thoughts, feelings and behaviours that is either nurturing (permission giving, but sets limits in a healthy way); critical (also sometimes called prejudiced); or rescuing (Berne, 1961; Solomon, 2003). For the context of doctoral supervision activity we have chosen to re-conceptualise this ego state as either the *Guide* identity position (which guards the values and ethics inherent to the particular scholarly community but at the same time facilitates enculturation into the community), or alternatively a *Warden* identity position (as a gate-keeper into the scholarly community who could ward off or isolate potential entrants). For example, from the Guide identity approach, a supervisor helps mirror the standards and rigour in the scientific process and acts as an objective monitor and guide helping the student towards the generation of a quality product. The supervisor could, however, be overly meticulous in their feedback and react in a rescuing mode – trying to fix the student's work, thus jeopardising independence and student ownership of their work.

The Child ego state involves emotions, thoughts and feelings which may be Free (or Natural, in which people are creative and playful in situations where they feel safe and have the opportunity to play and enjoy themselves), or Adapted (parts of people's personalities that has learned to comply with, or rebel against, messages received). Both responses are adaptive to parental messages in some way (Berne, 1961; Solomon, 2003). For supervisors of doctoral students the Child ego state could be re-conceptualised as an *Explorative* identity position (which facilitates, fosters and rewards innovation and original thought), or a *Pedestrian* position (which cautiously mitigates risk rather than encourages imaginative experimentation). For example the supervisor in the Explorative identity position shows enthusiasm and engages with the student and their project. From the Pedestrian position, the supervisor may resist the student taking risks in a quest to retain control and thus stifling creativity in the student.

The Adult ego state centres on data processing and problem solving based on facts rather than on pre-judged thoughts or childlike emotions, but could come across as cold. How we communicate from each ego state may be helpful or not – which also has implications for how doctoral supervisors and students communicate (Berne, 1961; Solomon, 2003). We have chosen to re-conceptualise this ego state as an *Autonomous* identity position (where independent thought is paramount), or a *Reliant* position (when policies and structures dictate practice). In the Autonomous identity position, the supervisor retains objectivity based on the students' current work and stage of the project. From the Reliant position, the supervisor may be overly reliant on existing discourses in the field, prejudiced towards novel approaches, and/or inflexible and cold in their interaction with the student. They may also be too desirous to comply with external policies and may be excessively cautious in interactions with the student.

Communication from these identity positions can either be complementary (between people in the same ego state, which can continue indefinitely), or crossed (originating from different ego states, which may lead to difficulties in communication). It follows that complementary communication will make the negotiation of a learning space much easier in doctoral education, but supervisors also need to understand that different ego states may be emphasised in the student and supervisor due to their earlier experiences. For the purposes of this chapter we have chosen to focus on how the dimensions of the above-mentioned ego states could be re-conceptualised as identity positions supervisors may take on in order to negotiate learning spaces. We acknowledge that the concept of negotiation may involve a conflict perspective and we therefore also account for supervisor identity positions that could hinder the negotiation of a productive learning space.

Understanding how people communicate based on such identity positions could help both doctoral supervisors and students negotiate more productive learning spaces (which we explore in greater depth later in this chapter). It can also help us to understand how different combinations of attitude, emotions and behaviour can affect learning, as well as how the working, interpersonal, thinking and communication styles of all participants affect learning. Supervisors have power in managing supervisor-student relationships. Ideally, such strategies should be used responsibly and creatively to facilitate learning, but Ernst (1972) warns that disruptive supervisor roles may also exist, which suggests that supervisors do not always operate from the positive dimensions of their ego states. In such cases the identity positions they take on may create disruptive learning spaces, based on a deficit approach to learning, as is also evident in the work of Cree (2012).

If we want to apply the notion of identity positions to how learning spaces may be negotiated in the doctoral context, it becomes necessary to explore how these identity positions may be conceptually applied to the dynamic doctoral student-supervisor relationship.

Relationship dynamics in negotiating a doctoral learning space

To visualise doctoral learning as a negotiated space, the various elements of this relationship need to be explored. We argue that dynamic flexibility of identity positions; relationship convergence and relationship enhancement are necessary elements in negotiating a doctoral learning space.

Dynamic flexibility

Even though students/supervisors have learned to have preferences for some identity position(s), as described above, these identity positions are not static but rather can develop over time and be used in various combinations. We see dynamic flexibility as a key concept in this process, which can only appear in a negotiated learning space. The identity positions we have proposed allow us the conceptual tools to visualise doctoral learning as a negotiated space, in which student-supervisor relationships are a prerequisite for learning and the student becomes an active participant in (rather than a passive consumer of) learning (Tudor, 2009). As such, *"the facilitation of significant learning rests upon certain attitudinal qualities which exist in the personal relationship between the facilitator and the learner"* (Rogers, 1969:106).

Although we agree with Rogers (1969) that the attitudinal qualities that both supervisors and students bring to the learning space are equally important, and that students should voice what they want and need from supervision (as echoed by Eley & Murray, 2009), it may be more difficult for students to shift supervisors' identity positions than *vice-versa* due to the differential power relationship typically found in doctoral education (Minor *et al.*, 2012). In this professional relationship the power dynamic is evident in an evaluative component whilst focusing on student development (Inman *et al.*, 2011). Students may furthermore not be aware or able to explicitly state what their needs will be throughout the process (Chinnock, 2011). Indeed, Fataar (2005) argues that the authority of the supervisor is paramount to the conversation and learning process. Therefore supervisors need to acknowledge the power dynamic inherent in the supervisory relationship, and plan strategies that will empower students to become independent and creative scholars (Frick *et al.*, 2010).

The supervisory relationship should ideally allow empowerment or emancipation of the student (Frick *et al.*, 2010; also see Lee, 2008). Students need to be aware of the ways in which empowerment or lack thereof impacts on the various aspects of their relationships (Albertyn *et al.*, 2002; Van der Merwe & Albertyn, 2010). Empowerment in doctoral education involves the development of the student's academic and professional identity, as well as the successful completion of the research. Empowerment of the student thus means enabling the student through a process of transformation where the supervisor acts as the facilitator of transformation through providing the context for learning, enculturation and identity formation to take place. Mastery of a new identity as researcher does not reside within the supervisor, but supervisors need to facilitate this process because becoming a researcher involves acquiring new ways of thinking, acting and being (Dysthe *et al.*, 2006; Frick *et al.*, 2010).

Wright and Cochrane (2000) emphasise that doctoral supervision involves a complex negotiation of students' identities, while Green (2005:162) argues that "[d]*octoral pedagogy is as much about the production of identity, then, as it is the production of knowledge. At issue is the (re)production of specific research identities*". Fataar (2005) adds that a student's sense of self may influence the type of intellectual questions they pose. The notion of doctoral (and supervisor) identity implies that these stakeholders' identity positions (according to our re-conceptualisation of transaction analysis theory) are involved in the transactions that take place during the supervision communication and relationship building processes. Identity positions and the communication that takes place between these positions are not static. Cree (2012) notes that a student may take on a (helpless) dependent identity position at the initial stages of the doctoral process, which demands a (nurturing) Guide response. As their study progresses the idea is that the student becomes more independent and therefore able to communicate from an Autonomous identity position. And so the supervisor's responses need to adapt accordingly, what Fataar (2005:38) calls "*reflexive adaptability of the supervisory process*". In doing so, both supervisor and student power is used to negotiate the doctoral learning space. Through this dialogue, knowledge is seen as a process and product of the interaction of voices and is concerned with the construction and transformation of understanding through the tension between multiple perspectives and opinions (Dysthe *et al.*, 2006). However, problems may arise if the student and/or supervisor get stuck in an identity position that does not contribute to a constructive learning space.

Anderson (1988) and Gatfield (2005) propose four, and Rowan (1983) five, possible positions a supervisor can take in the supervisory process based on the extent of support and structure provided by the supervisor, which are compared in Table 1. Linkages to the supervisors' identity position are indicated in each case.

Supervisory management styles (Gatfield, 2005:322)	Supervisor styles (Rowan, 1983:193)	Supervision styles Anderson (1988:41)	Supervisor identity position
Laissez-faire Low in both structure and support, where the doctoral candidate has limited motivation and management skills and the supervisor is non-directive and does not engage in much personal interaction with the candidate.	**Laissez-faire** The supervisor lets the supervisee make progress with little interference.	**Passive** Supervision is characterised by having no input and not responding to student's input.	Although the supervisor could think they are operating from an Autonomous identity position by letting the student get on with the work independently, few students are able to complete their doctoral studies with no support. Curr (2001:89) refers to this state as "benign neglect".
Pastoral Low in structure, but offering high support, where the doctoral candidate may have little management skills but uses all available support and the supervisor provides considerable personal care and support without being task-driven.	**Feelings-Oriented** The supervisor invites the supervisee to discover from his/her own experiences.		The supervisor can be nurturing (Guide position), which may be appropriate in especially the initial phases when the student may be unsure and require more support (which aligns to the supervisor pastoral and feelings-oriented styles described here). However, the supervisor could also be rescuing (with reference to the Warden and Pedestrian identity positions), which puts the student in a dependent and helpless position.

Directional	Insight-Oriented	Indirect passive	The supervisor could
High in structure, but low in support, where the doctoral candidate is highly motivated and works in self-directed, task-driven manner and the supervisor has an interactive but task-focused relationship with the candidate.	The supervisor allows the supervisee to think about and search for answers her/himself.	Supervisor listens and waits for student to process ideas and problem solve.	use positive input to elicit Autonomous transactions, but needs to take care not to come across as cold (indicative of the Reliant and Warden identity positions).
Contractual	**Didactic-Consultative**	**Indirect active**	The supervisor could
High in structure and support, where the doctoral candidate his highly motivated and can take independent initiative and the supervisor is able to balance management and interpersonal input into the process.	The supervisor offers advice, suggestions, and/or interpretations.	Supervisor asks for opinions and suggestions, accepting and expanding the student's ideas, or asking for explanations and justifications of the student's statements.	use positive input to elicit Autonomous transactions, but needs to take care not to move into a rescuing (Warden) position.
	Authoritative	**Direct Active**	The supervisor may
	The supervisor monitors and regulates the supervisee's work closely.	Supervision is characterised by initiating, criticising, telling and directing behaviour.	use either the rescuing (Warden), or an overly critical (Reliant) position, and need to take care that students do not rebel, or become dependent, helpless and disempowered.

Table 1: Supervisor styles (adapted from Anderson, 1988; Gatfield, 2005 and Rowan, 1983).

Despite the varied origins of the above-mentioned authors' work, the similarities in their conclusions on supervision styles are evident and can be linked to the different identity positions that we have proposed. The authoritative style may not be seen as appropriate to doctoral supervision where independent work is favoured, which may be a reason for its absence from Gatfield's typology. However, authors such as Anderson (1988), Cree (2012) and Curr (2001) suggest that this style is prevalent in doctoral supervision. It is interesting to note that Anderson (1988) did not include a supervisory style that could be aligned to the pastoral or feelings-oriented styles included by the other two authors. This may be attributed to either the context in which the work was produced, or the time period in which it was published when not much was written on the nature of the supervisor-student relationship in doctoral education.

Gatfield (2005) describes these positions as preferred operating styles. Although students' attitudes and responses may influence the supervisory management style, it is unlikely to be deterministic. Both Gatfield and Rowan found that supervisors may move between styles depending on the stage in the research process, which Gatfield (2005:324) termed operational flexibility. This idea is supported by the work of Erskine (1997) on practitioner development from beginning, through intermediate, to advanced stages, during which, supervisory styles needed to adapt to be appropriate to the different developmental stages. As such, the supervisor becomes *"an embedded participant in a mutually influencing supervisory process"* (Frawley-O'Dea & Sarnat, 2001:41), while *"honouring the emergence of 'implicit' experience"* (Sills, 2009:192). This illustrates the dynamic flexibility that is necessary in the relationship.

Relationship convergence

Whilst these typologies are useful in understanding supervisory styles, it does not take into account the role either supervisor or student identities play in negotiating the doctoral learning space. It also does not account for the power dynamic at play between supervisors and students throughout the candidature – especially not the potential influence doctoral students can have on determining the type of relationship (and thus learning space) that evolves. Minor *et al.* (2012) note that one of the major areas of dissonance for doctoral candidates is deciphering and managing multiple relationships. Lin *et al.* (2013) refer to 'power distance orientation', which represents individuals' values of power. A student with a higher power distance orientation may more readily passively accept the imbalance of power. Understanding the dynamics of their power may demystify and help to resolve dissonance in the student/supervisor relationship.

Foucault (1997) argues that power is never solely 'top down' – where there is power, there is resistance. Students therefore possess the power to change the supervisory relationship my means of resistance (Cree, 2012). Power imbalances could arise through conflicting expectations between the supervisor and the student, which could influence the style of and approach to the supervision process (Frick *et al.*, 2010). Lee (2008) takes the debate further by taking possible student reactions into account in her framework for concepts of research supervision (see Table 2 below).

Lee's (2008) work starts to touch on relationship building as a key element of creating a doctoral learning space. Fataar (2005, forthcoming) refers to this relationship as dynamic and formative at the intersection of the student's personal approaches to research and how such approaches may influence the knowledgeability necessary for work at the doctoral level. It emphasises the function of the supervisor in helping the student move from dependence to independence, and provides space for the interplay between supervisors' professional and personal roles in doctoral pedagogy. Gardner (2008) notes this transition to independence and refers to graduate student socialisation where interpersonal processes (together with academic and professional processes) are an integral part of the transition. However, the supervisor may facilitate or hinder students' independence and integration into the scholarly community – a notion underscored by Dison (2004). Understanding the function of the doctoral supervisor is therefore essential to understanding how the supervisor-student relationship may unfold, even if it lacks showing the complete picture of how a learning space is negotiated by both parties. Aside from these processes and relationships involved in doctoral education, the supervisor is required to understand how the task can be completed successfully within the parameters of the system in which they are working (Vilkinas, 2002). The functions of supervision to enhance the relationship (which we call relationship convergence) and to achieve the goals in the doctoral context are thus relevant.

	PROFESSIONAL ROLE			PERSONAL ROLE	
	Functional	Encultura-tion	Critical thinking	Emancipa-tion	Rela-tionship development
Supervisor's activity	Rational progression through tasks	Gate-keeping, encourages student to become a member of the disci-plinary community	Evaluation, challenge, encourages student to question and analyse their work	Mentoring, supporting construc-tivism, encourages student to question and develop themselves	Super-vising by experience, developing a relationship, enthuses, inspires and cares for student
Supervisor's knowledge and skills	Directing, project management	Diagnosis of deficiencies, coaching	Argument, analysis	Facilitation, reflection	Emotional intelligence
Possible student reactions	Obedience, organised	Role modelling	Constant inquiry, fight or flight	Personal growth, reframing	Emotional intelligence
Student dependence character-istics	Needs explanation of stages to be followed and direction through them	Needs to be shown what to do	Learns questions to ask and frameworks to apply	Seeks affir-mation of self-worth	Seeks approval
Student indepen-dence character-istics	Can programme own work, follow timetables completely	Can follow discipline's epistemolog-ical demands indepen-dently	Can critique own work	Autono-mous, can decide how to be, where to go, what to do, where to find information	Demon-strates appropriate reciprocity and has power to withdraw

Table 2: A framework for concepts of research supervision (adapted from Lee, 2008:268, 277).

Relationship enhancement

From a clinical perspective, Hawkins and Smith (2006), Kadushin (1976), Newton (2012) and Proctor (2000) all argue that supervision has three main functions, as described in Table 3 below.

Functions of supervision			Supervision philosophy	
Kadushin (1976)	*Proctor (2000)*	*Hawkins & Smith (2006)*	*Newton (2012)*	*Newton (2012)*
Administrative	Normative	Qualitative	**Accounting** Ensures appropriateness to context, ethical conduct and adherence to standards	**Behavioural / Technological** Emphasis on structure, competence, criteria and standards
Supportive	Restorative	Resourcing	**Nurturative** Offers recognition, encouragement and support	**Humanistic** Support and nurturing of personal growth
Educative	Formative	Developmental	**Transformative** Promotes reflection and exploration, which may include ways to implement theory, and develop practice and awareness	**Radical** Reflexive, theory-to-practice (praxis) Constructivist and co-creative approach to learning

Table 3: Functions of supervision (adapted from Newton, 2012:104).

These functions are also applicable to doctoral education to some extent. The supervisees (or doctoral students in our case) may utilise these functions of supervisors to develop their own way of working and how they want to develop. Newton (2012) extends her theory further to the supervisee/student as having a need for structure, recognition and stimulus (based on the earlier work of Berne in 1961, and Clarke & Dawson in 1998):

- *structure* would ideally be met by the *accounting* function of the supervisor (akin to Lee's functional type research supervision);

- *recognition* by the *nurturative* function (encapsulating Lee's enculturation and relationship development conceptions of research supervision); and

- *stimulus* by the *transformative* function (which could be aligned to Lee's critical thinking and emancipation conceptions of research supervision).

Newton (2012) argues that supervisors need to balance the above-mentioned functions in order to meet supervisees' needs. Over-emphasis of a particular function may result in the supervisee experiencing the learning process as too rigid (if the supervisor becomes authoritative for the sake of accountability), too comfortable (if the supervisor is too nurturing), or frightening (if the challenges faced are overwhelming). Too little emphasis on any of the three functions may result in a sense of abandonment, isolation, or lack of connection. Conflict in the relationship could have deleterious consequences (Tepper *et al.*, 2011) in the doctoral process, which Cree (2012) refers to as imbalance in the supervisor relationship. However, Cree (2012) also notes that increasing student numbers and pressures to boost student throughput and publications may be indicative of a lack of institutional interest in students' affective needs and ultimately the functioning of the supervisor-student relationship beyond productivity. As such, Tronto's (1993) notion of care as attentiveness, responsibility, competence and responsiveness are useful, as it conceptualises supervisory care as encapsulating the nurturative, accounting and transformative functions of supervision.

Breaking the bonds of performativity in order to negotiate a doctoral learning space characterised by care (Tronto, 1993), morality (Cree,

2012), kindness (Clegg & Rowland, 2010), and freedom and friendship (Waghid, 2006) is not easy. Wisker (2005:192) aptly points out that there are *"discourses of power in the supervisor-university-student relationship"* at play. Supervisors and students therefore need to be compatible, which Rugg and Petre (2004) refer to as a workable relationship (even if it needs to be worked at). It is thus important to make sure that the elements that constitute the doctoral student-supervisor relationship are understood so that effective functioning will benefit both parties. Effective functioning would culminate in successful completion of studies. Identity and power are key elements in the relationship between doctoral students and research supervisors, and these elements need to be negotiated in order to constitute an effectively functioning learning space – that which we refer to as relationship enhancement.

A framework for negotiating doctoral learning spaces

We have conceptualised the relationship between doctoral students and their research supervisors as a negotiated learning space. This conceptualisation proposes this learning space as a negotiation between the self and others based on identity and power within the doctoral student-supervisor relationship that facilitates compassionate rigour (Manathunga, 2005:24) and reflexivity (Cree, 2012). All supervisory relationships contain aspects of both parties' conscious and unconscious present and past (Chinnock, 2011). Being mindful of these relational complexities may allow supervisors and students to co-create relational experiences (Chinnock, 2011), which allows for a constructive negotiated learning space to emerge.

However, the literature cited in our introduction suggests that this learning space is not always negotiated and/or constructive, which could result in a potentially deficient relationship where the potential negative effects of identity positions become manifest (as transaction analysis theory also suggests that each ego state/identity position has both a positive and negative side). Figure 1 provides a conceptualisation of the possible negative dimensions of supervisors' identity positions and how this may influence the learning space and ultimately the learning outcomes.

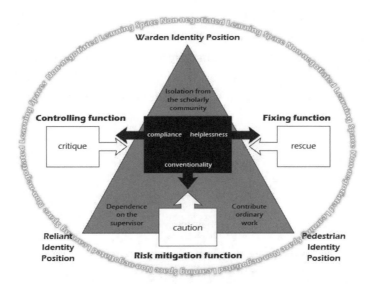

Figure 1: Doctoral supervisor-student relationship as a non-negotiated learning space.

As Figure 1 indicates, supervisors may take on identity positions that do not foster a negotiated learning space. Supervisors who take on Warden and Reliant identity positions fulfil a controlling function and offer overly critical comments on their students' work. Such students may comply with their supervisors' instructions, but remain dependent on receiving instructions. If the supervisor takes on the Warden and Pedestrian identity positions, the fixing function is performed – rescuing students from difficult situations or problems, but does not enhance their ability to become encultured into the scholarly community as responsible scholars themselves. The risk mitigation function is performed when the supervisor moves between Pedestrian and Reliant identity positions in which the supervisor enacts caution that may inhibit creativity and breed conventionality.

If students are merely compliant and exhibit helplessness, they may find it difficult to become encultured into the scholarly community. A helpless attitude coupled with conventional work may result in ordinary (non-original) contributions. Conventionality and compliance does not set the scene for students' movement towards independence. Supervisors can thus also inhibit their students' development based on the identity positions they occupy.

Such non-negotiated learning spaces may result in conflict; however, conflicts do not have to be destructive if they are solved constructively. Figure 2 provides doctoral supervisors with a conceptual framework for understanding doctoral supervision interpersonal relationships so as to guide supervisors to more effective interactions while supervising doctoral students.

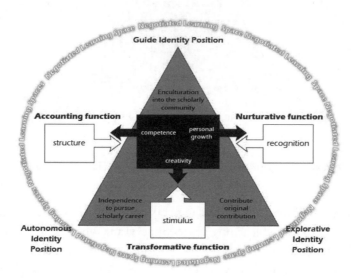

Figure 2: Doctoral supervisor-student relationship as a negotiated learning space.

In figure 2 we suggest that supervisors need to achieve synchronicity between their own and students' identity positions and facilitate mutual sensitivity towards each other's backgrounds (as the work of Fataar (2005) suggests) in order to negotiate a mutually satisfying and beneficial learning space. If there is synchronicity between the supervisor and the student, the student will develop competence, personal growth and creativity. The supervisor who is able to balance the Guide and Autonomous identity positions will be able to activate the accounting function and provide structure to the student and develop their competence. If the supervisor takes on the Guide and Explorative identity positions, the nurturative function is performed that gives students recognition and encourages students' personal growth. The transformative function is realised when the supervisor moves between Explorative and Autonomous identity positions, thus providing a stimulus for students' creativity. If such synchronicity is achieved, relationship convergence emerges.

If students' competence and personal growth are enhanced, their enculturation into the scholarly community through the recognition of their doctoral work may be facilitated. A combination of personal growth and creativity may lead students towards making an original contribution to their field of study through their doctoral work. If students are both competent and creative, it may facilitate their transformation into independent scholars.

Supervisors need to recognise their own identity positions (which we have conceptualised as Guide / Warden, Autonomous / Reliant, and Explorative / Pedestrian) and how this influences their supervisory function. Knowledge of the identity positions of their students at a specific stage will help supervisors to negotiate, be responsive and adapt to these relative positions. We furthermore make the proposition that supervisors do not often position themselves only within one of these positions, as supervision requires dynamic flexibility in the supervisor's own identity positions in order to fulfil their supervisory functions. As such, a supervisor may move between identity positions in order to fully facilitate student learning. Knowledge of the opposing dimensions could guide supervisors in adapting and negotiating learning spaces, especially since supervisors have the power to change and move between identity positions more readily than do their students.

Supervisors thus need to be flexible in moving between identity positions when necessary in order to be accounting, nurturative and/or transformative as the relationship and stage of study requires. By enhancing the relationship between the supervisor and student – where the structure, stimulus and recognition a supervisor provides can be met by student competence, creativity and personal growth in return – supervisors can negotiate constructive, caring, and empowering learning spaces. Such learning spaces foster students' enculturation into scholarly communities, enhance their ability to contribute original work, and provide opportunities for them to develop into independent scholars.

Future research could focus on applying the conceptual framework presented here to empirical studies, and broadening our understanding of how such negotiated learning spaces operate in joint supervision contexts.

Although our contribution in this chapter focused on a notional singular supervisor-student relationship, the application of our conceptualisation would also apply to joint and co-supervision contexts where supervisors (and students) can jointly negotiate their positions.

About the authors

Liezel Frick is a senior lecturer at the Centre for Higher and Adult Education, Faculty of Education, Stellenbosch University, South Africa. She can be contacted at this e-mail: blf@sun.ac.za

Eva Brodin is a lecturer at the Department of Psychology at Lund University, Sweden. She can be contacted at this e-mail: Eva.Brodin@psy.lu.se

Ruth Albertyn is a research associate at the Centre for Higher and Adult Education, Faculty of Education, Stellenbosch University, South Africa. She can be contacted at this e-mail: rma@sun.ac.za

Using the Theory and Practice of 'Built Pedagogy' to Inform Learning Space Design

Eva Dobozy

Introduction

This chapter contributes to the anthology on learning space design in higher education by focusing primarily on design decisions regarding non-formal learning. As inspiration for my conceptualisation of learning spaces I utilise Thody's (2008:13) definition of a related term: 'learning landscapes', which she describes as being *"conceptually holistic, loosely-coupled interconnections of all formal and informal, on- and off-campus, virtual and physical facilities, sites and services and how stakeholders use them."* I also take the concept of *built pedagogy* as a starting point, which according to Oblinger (2006) is the ability of space to define how we teach. Consideration of these wider notions of 'learning spaces' enables me to explore how, through deliberate design decisions, first-year teacher education students at Curtin University studying the same learning material in different learning modes have been encouraged to engage in 'border-crossing' practices. The concept of 'border-crossing' is related to the idea of making possible free and unrestricted movement between learning spaces that are conventionally separate, such as learning spaces created for different student groups. My exploration of the learning design decisions made in the construction of the joint occupation of a virtual learning space by learners studying the same learning material in either an on-campus or off-campus mode attempts to illustrate how consideration of learning spaces should be factored in as important component of the support given to students' learning engagement and subsequent learning outcomes. Therefore, the purpose of this chapter is to explore the concept of *built pedagogy* from a theoretical and practical view point. Specifically, it illustrates how design decisions are explicitly linked to a designer's educational philosophy and pedagogical practice. Hence, Biggs' (2003) often quoted model of constructive alignment of a designer's educational philosophy, teaching and learning methods, assessment practices and intended learning outcomes will require the inclusion of learning space or landscape design, which I refer to here as *built pedagogy*. Reading this chapter, you will:

1. have a clear understanding of *built pedagogy* as an underlying concept for learning space design;

2. have reviewed an example of a shared virtual learning space designed (built) to facilitate collaborative learning between students engaging via different study modes; and

3. have a developed awareness of the importance of allowing the design of learning spaces to facilitate elective informal learning engagement.

It is not surprising that design decisions concerning learning spaces can support or hinder certain forms of learning, such as formal, non-formal, informal or incidental. As stated above, I focus primarily on design decisions concerning the realm of non-formal learning, which is contrasted by Scott-Webber (in this volume), who focuses on the formal teaching and learning environment, the classroom, and discusses the impact of spatial design on student success. Scott-Webber and I agree that traditional teacher-centric education is firmly situated within the realm of formal learning and can be perceived as unidirectional input education, flowing from the teacher, as the 'sage on the stage', to the student as recipient of the teacher's wisdom. Hence, the lecture held in a physical learning space, the classical lecture theatre, or the virtual lecture uploaded to an online learning platform and consumed by the learner in an anywhere and anytime fashion, are both physical manifestations of the unidirectional input education tradition. By contrast, non-formal education is often designed to shift the focus from teaching to learning and from content-centric learning outcomes to process-centric learning outcomes. Informal and incidental learning differ from non-formal learning insofar that they are seldom pre-planned and do not have predesigned learning outcomes. According to Werquin (2010), informal and incidental learning can happen anytime, anywhere and with anyone (see below for a more detailed discussion on the different forms of learning design).

A holistic view of learning design, which includes learning space considerations, is important and Scott-Webber (2011:15) aptly notes: *"It's easy to dismiss design – to relegate it to mere ornament, the prettifying of [learning spaces] to disguise their banality. But that is a serious misunderstanding of what design is and why it matters – especially now."*

Although it would be interesting to capture student perceptions and experiences of the joint learning space that forms a focus for this chapter, I have chosen to only document design decisions, focusing on the idea of *built pedagogy*. Hence, the chapter takes forward the notion that through deliberate planning and design, it is possible to prepare learning spaces that provide opportunities for formal, non-formal, informal and incidental learning. However, it is not possible to make learners use the learning spaces in the way they were envisioned and designed. We may assume students come into a specific learning space with preconceived ideas and expectations, but foremost with agency and an understanding that they are able to inhabit a learning space in a manner that suits their ideas and intentions, which may or may not be the way it was designed.

Similar to Scott-Webber (2011), I argue that there is a need to pay close attention to the way design decisions are made when constructing new and innovative physical and/or virtual learning spaces prior to the investigation of how these spaces are perceived as conducive to learning and how they are utilised differently by learners and teaching staff not involved in the design. Although it is outside the scope of this chapter to do so, I acknowledge that there is great value in investigating learner and tutor perspectives in relation to agency and how effective *use, non-use, mis-use* and/or *ab-use* of learning spaces and how consideration of such can lend insight into how students learn differently and what design decisions need to be adopted and what adaption made to enhance the learning engagement of diverse learners and cater effectively for student variability (see Frick *et al.* in this volume for a discussion of how doctoral students and supervisors perspectives in relation to agency constitutes relational learning spaces).

Below, I continue the chapter by exploring the concept of *built pedagogy* and link it to the development of learners' 21st century competencies.
Next, the concepts of formal, non-formal and informal learning are
explored from a Bourdieuian dispositional theory of action perspective
and connected to learner agency and decision-making power. The chapter
continues with the case of teacher education at Curtin University, which
illustrates how traditionally disparate learning spaces have been recon-
ceptualised to facilitate the ideas of 'border crossing' and agency. Finally,
some implications for future designs of virtual learning spaces are
outlined, focusing on the need to plan for non-formal learning and the
design of social learning spaces.

Built pedagogy

Architecture has often been linked to philosophy in the sense that value
is ascribed to method. Foucault (1977) argued that knowledge and power
are interrelated. Thus, power is exerted through the possibility *to choose*
certain actions or inactions based on a set of beliefs or knowledge. Wherever power is exerted, knowledge is involved and vice versa – wherever
knowledge is involved, power is exerted. In other words, it is through
design decisions that particular actions are made possible or impossible.
A classical and well-known example is the case of Robert Moses, a city
planner in New York from the 1920s to the 1960s, who decided to focus
on a specific design feature of a bridge to promote certain personal and
professional values. Leigh Star (1999:387) explains: *"[Moses] made a
behind the scene policy decision to make the automobile bridge over the Grand
Central Parkway low in height. The reason? The bridge would then be too low
for public transport-buses to pass under them. The result? Poor people would
be effectively barred from the richer Long Island suburbs, not by policy, but
by design."*

This example illustrates that there exists an explicit relationship
between the personal and professional values and beliefs that a designer,
such as Robert Moses, holds and the design features of a product, in
this case, the automobile bridge over the Grand Central Parkway. Thus,
the choice of bridge design corresponds to his personal and professional
values, much the same way as a university educator's choices of learning

design are to some extent consistent with, and supportive of, the educator's personal and professional values. Hence, learning design, similar to bridge design, is deeply imbued with the designer's philosophy.

Understanding the power of architectural design means accepting the idea that built pedagogy can, on the one hand, restrict learners' ability to act independently and, on the other hand, compel or even demand that learners take charge and appropriate the learning space to their perceived needs (Mohanan, 2002). To put it more simply, the continuum between learner discipline and autonomy, the objectification of learners and the regarding of learners as autonomous decision-makers, can be illustrated through the documentation of built pedagogies (Figure 1).

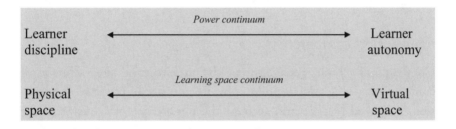

Figure 1: Built pedagogy as continuum from learner discipline to learner autonomy across Physical spaces and Virtual spaces.

Considerations of power and agency have to be at the centre of pedagogical design decisions. People who are unable to choose are *objects of power* who are denied free will, whereas people, who are able to choose, are *subjects of power* or agents of power. School children in Australia and elsewhere, including high-school students, are closely monitored and supervised. Teachers make regular decisions for them, which content to study, for example, which worksheet to complete and when and how long to engage in discussions with peers. They are, more often than not, *objects of power* in schooling situations. They are compelled to attend each class and strict attendance records are kept of each student.

By contrast, first-year university students are *subjects of power*. Australian university policy in most cases dictates that adult learners cannot be compelled to attend classes or participate in learning activities

(Rodgers, 2002). Hence, university students in contrast to school children have freedom of choice. Thus, there is no getting around having to choose certain actions (or inactions) based on personal judgement. Accordingly, whenever people are free to choose certain actions or inactions, they are agents of power.

Adult learners are subjects of power and agency. Whenever they encounter learning activities, they can either accept or reject the opportunity to engage with it. Consequently, the first step of learning in higher education involves the process of acceptance and/or rejection. This is a value-laden process as it involves power or agency. Within this process of evaluation, adult learners cannot help but be influenced by their personal viewpoints, prior school and life experiences and motivational and epistemological readiness for learning.

Agency and competency

Contemporary built pedagogy, as the architectural embodiment of contemporary educational philosophy, irrespective of the level of education, will need to take into account the importance of agency and the provision of opportunities to choose appropriate actions, which is one of the desired 21st century competencies or learning outcomes of university graduates all over the world. A competency is *"more than just knowledge and skills. It involves the ability to meet complex demands, by drawing on and mobile[s]ing psychosocial resources"* (OECD, 2005:4). Therefore, competencies include personal characteristics, such as motivation, attitude and values besides narrow technical skills. No longer is it sufficient for 21st century adult learners to acquire narrow technical knowledge and skills, to be employable, they will need to demonstrate an array of specific competencies that have also been referred to as intangible assets (Levy et al., 2011).

Most important for the present discussion is the recent survey of US employers conducted by Millennial Branding (2012), which found that narrow technical knowledge and skills (commonly tested in end-of-semester examinations at university and international or national testing regimes in school education) did not feature high on the list of important competencies. When asked: "What skills are you looking for when you hire", the top three competencies identified were: communication (98%), positive attitude (97%) and adaptable to change (92%). On fourth and fifth position were teamwork (92%) and goal orientation (88%). Given the great variety of terms using and meaning attributed to these competencies, a number of scholars and organisations have proposed taxonomies of 21st century competencies. Finegold and Notabartolo's (2008) taxonomy is useful in designing effective learning landscapes that allow ample opportunities for learners to develop 21st century competencies during the course of their study (see Table 1).

Analytic skills	Interpersonal skills	Ability to execute	Information processing	Capacity for change
Critical thinking	Communication	Initiative/ self- direction	Information literacy	Creativity/ innovation
Problem solving	Collaboration	Productivity	Media literacy	Adaptive learning/ learning-to-learn
Decision making	Leadership / responsibility		Digital citizenship	Flexibility
Research/ inquiry			ICT operations/ concepts	

Table 1: Taxonomy of 21st century competencies.

Given the increased importance of and demand for process skills of higher education graduates, it is vital that learning space design supports students' process skills development during the course of their studies. Therefore, built pedagogy needs to allow maximum possibility of people with different backgrounds, skills and mindsets to mingle and interact with each other. The building of a designated communal space ought to have the potential to assist in the formation of synergies and allow for greater student engagement, leading to improved student learning outcomes (Parker, 2003).

Now that the concept of built pedagogy has been explained, which links contemporary educational philosophy with architectural design, the next section clarifies the use of the terms formal, non-formal, informal and incidental learning. Understanding the move away from the formal, teacher-centric education model to more informal, student-centric learning designs based on social constructivist and/or connectivist learning theories (see Nygaard *et al.*, 2014) is important in appreciating the push for the design of learning spaces that provide opportunities for non-formal, informal and incidental learning. The discussion of inter-activity and possibilities of 'border-crossing' behaviours as non-formal learning activities will set the stage for the practical example I present, which illustrates how *the present conceptualisation of built pedagogy* has been enacted in a particular context.

Formal, non-formal, informal and incidental learning

In a typical Australian undergraduate teacher education course the most common pedagogical approach, which is utilised to introduce students to new knowledge and develop their skills, is through well-structured lectures and tutorial sessions (Phillips, 2005; Webster, 2009). Although formal education is the norm in traditional university education, the value of informal, non-formal and incidental learning and teaching seems to have gained traction, and much effort is placed on creating spaces that support these alternative ways of learning, such as problem, scenario or inquiry-based learning and teaching (Werquin, 2010).

Whereas traditional formal teaching and learning is mainly unidi-rectional, non-formal education is multidirectional and fluid, similar to informal and incidental learning. Dissimilar to informal learning, designing non-formal learning provisions requires intention and clearly stated learning outcomes (see Table 2).

Changing formal and entrenched learning and teaching cultures in school, higher and further education is not easy, because socio-cultural practices are habitualised and taken for granted (Arora, 2010; Walker & Creanor, 2012). Putting someone into traditional formal teaching and learning provisions who expects non-traditional learning spaces might cause her/him to experience anxiety and frustration to the point that they are unable and/or unwilling to engage in meaningful learning (Dobozy, 2011, 2012). From a Bourdieuian dispositional theory of action perspec-tive, commonly referred to as the study of habitual action or *habitus*, this does not seem to be such a surprising proposition. I see Pierre Bourdieu's (1977, 1990) work as most useful in understanding psychosocial reactions of learners to new and unfamiliar learning spaces and the resistance to cultural change by teacher educators and trainee teachers. Why? Because, according to Bourdieu, there is a dialectical relationship between the learner and the learning environment. The learner is socialised into particular ways of being a student, which means that the cultural experiences as forms and habits of cultural behaviours and role expectations of learners and teachers are formed and cemented into taken-for-granted expectations. The dialectic relationship as outlined by Bourdieu (1977) refers to this mutual influence between the individual, the situation and past experiences, and the presence or absence of certain characteristics of the learning environment. Bourdieu (1977:261) explains: *The product of a dialectical relationship between a situation and the habitus, understood as a system of durable and transposable dispositions which, integrating all past experiences, functions at every moment as a matrix of perceptions, appreciations, and actions.*

Attributes	Formal learning	Non-formal learning	Informal learning	Incidental learning
Stated learning outcomes	◆	◆		
Intentional and systematic	◆	◆		
mainly unidirectional	◆			
Tightly structured	◆			
Loosely structured		◆	◆	
Unstructured				◆
mainly multidirectional		◆	◆	◆
Fluid		◆	◆	◆

Table 2: Attributes of formal, non-formal, informal and incidental learning.

These expectations of actions and behaviours, underpinned by past experiences are deeply influential in shaping perceptions of quality teaching and learning experiences and role expectations. For example, in a traditional learning space, the classes are divided and strictly organised; and the expectation is for a teacher, as the expert, to *teach* . . . to tell the class what, when, how and how much to do. Hence, developing a different mindset concerning the value of non-formal teaching and informal or incidental peer-supported learning requires not simply a carefully prepared learning space, but more importantly it requires the development of new cognitive structures and role expectations of both students and teachers (Fullan, 2008). In other words, students and teachers need to be educated about the link between the designs of built pedagogy and underpinning educational philosophy that guide design decisions.

A virtual learning landscape was designed to assist students move cognitively and emotionally from the pre-formed expectation and value of traditional formal learning, which focuses on passive information consumption in a formal designated place. Positive engagement with the virtual learning environment entails a consideration of the value-adding nature of non-formal education, accepting the invitation to be an actor with power and agency and to choose to engage (or not) in non-formal learning through 'border-crossing' practices. The next section will provide a case example of the application of built pedagogy thinking.

Case example of implementing built pedagogy

The joint virtual learning space created for on-campus and off-campus students within *Blackboard*, the university's official learning management system, was permeated with socio-cultural values, based on contemporary social constructivist educational philosophy. It aimed to play on students' curiosity and invite active learner engagement with the learning material and with each other. More specifically, the design intended to prompt students to engage in 'border-crossing' behaviours and become involved in non-formal learning through engaged inquiry (see Rowley, in this volume). It attempted to adhere to specific design principles, one of which was fluidity, enabling students to move, effortlessly, in and out of public, social and private spaces, emphasising openness, flexibility as well as intimacy. The plan was to provide a multi-zoned learning landscape that triggered inquisitiveness and interest in learners about the learning experiences of *The Other*, meaning students who chose to enrol in a different study mode (see Figure 2).

Home group	On-campus study mode	Off-campus study mode	The other
	Off-campus study mode	On-campus study mode	

Figure 2: Home group and 'The Other'.

To minimise or alleviate student anxiety about an unfamiliar virtual learning landscape, it needed to be designed for optimal *"Proxemic interaction"* (Ballendat *et al.*, 2010) [Proxemic zones first identified by E.T. Hall, 1969]. This meant to design a learning landscape that provided a balance between openness, flexibility and intimacy. The design needed to encourage interpersonal interaction and communication as a form of non-formal education. Hence, a zoned virtual learning space was created, which provided explicit signals concerning interpersonal special relationships and allowed for various levels of personal proximity (see Figure 3).

1. The Public Zone: Course-related information *Ungated*	2. The Social Zone: Discussion board *Ungated*
3. The Private or Social Zone (Home Group/The Other): Group-specific information *Gated* (open gates)	

Figure 3: Proxemic zones of interaction design.

This zone-based *Blackboard* site development requires *"a notable change in the collective mindset of diverse actors"* (Moilanen, 2012:100) as tutors and learners adjusted to the design of learning zones. In other words, this three-zone Blackboard site design (zone 1: public; zone 2: social (gated/ungated); zone 3: private) incorporated Proxemic cues, helping students to assimilate to the new virtual learning environment, which included new features and behavioural rules.

The personal zone signified by the use of a designated folder is important to signify nearness. The personal zone for learners, studying in either off-campus or on-campus modes, is referred to here as *Home*

Group. By contrast, the social zone is intended to signal communal learning spaces, which are either gated (designated folder), or ungated spaces (discussion board) (Scott-Webber, 2011). The personal zone of *The Other*, although designed as a gated learning space, is accessible by everyone. The purpose of open access to social and private spaces aimed to fulfil the function of intimacy and openness, focusing on personal need and adhering to a democratic and social learning philosophy. Finally, the public zone provided standard course-related information, such as e-texts, multimedia resources, online lectures, and public announcements (see Figure 4).

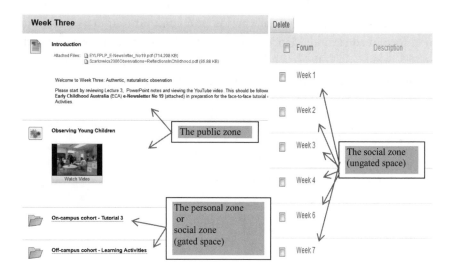

Figure 4: Implementation of a zone-based virtual learning environment.

The Proxemic zones (Hall, 1969) of interaction design intended to invite 'border-crossing' behaviours, based on student agency, driven by curiosity and a feeling of security. In traditional segregated learning environments, there is limited interaction among students studying in different learning modes. The combining of the *Blackboard* site for the two student groups (studying in on-campus and off-campus mode) was an intention to break free from the traditional learning design mould and invite spontaneous interaction among different student groups, aiding non-formal, informal and incidental learning.

Openness (the social and public zones)

Built pedagogy supports the notion that a culture of deep learning, creativity and active participation can be deliberately designed to counterbalance spatial distance and enable constructive dialogue between individuals who are, for example, expected to work through the same learning content, but experience learning and teaching differently through their choice of delivery mode. Bringing voices from different places together allows people to share in a joint experience and co-create their knowledge and understanding of the learning activities. This practice is variably referred to as space shifting or communicating over distance, which is essential in today's knowledge-based society and economy (Forrester Research, 2010). Hence, openness was seen as vital to trigger 'border-crossing' behaviours through the engagement with learners and learning resources from *The Other*.

Intimacy (the personal zone)

Intimacy was seen as important to enhance learner well-being and confidence. Providing zoned learning spaces, but with open gates was intended to enhance learner well-being and self-confidence. It was important to design an environment that allows for the development of self-disclosure behaviour in students, such as the sharing of personal and affective information. This sharing behaviour would then serve as a trigger for learning communications among diverse students, leading to deep approaches to learning and information processing.

Intimacy was important to ensure a feeling of safety, well-being and control, contributing to learner agency and a willingness to engage in 'border-crossing' behaviours. Hence, openness needed to be balanced with closed or gated spaces to ensure that openness would not be experienced as oppressive in its expansiveness as was the emotional reaction of some students with past designs (Dobozy, 2012) and as Shulman (2005:11) notes: "*What happens when people who are used to being invisible ... suddenly or regularly find themselves visible, accountable, and ... vulnerable? You (as the teacher) inevitably begin to experience higher levels of emotion in a classroom. There's a sense of risk. There's a sense of unpredictability. There's a sense of – dare I say – anxiety. And for some, anxiety morphs into terror*". Utilising Proxemic interaction design principles (see Marquardt & Greenberg, 2012; Hall, 1969), private/separate and public/communal spaces were made clearly visible to not only assist students in dealing with feelings of anxiety, but to also aid 'border-crossing behaviours' and the development of a community of learners. Cognitive and psychosocial diversity are key ingredients for the development of a productive learning community and the building of learning networks. Bielaczyc and Collins (1999:18) note: "*A learning community continually discusses ideas and examines its progress in understanding ... what occurs in a learning community is 'collective learning by doing', where participants learn from what others do. What is learned by individuals is what 'gets into the air' of the community.*"

Yet, one cannot be cognitively or affectively involved in learning situations and contribute to the building of collective knowledge if one is absent altogether. A phenomenon pertaining to technology-enhanced communication and social networking is lurking. Therefore, it was important to include design features that would enhance students' understand of the significance of *showing up* in social learning zones. The signaling of social presence in any learning environment, even if there are no intentions to actively engage in knowledge sharing behaviour, is important, but more so in technology-enhanced learning.

Social presence

Social presence has been variously defined in the literature and there is no agreed upon conceptualisation. Nevertheless, many contemporary researchers utilise a 1976 conceptualisation presented by Short and colleagues agreeing that social presence is "*the degree of salience of the person in the interaction and consequent salience of the interpersonal relationships*" (Aragon, 2003:59), indicating the willingness of a person to initiate or participate in group-based discussions.

The lurking phenomenon is well documented in the technology-enhanced learning literature. A lurker is an unidentified visitor, someone who is socially present in a virtual learning environment, but her/his identity is unknown or the visit is unacknowledged (Soroka & Rafaeli, 2006). Explanations for lurking behaviours include a need to learn community conventions, lack of academic self-efficacy, and anxiety concerning self-disclosure (Preece *et al.*, 2004). Hence, rather than being completely absent from the learning situation, lurkers are socially present.

Consequently, a deliberate design decision was to enable the self-enrolment feature within *Blackboard* and not automatically enrol all students in the discussion board. As agents of power, students can choose to show up and, therewith, signal social presence. To commit to interactive and collaborative learning, one must first be socially present prior to cognitively and affectively investing in learning tasks. Hence, the promise of high interactivity and active participation may be contributing to feelings of anxiety in students more comfortable in a traditional learning environment where they can remain passive and invisible. To assist students break with habitual passive learning behaviour, lurking was encouraged and factored into the design of the discussion board. Students needed to commit to specific discussion-based learning activities by self-enrolling into each discussion topic on the discussion board. Learners not intending to actively contribute to the discussion, but intending to read the posts, needed to indicate their social presence, hence they would break the mould of the 'invisible participant' and can be identified.

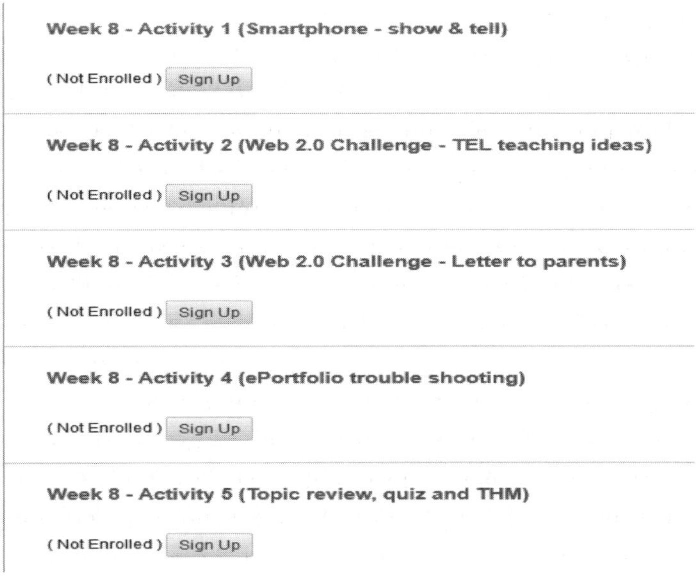

Week 8 – Activity 1 (Smartphone – show & tell)

(Not Enrolled) Sign Up

Week 8 – Activity 2 (Web 2.0 Challenge – TEL teaching ideas)

(Not Enrolled) Sign Up

Week 8 – Activity 3 (Web 2.0 Challenge – Letter to parents)

(Not Enrolled) Sign Up

Week 8 – Activity 4 (ePortfolio trouble shooting)

(Not Enrolled) Sign Up

Week 8 – Activity 5 (Topic review, quiz and THM)

(Not Enrolled) Sign Up

Figure 5: Self-enrol feature to signal social presence.

The aim of this deliberate design decision was to enable re-socialisation of students familiar with passive roles and invisibility in online learning environments. An example of tacit knowledge and intangible asset development is to understand how social presence constitutes a precondition for cognitive and affective learning engagement and knowledge sharing. Hence, students will need to become comfortable with being seen in social learning spaces, such as discussion boards. The close relationship between intimacy and social presence has been recognised as an important factor in improving students' learning engagement and the development of a community of learners (Aragon, 2003; Bielaczyc & Collins, 1999).

The next section will synthesise the information presented above. In particular, it will discuss the significance of the design decisions made in the creation of a joint virtual learning space for students studying the same unit during the same time period in either on-campus or off-campus mode, with the aim of aiding 'border-crossing' behaviours in students to enhance their learning engagement and learning outcomes.

Discussion

Learning space design is increasingly recognised as important. Linking learning space design decisions with contemporary educational philosophy enables the creation of different power relationships and forms of personal interaction, based on intent and habitual behaviour. By way of making the power of architectural design explicit – I am arguing that the creation of a jointly occupied virtual learning space aimed to move students' habitual action from passive information consumption to active learning engagement and collaboration motivated by curiosity and a desire to connect with *The Other* constitutes a designed (built) pedagogy. As subjects of power, students are, in this joint learning space, invited to make choices to either stay in the familiar gated personal and public zones or venture into the social zones, exemplified by the open access discussion board, primarily designed for students studying fully online, and gated folders of *The Other* – which includes learning materials specific to the study mode.

The centrality of agency within this learning space becomes visible as the architectural embodiment of contemporary educational philosophy through the invitation to engage in non-formal, multi-directional learning. In other words, the decision to focus on the design of non-traditional social places within the unit *Blackboard* site was intended to enhance students' willingness to engage in non-formal learning. The power of choice is illustrated when students move into social places as they signal a desire to interact and learn from and with others, not traditionally perceived as their learning peers. Hence, the junction between learning space design and educational intent is important in changing traditional unidirectional information delivery and consumption associated with *Blackboard* (see Dobozy & Reynolds, 2012) so as to increase the focus on non-formal learning opportunities of students. The dialectical relationship between learning space, learner habitual action and learning opportunity is not yet well understood. However, educational research, notably Pierre Bourdieu's (1977, 1990) work, has established the influence habitual action has on student learning engagement and the influence learning structures have in enabling or hindering certain practices and relationships to emerge (Guzzini, 2006). Hence, a key goal of this example of built pedagogy was to increase student interaction and collaboration through the provision of new environmental cues that trigger 'border-crossing' behaviours and therewith disrupt habitual student passivity (see also Drew & Koppler, this volume). As Verplanken and Wood (2006:95) explain: *"Because habits are triggered by the environment, successful interventions must focus on changing the environmental features that maintain those habits."* In other words, the impact of the learning environment on learner action and engagement with learning for the benefit of shared knowledge creation and the development of 21st century competencies should not be underestimated.

So, a key design decision was to divide the *Blackboard* site into three major zones. In an attempt to disrupt passive learning behaviour and balance openness with intimacy, the unit *Blackboard* site was designed with the aim to create spaces for non-formal learning and entice students to increase collaboration and knowledge sharing.

The creation of a personal zone, *The Home Group*, designated to the specific student groups (studying in on-campus or off-campus mode) is a gated environment, exemplified by the two folders. However, there is open access to gated private and social spaces, enabling students to choose to explore these spaces or completely stay away.

The discussion board is an important social zone, which may be regarded as the *unit hot spot*. It is classified as a social zone for two reasons: firstly, it is an interaction space linked to the learning activities for the off-campus student group, but again invites 'border-crossing' behaviours of students from the on-campus group; and secondly, it is designed as the metaphorical garden or park of the virtual learning space, encouraging students to become involved in knowledge sharing and the creation of a community of learners. Hence, it is a multi-purpose space, allowing for a variety of non-formal learning participation, from lurking to responding to learning activity questions to framing of learning problems or scenarios.

Conclusion

The concept of *built pedagogy* was explored in this chapter from a theoretical and a practical viewpoint. It illustrated that design decisions in the construction of a joint *Blackboard* site for students studying the same unit in different modes must be taken seriously. But more importantly, it needs to be recognised that there is a requirement to document carefully design decisions to help align learning theory with pedagogical decision-making and space design. The design considerations and decisions outlined here reflect the roots of my interpretation of built pedagogy thinking as the interrelationship between learning space and educational philosophy. Documenting design decisions in education is not new. However, *built pedagogy*, as the nexus between contemporary educational philosophy and architectural design will need to be better understood. Exploring specific design decisions in the creation of learning opportunities for students that assist in the accumulation of intangible assets, such as team-building and communication skills in theory and practice is urgently needed as universities prepare graduates ready to contribute to the global knowledge economy.

There is a clear demand for carefully designed non-formal learning spaces, illustrating how ideas of built pedagogy can be enacted in various contexts and with diverse learners. A possible implication of this case example is that design decisions that render students visible, enabling 'border-crossing' behaviours, will need to be approached systematically, taking cross-cultural factors and habitual actions into consideration. Therefore, it is important to understand psychosocial reactions of learners to new and unfamiliar learning spaces. Changing cultural practices and entrenched student and staff roles requires not simply an acknowledgement of diverse pedagogical possibilities, but rather it requires a heightened appreciation of informal, non-formal and incidental learning in higher education and elsewhere.

About the author

Eva Dobozy is Senior Lecturer in the School of Education at Curtin University, Australia. She can be contacted at this e-mail: eva.dobozy@ curtin.edu.au

Collected Bibliography

Aaragon, S. (2003) Creating social presence in online environments. *New Directions for Adult and Continuing Education*, Vol. 100, No. 1, pp. 57-68.

Adamopoulos, J. & W. J. Lonner (1994) Absolutism, relativism and universalism in the study of human behavior. In W. J. Lonner & R. S. Moypass (eds) *Psychology and Culture*. Boston: Allyn & Bacon, pp. 129-134.

Adult Mental Health Division and COSIG Team, The Therapeutic Alliance (undated) Department of Health, State of Hawaii.

Åkerlind, G. (2005) Variation and commonality in phenomenographic research methods. *Higher Education Research & Development*, Vol. 24, No. 4, pp. 321-334.

Albertyn, R. M., Kapp, C. A. & Groenewald, C. (2002) Patterns of empowerment in individuals through the course of a life-skills programme in South Africa. *Studies in the Education of Adults*, Vol. 33, No. 2, pp. 180–200.

Ally, M. (2004) Foundations of educational theory for online learning. In T. Anderson & F. Elloumi (eds) *Theory and practice of online learning*. Athabasca, Alberta: Athabasca University, pp. 3-32.

Altman, I. (1970) Territorial behavior in humans. An analysis of the concept. In L. Pastalan & D. Carson (eds) *Spatial behavior of older people*. Michigan: The University of Michigan, pp. 1-24.

Altman, I. (1975) *The environment and social behavior*. California: Wadsworth.

Anderson, J. (1988) *The supervisory process in speech language pathology and audiology*. Boston: College Hill Press & Little.

Applegate, J. L. (2011) *Graduating the 21st century student: Advising as if their lives (and our future) depended on it*. Keynote address at the 35th Annual Conference on Academic Advising, Denver, CO.

Arora, P. (2010) Hope-in-the-wall? A digital promise for free learning. *British Journal of Educational Technology*, Vol. 41, No. 5, pp. 689-702.

Austerlitz, N. (ed) (2008) *Unspoken interactions: Exploring the unspoken dimension of learning and teaching in creative subjects*. London: Centre for Learning and Teaching in Art and Design.

Austin, Z. & M. Rocchi Dean (2006) Impact of facilitated asynchronous distance education on clinical skills development of international pharmacy graduates. *The American Journal of Distance Education*, Vol. 20, No. 2, pp. 79-91.

Ballendat, T.; N. Marquardt & S. Greenberg (2010) Proxemic interaction: Designing for a proximity and orientation-aware environment. In *Proceedings of the ACM conference on interactive tabletops and surfaces - ACM ITS 2010*. Saarbruecken, Germany:ACM Press, pp. 121-130, November 7-10.

Bandura, A. (1977) *Social learning theory*. Englewood Cliffs: Prentice Hall.

Bandura, A. (1994) Self-efficacy. In V. S. Ramachaudran (ed) *Encyclopedia of Human Behavior*, Vol. 4, pp. 71-81. New York: Academic Press.

Barkley, E. F.; K. P. Cross & C. H. Major (2005) *Collaborative learning techniques: A handbook for college faculty*. San Francisco: Jossey-Bass.

Barnett, H. (ed) (2012) *Broad vision: Inspired by... images from science*. London: University of Westminster.

Barnett, H. & J. R. A. Smith (ed) (2011) *Broad Vision: The art & science of looking*. London: University of Westminster.

Barnett, R. & K. Coate (2005) *Engaging the curriculum in higher education*. Maidenhead: Society for Research into Higher Education/Open University Press.

Barnett, R. & P. Temple (2006) Impact on space of future changes in higher education. *Space Management Group*.

Barrett, H. C. (2007) Researching electronic portfolios and learner engagement: The REFLECT initiative. *International Reading Association*, pp. 436-449.

Bartholomae, D. (1986) Inventing the university. *Journal of Basic Writing*, Vol. 5, pp. 4-23.

Beachboard, M.; J. C. Beachboard; W. Li & S. R. Atkinson (2011) Cohorts and relatedness: Self-determination theory as an explanation of how learning communities affect educational outcomes. *Research in Higher Education*, Vol. 52, No. 8, pp. 853-874.

Beaudoin, M. F. (2002) Learning or lurking? Tracking the "invisible" online student. *Internet and Higher Education*, No. 5, pp. 147-155.

Beauvois, M. H. (1998) Write to speak: The effects of electronic communication on the oral achievement of fourth-semester French students. In J. A. Muykens (ed) *New ways of learning and teaching: Focus on technology and foreign language education.* Boston: Heinle & Heinle, pp. 93-116.

Becher, T. (1989) *Academic tribes and territories.* Milton Keynes: SRHE/Open University Press.

Beery, T. A.; D. Shell; G. Gillespie & E. Werdman (2013) The impact of learning space on teaching behaviors. *Nurse Education in Practice*, Vol. 13, No. 5, September 2013, pp. 382-387.

Bemer, A.; R. Moeller & C. Ball (2009) Designing collaborative learning spaces: Where material culture meets mobile writing processes. *Programmatic Perspectives*, Vol. 1, No. 2, pp. 139–166.

Bergsagel, V.; T. Best; K. Cushman; L. McConachie; W. Sauer & D. Stephan (2007) *Architecture for achievement: Building patterns for small school learning.* Mercer Island, WA: Eagle Charter Press, LLC.

Berne, E. (1961) *Transactional analysis in psychotherapy.* New York: Grove Press.

Bickford, D. J. & D. J. Wright (2006) Community: The hidden context for learning. In D. G. Oblinger (ed) *Learning Spaces, EDUCAUSE*, pp. 4.1-4.22.

Bielaczyc, K. & Collins, A. (1999) Learning communities in classrooms: A reconceptualization of educational practice. In C. M. Reigeluth (ed) *Instructional design theories and models, Vol. II.* Mahwah, N.J.: Lawrence Erlbaum Associates.

Bielaczyc, K. & Collins, A. (2007) Design research: Foundational perspectives, critical tensions, and arenas for action. In J. Campione, A. Palincsar & K. Metz (eds) *Children's learning in laboratory and classroom contexts: Essays in honor of Ann Brown.* Mahwah NJ: Lawrence Erlbaum Associates.

Biggs, J. (2003) *Teaching for quality learning at university (second edition).* Berkshire, England: Society for Research into Higher Education, Open University Press.

Biggs, J. & C. Tang (2007) *Teaching for quality learning at university: What the student does (third edition).* Maidenhead, Berkshire: Open University Press.

Biggs, J. B. (1989) Approaches to the enhancement of tertiary teaching. *Higher Education Research & Development*, Vol. 8, No. 1, pp. 7-25.

Biggs, J. B. (1999) *Teaching for quality learning at university (first edition).* Berkshire, UK: Open University Press.

Billett, S. (1996) Situated learning: Bridging sociocultural and cognitive theorising. *Learning and Instruction*, Vol. 6, No. 3, pp. 263-280.

Blair, B. (2011) Elastic minds? Is the interdisciplinary/multidisciplinary curriculum equipping our students for the future: A case study. *Art, Design, & Communication in Higher Education*, Vol. 10, No. 1, pp. 33–50.

Blatchford, P.; P. Kutnick; E. Baines & M. Galton (2003) Toward a social pedagogy of classroom group work. *International Journal of Educational Research*, Vol. 39, pp. 153-172.

Blink, C. van den (2009) Uses of labs and learning spaces. *EDUCAUSE*.

Boddington, A. & J. Boys (eds) (2011) *Reshaping learning: A critical reader. The future of learning spaces in post-compulsory education*. Rotterdam: Sense Publishers.

Bordin, E. S. (1979) The generalizability of the psycho-analytic concept of the working alliance. *Psychotherapy: Theory, Research and Practice*, No. 16, pp. 252-260.

Bordo, S. (1987) *The flight to objectivity: Essays on cartesianism and culture*. Albany, NY: State University of New York Press.

Boud, D.; R. Cohen & J. Sampson (1999) Peer learning and assessment. *Assessment & Evaluation in Higher Education*, Vol. 24, No. 4, pp. 413-426.

Bourdieu, P. (1977) *Outline of a theory of practice*. Cambridge, UK: Cambridge University Press.

Bourdieu, P. (1984) *Distinction: a social critique of the judgment of taste*. London: Routledge.

Bourdieu, P. (1990) *The logic of practice*. Cambridge, UK: Polity Press.

Bourdieu, P.; J. Passeron & M. De Saint Martin. (1996) *Academic discourse: Linguistic misunderstanding and professorial power*. Cambridge, UK: Polity Press in association with Blackwell Publishers Ltd.

Boys, J. (2009) *Beyond the beanbag? Towards new ways of thinking about learning spaces*. In Networks 8, September (HEA-ADM publication).

Boys, J. (2010) *Towards creative learning spaces: Re-thinking the architecture of post-compulsory education*. Abingdon: Routledge.

Boys, J. (2011) *Towards creative learning spaces: Re-thinking the architecture of post-compulsory education*. New York: Routledge.

Boys, J. (2011) Where is the theory? In Boddington, A. & J. Boys (eds) *Reshaping learning: A critical reader. The future of learning spaces in post-compulsory education*. Rotterdam: Sense Publishers, pp. 49-66.

Boys, J.; C. Melhuish & A. Wilson (forthcoming). *Developing research methods for analyzing learning spaces that can inform institutional missions of learning and engagement*. Ann Arbor, MI: Perry Chapman Learning Spaces Research Prize, Society of College and University Planners (SCUP).

Brettell, C. & J. Hollifield, (eds) (2008) *Migration Theory: Talking Across Disciplines*, London: Routledge.

Broadfoot, O. & R. Bennett (2003) Design studios: Online? *Apple university consortium academic and developers conference proceedings 2003*, pp. 9–21.

Broadfoot, P. (2002) Editorial: Structure and agency in education: The role of comparative education. *Comparitive Education*, Vol. 38, No. 1, pp. 5-6.

Brookfield, S. D. & Preskill, S. (1999) *Discussion as a way of teaching*. Buckingham: Open University Press.

Brooks, D. C. (2012) Space and consequences: The impact of different formal learning spaces on instructor and student behavior. *Journal of Learning Spaces*, Vol. 1, No. 2, pp. 1-10.

Brooks, W. & J. Rowley (2013) Music students' perspectives on learning with technology. *XIX National conference of the Australian society for music education*. Canberra, September 2013, pp. 38-41.

Brown, J. S.; A. Collins & P. Duguid (1989) Student cognition and the culture of learning. *Educational Researcher*, Vol. 18, No. 1, pp. 32-42.

Brown, M. (2005) Learning spaces. In D. Oblinger & J. Oblinger (eds) *Educating the Net. Gen.* 12.2.-12.22.

Brown, M. & P. Long (2006) Trends in learning space design. In DG Oblinger (ed) *Learning Spaces, EDUCAUSE*, pp. 9.1-9.11.

Browne of Madingley, J. (2010) *Securing a sustainable future for higher education*. London: Department for Business, Innovation and Skills.

Brownstein, E. & R. Klein (2006) Blogs: Applications in science education. *Journal of College Science Teaching*, Vol. 35, No. 6, pp. 18-22.

Bruner, J. (1977) *The Process of education*. Cambridge: Harvard University Press.

Brush, T. & J. Saye (2002) A summary of research exploring hard and soft scaffolding for teachers and students using a multimedia supported learning environment. *The Journal of Interactive Online Learning*, Vol. 1, No. 2, pp. 1-12.

Bullen, M.; T. Morgan & A. Qayyum (2011) Digital learners in higher education: Generation is not the issue. *Canadian Journal of Learning and Teaching*, Vol. 37, No. 1, pp. 1-24.

Carbone, A.; K. Lynch; D. Arnott & P. Jamieson (2000) Introducing a studio-based learning environment into information technology. Paper presented at the *ASET-HERDSA 2000, Flexible Learning for a Flexible Society* conference, University of Southern Queensland, Toowoomba.

Carlile, O. & A. Jordan (2005) It works in practice but will it work in theory? The theoretical underpinnings of pedagogy. *Emerging Issues in the Practice of University Learning and Teaching*. Dublin: AISHE, 11-26.

Chan, J. & G. Cheng (2010) Towards understanding the potential of e-portfolios for independent learning: A qualitative study. *Australasian Journal of Educational Technology*, Vol. 27, No. 7, pp. 932-950.

Chandramohan, B. & S. Fallows (eds) (2009) *Interdisciplinary learning and teaching in higher education*. London: Routledge.

Chickering, A. W., & Z. F. Gamson (1991) *Seven principles for good practice in undergraduate education*. San Francisco, CA: Jossey-Bass.

Chinnock, K. (2011) Relational transactional analysis supervision. *Transactional Analysis Journal*, Vol. 41, No. 4, pp. 336-350.

Chism, N. V. (2006) Challenging traditional assumptions and rethinking learning Sspaces, in D.G. Oblinger (ed) *Learning Spaces, EDUCAUSE*.

Chism, N. V. N. (2006) Challenging traditional assumptions and rethinking learning spaces. In D. G. Oblinger (ed) *Learning Spaces, EDUCAUSE*, pp. 2.1-2.12.

Christensen, C. M. (2006) The ongoing process of building a theory of disruption. *Journal of Product Innovation Management*, Vol. 23, No. 1, pp. 39-55.

Chun, D. (1994) Using computer networking to facilitate the acquisition of interactive competence. *System*, No. 22, pp. 17-31.

Clarke, J. I. & Dawson, C. (1998) *Growing up again (second edition)*. Center City: Hazelden.

Clegg, S. & Rowland, S. (2010) Kindness in pedagogical practice and academic life. *British Journal of Sociology of Education*, Vol. 31, No. 6, pp. 719-735.

Coffield, F. & B. Williamson (2011) *From exam factories to communities of discovery*. London: Institute of Education, University of London.

Connell, R. W. (1985) How to survive a PhD. *Vestes*, Vol. 2, pp. 38-41.

Cortese, A. (2003) The critical role of higher education in creating a sustainable future. *Planning for Higher Education*. Vol. 31, No. 3, pp. 5-22.

Cranton, P. & E. Carusetta (2002) Reflecting on teaching: The influence of context. *International Journal for Academic Development*, Vol. 7, No. 2, pp. 167-176.

Cree, V. E. (2012) 'I'd like to call you my mother.' Reflections on supervising international PhD students in social work. *Social Work Education*, Vol. 31, No. 4, pp. 451-464.

Curr, G. M. (2001) Negotiating the "Rackety Bridge" – a dynamic model for aligning supervisory style with research student development. *Higher Education Research and Development*, Vol. 20, No. 1, pp. 81-92.

Danvers, J. (2003) Towards a radical pedagogy: Provisional notes on learning and teaching in art & design. *International Journal of Art & Design Education*, Vol. 22, No. 1, pp. 47-57.

Deacon, R. (2006) Michael Foucault on education: A preliminary theoretical overview. *South African Journal of Education*, Vol. 26, No. 2, pp. 177-187.

Dede, C. (2010) Comparing frameworks for 21st century skills. In J. Bellanca, & R. Brandt (eds) *21st century skills: Rethinking how students learn*, Bloomingtonn, IN: Solution Tree Press, pp. 51-76.

Delamont, S., Parry, O. & Atkinson, P. (1998) Creating a delicate balance: The doctoral supervisor's dilemmas. *Teaching in Higher Education*, Vol. 3, No. 2, pp. 157-172.

Deng, L. & A. H. K. Yuen. (2009) Blogs in higher education: Implementation and issues. *TechTrends*, Vol. 53, No. 3, pp. 95-98.

Department for Business, Innovation and Skills (BIS) (2011) *Students at the heart of the system: Consulting on the future of higher education*. London.

Descartes, R. (1993) *Meditations on first philosophy in which the existence of God and the distinction of the soul from the body are demonstrated.* Indianapolis, IN: Hackett Publishing Company, Inc. (Original work published in 1641).

Design Council (2005) The business of design. Design Institute of Australia (2009). *Structure of the design industry: A structural view of design disciplines.* Online resource: http://www.dia.org.au/index.cfm?id=248 [Accessed October 23, 2013].

Designshare (2001) *Aesthetic codes in early childhood classrooms, section 3: Reggio Emilia.* Online resource: http://www.designshare.com/Research/Tarr/Aesthetic_Codes_3.htm [Accessed October 23, 2013].

Devlin, M. & G. Samarawickrema (2010) The criteria of effective teaching in a changing higher education context. *Higher Education Research & Development*, Vol. 29, No. 2, pp. 111-124.

Dewdney, A.; D. Dibosa & V. Walsh (2013) *Post-critical museology; Theory and practice in the art museum.* London: Routledge.

Dewey, J. (1929). My pedagogic creed. *Journal of the National Education Association*, 18(9), 291:295.

Dewey, J. (1933) *How we think.* Boston: D. C. Heath & Co.

Dillenbourg P. (1999) What do you mean by collaborative learning? In P. Dillenbourg (ed) *Collaborative-learning: Cognitive and computational approaches.* Oxford: Elsevier, pp.1-19.

Dison, A. (2004) *Finding her own academic self: Research capacity development and identity.* Paper presented at the Spencer doctoral students' colloquium. Johannesburg, 20 August.

Dobozy, E. (2011) Resisting student consumers and assisting student producers. In C. Nygaard; C. Holtham & N. Courtney (eds) *Beyond transmission: Innovations in university teaching.* Oxfordshire: Libri Publishing Ltd., pp. 11-16.

Dobozy, E. (2012) Failed innovation implementation in teacher education: A case analysis. *Problems of Education in the 21st Century,* Vol. 40, No. 3, pp. 35-44.

Dobozy, E. & P. Reynolds (2012) The tele-learning airport model: Serving consumer and producer students'. *Proceedings of Internet Technologies & Society* (ITS), pp. 222-226.

Doorley, S. & S. Witthoft (2012) *Make space: How to set the stage for creative collaboration.* Hoboken, NJ: John Wiley and Sons, Inc.

Doorley, S. & S. Witthoft (2012) Making space for change. In S. Doorley & S. Witthoft (Eds.) *Make space: How to set the stage for creative collaboration.* Hoboken, NJ: John Wiley & Sons, Inc., pp. 12-53.

Drew, L. (2007) Designing the interface between research, learning and teaching. *Design Research Quarterly,* Vol. 2, No. 3.

Drew, S. & C. Klopper (2013) *PRO-Teaching - Sharing Ideas to Develop Capabilities.* Paper presented at the International Conference on Higher Education 2013, Paris, France.

Duggan, B. & B. Dermody (2005) Design education for the world of work: A case study of a problem-based learning (PBL) approach to design education at Dublin Institute of Technology (DIT). In Barrett (et al.) (ed), *Handbook of Enquiry & Problem Based Learning,* CELT, Galway, pp. 137-145.

Dysthe, O., Samara, A. & Westerheim, K. (2006) Multivoiced supervision of master's students: A case study of alternative supervision practices in higher education. *Studies in Higher Education,* Vol. 31, No. 3, pp. 299-318.

Earthman, G. I. (2004) *Prioritization of 31 criteria for school building adequacy.* Baltimore, MD: American Civil Liberties Union Foundation of Maryland.

Efimova, L. (2003) Blogs: The Stickiness Factor. Paper presented at *BlogTalk: A European conference on weblogs,* Vienna, May 23-24. Enomoto, K. & R. Warner (2013) Building student capacity for reflective learning. In C. Nygaard; J. Branch & C. Holtham (eds) *Learning in higher education: Contemporary standpoints.* Oxfordshire: Libri Publishing Ltd., pp.183-202.

Elden, S. (2004) *Understanding Henri Lefebvre.* London: Continuum.

Eley, A. & Murray, R. (2009) *How to be an effective supervisor*. Berkshire: Open University Press.

Ellmers, G. (2005) *A re-examination of graphic design pedagogy, and its application at the University of Wollongong: Towards a PhD study in design education*. Paper presented at the ACUADS 2005, Edith Cowan University, Perth.

Ellmers, G. (2006) Reflection and graphic design pedagogy: Developing a reflective framework to enhance learning in a graphic design tertiary environment. Paper presented at the *ACUADS 2006* conference, Monash University, School of Art, Victorian College of the Arts, Melbourne.

Emilsson, U. M. & Johnson, E. (2007) Supervision of supervisors: On developing supervision in postgraduate education. *Higher Education Research & Development*, Vol. 26, No. 2, pp. 163-179.

Epling, M.; S. Timmons & Wharrad, H. (2003) An educational panopticon? New technology, nurse education and surveillance. *Nurse Education Today*, No. 23, pp. 412-418.

Erlauer, L. (2003) *The brain-compatible classroom. Using what we know about learning and improve teaching*. Virginia: Association for Supervision and Curriculum Development (ASCD).

Ernst, K. (1972) *Games students play (and what to do about them)*. Berkeley: Celestial Arts.

Erskine, R. G. (1997) Supervision of psychotherapy: Models for professional development. In R.G. Erskine (ed). *Theories and methods of an integrated transactional analysis*. San Francisco: TA Press, pp. 217-226.

Ertmer, P. A. & T. J. Newby (1993) Behaviorism, cognitivism, constructivism: Comparing critical features from an instructional design perspective. *Performance Improvement Quarterly*, vol. 6, no. 4, pp. 50-72.

Farmer, J. & A. Bartlett-Bragg (2005) Blogs@anywhere: High fidelity online communication. In Balance, fidelity, mobility: Maintaining the momentum? *Proceedings of ASCILITE 2005*, Brisbane, December 4-7, 2003, pp. 197-203.

Fataar, A. (2005) Negotiating student identity in the doctoral proposal development process: A personal reflective account. *Journal of Education*, No. 36, pp. 37-58.

Fataar, A. (2013 *forthcoming*) A pedagogy of supervision: 'Knowledgeability' through relational engagement. *Journal of Education*.

Felix, E. (2011) Learning space service design. *Journal of Learning Spaces*, Vol. 1, No. 1.

Ferris, T. L. & S. Aziz (2005) *A psychomotor skills extension to Bloom's taxonomy of education objectives for engineering education.* Tainan, Taiwan: National Cheng Kung University.

Finegold, D. & A. Notabartolo (2008) 21st century competencies and their impact: An interdisciplinary literature review. Working paper.

Fink, L. D. (2005) *Self-directed guide to designing courses for significant learning.* Online resource: http://www.ou.edu/idp/significant/Self-DirectedGuidetoCourseDesignAug%2005.doc [Accessed November 23, 2013].

Fleischmann, K. & R. Daniel (2010) Enhancing employability through the use of real-life scenarios in digital media design education. In Errington (ed) *Preparing graduates for the professions using scenario-based learning,* Mt Gravatt: PostPress, pp. 85-96.

Ford, C. (2012) Building a runway for entrepreneurs. In S. Doorley & S. Witthoft (eds) *Make space: How to set stage for creative collaboration.* Hoboken, New Jersey: John Wiley & Sons, Inc., pp. 186-205.

Forrester Research. (2010) Making collaboration work for the 21st century's distributed workforce: Workers need natural ways to interactively communicate over distance. Cambridge, MA: Forrester Research Inc.

Forret, M.; C. Eames; R. Coll; A. Campbell; T. Cronje; K. Stewart; D. Dodd; H. Stonyer; J. Clark; C. Maclean; R. Kunnemeyer & M. Prinsep (2012) *Understanding and enhancing learning communities in tertiary education in science and engineering.* Online Resource: http://www.tlri.org.nz/sites/default/files/projects/9223_summaryreport_0.pdf [Accessed November 23, 2013].

Foucault, M. (1977) Discipline and punish, panopticism. In *Discipline & punish: The birth of the prison.* A. Sheridan (ed). New York: Vintage Books, pp. 195-228.

Foucault, M. (1977) *Discipline and punish: The birth of the prison.* New York, N.J.: Pantheon Books.

Frawley-O'Dea, M. G. & Sarnat, J. E. (2001) *The supervisory relationship: A contemporary psychodynamic approach.* New York: Guilford Press.

Freire, P. (1972) *Pedagogy of the oppressed.* Harmondsworth: Penguin.

Frick, B. L. (2010) Creativity in doctoral education: Conceptualising the original contribution. In C. Nygaard, N. Coutney & C.W. Holtham (eds). *Teaching creativity – Creativity in teaching.* Oxfordshire: Libri Publishing.

Frick, B. L., Albertyn, R. M. & Rutgers, L. (2010) The socratic method: Exploring theories underlying critical questioning as a pathway in student independence. *Acta Academica,* Supplementum 1, pp. 75-102.

Fry, H.; S. Ketteridge & S. Marshall. (2000) *A Handbook for teaching and learning in higher education; Enhancing academic practice.* London: Kogan Page.

Fullan, M. (2008) *The six secrets of change.* San Francisco, C.A.: Jossey-Bass.

Furman, R. (2009) *Brain compatible classroom.* Online Resource: www.robinfogarty.com/brain-compatible-classrooms-21.html [Accessed November 12, 2013].

Guzzini, S. (2006) Applying Bourdieu's framework of power analysis to IR: opportunities and limits. *Proceedings of the 47th Annual International Studies Association. 22-25 March, 2006.* pp. 1-21.

Gagne, R. (1985) *Conditions of learning.* Online Resource: http://www.instructionaldesign.org/theories/conditions-learning.html [Accessed November 30, 2013].

Gardner, S. K. (2008) 'What's too much and what's too little?': The process of becoming an independent researcher in doctoral education. *The Journal of Higher Education,* Vol. 79, No. 3, pp. 327–350.

Garfinkel, H. (1967) *Studies in ethnomethodology.* Englewood Cliffs, NJ: Prentice–Hall.

Garrison, D. R.; T. Anderson & W. Archer. (2000) Critical inquiry in a text-based environment: Computer conferencing in higher education. *Internet and Higher Education,* Vol. 11, No. 2, pp. 1–14.

Gatfield, T. (2005) An investigation into PhD supervisory management styles: Development of a dynamic conceptual model and its managerial implications. *Journal of Higher Education Policy and Management,* Vol. 27, No. 3, pp. 311-325.

Geertz, C. (1973) *The interpretation of cultures.* New York: Basic Books.

Gibbs, G. (1995) *Assessing student centred courses:* Oxford: Oxford Centre for Staff Development.

Gibbs, G. & C. Simpson (2004-05) Conditions under which assessment supports students' learning. *Learning and Teaching in Higher Education,* Issue 1.

Glaser, B. G. & A. Strauss (1967) *Discovery of grounded theory. Strategies for qualitative research.* Mill Valley, CA: Sociology Press.

Glowacki-Dudka, M., & M. Brown (2007) Professional development through faculty learning communities. *New Horizons in Adult Education and Human Resource Development,* Vol. 21, No. 1/2, pp. 29-39.

Golde, C. M. (2005) The role of the department and discipline in doctoral student attrition: Lessons from four departments. *The Journal of Higher Education,* Vol. 76, No. 6, pp. 669–700.

Gonzalez, C. (2009) Conceptions of, and approaches to, teaching online: A study of lecturers teaching postgraduate distance courses. *Higher Education*, Vol. 57, No. 3, pp. 299-314.

Goodwin, L.; J. E. Miller & R. D. Cheetham (1991) Teaching freshmen to think: Does active learning work?, *Bioscience*, No. 41, pp. 719-722.

Goodyear, P. (2001) *Effective networked learning in higher education: notes and guidelines*. Networked Learning in Higher Education Project (JCALT); January 2001. (Vol. 3 of the Final Report) Lancaster: Lancaster University.

Gorbis, M. (2013) *The Nature of the future: Dispatches from the socialstructured world*. New York, NY: Free Press.

Graff, G. (2004) *Clueless in academe: How schooling obscures the life of the mind*. New Haven, CT: Yale University Press.

Grant, B. (2003) Mapping the pleasures and risks of supervision. *Discourse: Studies in the Cultural Politics of Education*, Vol. 24, No. 2, pp. 175-190.

Grant, B. (2011) The bothersome business of curriculum in doctoral education. In E. Bitzer and N. Botha (eds). *Curriculum inquiry in South African higher education: Some scholarly affirmations and challenges*. Stellenbosch: SunMedia.

Green, B. & Lee, A. (1995) Theorising postgraduate pedagogy. *Australian Universities' Review*, Vol. 38, No. 2, pp. 40–45.

Green, W. (2005) Unfinished business: Subjectivity and supervision. *Higher Education Research and Development*, Vol. 24, No. 2, pp. 151-163.

Greenfield, S. (2013) *Modern technology is changing the way our brains work says neuroscientist*. Adapted from ID: The quest for identity in the 21st century. Online Resource: http://www.dailymail.co.uk/sciencetech/article-565207/Modern-technology-changing-way-brains-work-says-neuroscientist.html [Accessed Novemebr 23, 2013].

Greenhow, C.; B. Robelia & J. E. Hughes (2009) Learning, teaching, and scholarship in a digital age. *Educational Researcher*, No. 38, pp. 246.

Gruenewald, D. (2003) Foundations of place: A multidisciplinary framework for place-conscious education. *American Educational Research Journal*, Vol. 40, No. 3, pp. 619-654.

Grummon, P. T. (2009) Best practices in learning space design: Engaging users. *EDUCAUSE Quarterly*, Vol. 32, No.1.

Hagen, S. (1997) *Buddhism: plain and simple*. New York: Broadway Books.

Hailikari, T., A. Nevgi & S. Lindblom-Ylänne (2007) Exploring alternative ways of assessing prior knowledge, its components and their relation to student achievement: A mathematics based case study. *Studies in Educational Evaluation*, Vol. 33, No. 3-4, pp. 320-337.

Hale, L. S.; E. A. Mirakian & D. B. Day. (2009) Online vs classroom instruction: Student satisfaction and learning outcomes in an undergraduate allied health pharmacology course. *Journal of Allied Health*, Vol. 38, No. 2, pp. 36-42.

Hall, C. & A. Johnson (1994) SLOs, Bloom's taxonomy, cognitive, psychomotor, and affective domains. Module A5: Planning a test or examination. In B. Imrie & C. Hall (eds), *Assessment of student performance*. Wellington, New Zealand: University Teaching Development Centre, Victoria University of Wellington.

Hall, E. T. (1969) *The hidden dimension*. Garden City, N.Y.: Anchor.

Hall, K.; M. Horgan; A. Ridgway; R. Murphy; M. Cuneen & D. Cunningham (2010) *Loris Malaguzzi and the Reggio Emilia experience (continuum library of educational thought)*. New York, NY: Continuum International Publishing Group.

Hammersley, M. (2004) Action research: A contradiction in terms? *Oxford Review of Education*, Vol. 30, No. 2, June 2004, pp. 166-181.

Harrhy, K.; J. Coombes; T. McGuire; G. Fleming; D. McRobbie & J. Davies (2003) Piloting an objective structured clinical examination to evaluate the clinical competency of pre-registration pharmacists. *Journal of Pharmacy Practice and Research*, Vol. 33, No. 3, p. 194.

Hart, J.; T. Zamenopoulos & S. Garner (2011) The learningscape of a virtual design atelier. *Compass: The Journal of Learning and Teaching at the University of Greenwich*, No. 3, pp. 1-15.

Hawkins, P. & Smith, N. (2006) *Coaching, mentoring and organisational consultancy: Supervision and development*. Maidenhead: Open University Press.

Heagney, M. (2009) Australian higher education sector on the brink of a major shake up. *Widening Participation and Lifelong Learning*, Vol. 11, No. 1, pp. 1-5.

Heidegger, M. (1962) *Being and time*. New York: Harper & Rows Publishers, Inc.

Heller, S. & L. Talarico (2011) An education manifesto for Icograda. In Bennett & Vulpinari (eds) *ICOGRADA Design Education Manifesto*. Tapei: International Council of Graphic Design Associations, pp. 82-85.

Helms, S. A. (2012) Blended/hybrid courses: A review of the literature and recommendations for instructional designers and educators. *Interactive Learning Environments*, pp. 1-7.

Henri, F. (1992) Computer conferencing and content analysis. In A. R. Kaye (ed) *Collaborative learning through computer conferencing*. Berlin: Springer-Verlag, pp.117–136.

Hoffman, K. G. & J. F. Donaldson (2004) Contextual tensions of the clinical environment and their influence on teaching and learning. *Medical Education*, Vol. 38, No. 4, pp. 448-454.

Holtham, C. & N. Courtney (2004) *Barriers to innovation in management education – an international perspective.* National Teaching Fellows Conference, Nottingham, May 2004.

Hrastinski, S. (2008) Asynchronous and synchronous e-learning. *Educause Quarterly*, Vol. 4, pp. 51-55.

Huffington Post (2012) *The cost of college degree in U.S. has increased 1,120 percent in 30 years.* Online Resource: http://www.huffingtonpost. com/2012/08/15/cost-of-college-degree-increase-12-fold-1120-percent-bloomberg_n_1783700.html [Accessed November 12, 2013].

Hughes, J. E. (2005) The role of teacher knowledge and learning experiences in forming technology-integrated pedagogy. *Journal of Technology and Teacher Education*, No. 13, pp. 277-302.

Hunt, J. (2011) Icograda design education manifesto. In A. G. Bennett & O. Vulpinari (eds) *ICOGRADA Design Education Manifesto*. Tapei: International Council of Graphic Design Associations, pp. 86-89.

Hunt, L.; H. Huijser & M. Sankey (2011) Learning spaces for the digital age: Blending space with pedagogy. In M. Keppell; K. Souter & M. Riddle (eds) *Physical and virtual learning spaces in higher education: Concepts for the modern learning environment*, Hershey, Pennsylvania: IGI Global, pp.182-195.

Huxham, M. (2005) Learning in lectures. *Active Learning in Higher Education*. Vol. 6, pp.17-31.

Icograda (2011) *ICOGRADA Design Education Manifesto*, Tapei.

Ingold T. (2011) *Being alive: Essays on movement, knowledge and description.* London: Routledge.

Ingold, T. (2000) *The perception of the environment: Essays on livelihood, dwelling and skill.* London: Routledge.

Inman, A. G., Ladany, N., Boyd, D. L., Schlosser, L. Z., Howard, E. E., Altman, A. N. & Stein, E. P. (2011) Advisee nondisclosures in doctoral–level advising relationships. *Training and Education in Professional Psychology*, Vol. 5, No. 3, pp. 149-159.

Jamieson, P. (2008) *Creating new generation learning environments on the university campus.* Melbourne: Woods Bagot Research Press.

Jamieson, P. (2009) The serious matter of informal learning. *Planning for Higher Education*, January–March 2009, pp. 18-25.

Jamieson, P.; P. G. Taylor; K. Fisher; A. C. Trevitt, F. & T. Gilding (2000) Place and space in the design of new learning environments. *Higher Education Research & Development*. Vol. 19, No. 2, pp. 221-237.

Jara, M. & F. Mohamad (2007) *Pedagogical templates for e-learning*. WLE Center, London.

Jessop, T. & A. Smith (2008) *Spaces, pedagogy and power: A case study*. Paper presented at the HEA Annual Conference, Harrogate, July 2008.

JISC (2006) *Designing spaces for effective learning: A Guide to 21st century learning space design*. Bristol, UK: JISC Development Group, University of Bristol.

Johnson, C. & C. Lomas (2005) Design of the learning space: Learning & design principles. *Educause Review July/August*, pp. 16-28.

Johnson, P. (2009) 21st century skills movement. *Teaching for the 21st Century*, Vol. 67, No. 1, p. 11.

Kerawalla, L., S. Minocha & G. Conole (2008). An empirically grounded framework to guide blogging in higher education. *Journal of Computer Assisted Learning*. Vol.25, pp. 31-42.

Kadushin, A. (1976) *Supervision in social work*. New York: Columbia University Press.

Kefela, G. (2010) Knowledge-based economy and society has become a vital commodity to countries. *International NGO Journal*, Vol. 5, No. 7, pp. 160-166.

Kekkonen-Moneta, S. & Moneta, G. B. (2002) E-Learning in Hong Kong: Comparing learning outcomes in online multimedia and lecture versions of an introductory computing course. *British Journal of Educational Technology*. Vol. 33, No. 4, pp. 423-433.

Kelly, D. (2012) Foreword. In S. Doorley & S. Witthoft (eds) *Make space: How to set stage for creative collaboration*, Hoboken, NJ: John Wiley & Sons, Inc., pp. 4-5.

Kennedy, G. E.; T. S. Judd; A. Churchward; K. Gray & K. Krause (2008) First year students' experiences with technology: Are they really digital natives. *Australasian Journal of Educational Technology*, Vol. 24, No. 1, pp. 108-122.

Kerlow, I. (2001) Ten career tips for digital artists, designers, and animators. In S. Heller (ed) *The education of an e-designer*, New York: Allworth Press, pp. 238-243.

Klebsedel, H. & L. Kornetsky (2009) Critique as signature pedagogy in the arts. In R. A. R. Gurung; N. L. Chick & A. Haynie (eds) *Exploring signature pedagogies: Approaches to teaching disciplinary habits of mind.* Sterling VA: Stylus, pp. 99-120.

Klopper, C. & S. Drew (2013) Teaching for learning, learning for teaching: Triangulating perspectives of teaching quality through peer observation and student evaluation. In C. Nygaard; N. Courtney & P. Bartholomew (eds) *Quality enhancement of university teaching and learning: theories and cases.* Oxfordshire: Libri Publishing Ltd.

Knight, P. T. & P. R. Trowler (2000) Department-level cultures and the improvement of learning and teaching. *Studies in Higher Education,* Vol. 25, No. 1, pp. 69-83.

Knowles, M.S. & Associates (1985) *Andragogy in action.* San Francisco: Jossey-Bass.

Kolb, A. Y. & D. A. Kolb (2005) Learning styles and learning spaces: Enhancing experiential learning in higher education. *Academy of Management Learning & Education,* Vol. 4, No. 2, pp. 193-212.

Kolb, D. (1984) *Experiential learning: Experience as the source of learning and development.* New Jersey: Prentice-Hall.

Kolb, D. A. & Fry, R. (1975). Towards an applied theory of experiential learning. In C. Cooper (Ed.) *Theories of Group Process.* London: John Wiley.

Krause, S. (2004) *When blogging goes bad: A cautionary tale about blogs, email lists, discussion and interaction.* Online Resource: http://english.ttu.edu/kairos/9.1/praxis/krause/ [Accessed November 1, 2013].

Krupnick, J. L.; I. Elkin; J. Collins; S. Simmens; S. M. Sotsky; P. A. Pilkonis & J. T. Watkins (1994) Therapeutic alliance and clinical outcome in the NIMH treatment of depression collaborative research program: Preliminary findings. *Psychotherapy.* No. 31, pp. 28-35.

Kuh, G.; J. Kinzie; J. Schuh & E. Whitt (2005) *Student success in college: Creating conditions that matter.* San Francisco, CA: Jossey-Bass.

Kuhn, S. (2001) Learning from the architecture studio: Implications for project-based pedagogy. *International Journal of Engineering Education,* Vol. 17, No. 4 & 5, pp. 349-352.

KWP (2010) *Creating a 21st Century Curriculum: The King's-Warwick Project.* HEFCE.

Lacoss, J. & Chylak, J. (1999) *In their words: Students' ideas about teaching.* Online Resource: http://trc.virginia.edu/Publications/Teaching_Concerns/Spring_2000/TC_Spring_2000_Lacoss_Making.htm [Accessed December 4, 2013].

Lake, D.A. (2001) Student performance and perceptions of a lecture-based course compared with the same course utilizing group discussion. *Physical Therapy*, Vol. 8, pp. 896-903.

Lange, S. & J. Dinsmore (2012) *Collaborative chaos in the studio and the laboratory: promoting engagement via student-led extracurricular art/science research and practice.* Co-presentation at RAISE Conference: Student Engagement as a Shared Agenda: People, Places, Practices; University of Southampton.

Latour, B. (2007) *Reassembling the social: An introduction to actor-network-theory.* Oxford: Oxford University Press.

Latour, B. (2013) *An enquiry into modes of existence.* Cambridge: Harvard University Press.

Lave, J. (1991) Situating learning in communities of practice. *Perspectives on Socially Shared Cognition*, Vol. 2, pp. 63-82.

Lave, J. (2009) The practice of learning. In Illeris, K. (ed) *Contemporary theories of learning: Learning theorists in their own words*, London: Routledge, pp. 200-208.

Lave, J. & E. Wenger (1991) *Situated learning: Legitimate peripheral participation.* Cambridge: Cambridge University Press.

Lave, J. & E. Wenger (1998) *Communities of practice: Learning meaning and identity.* Cambridge: Cambridge University Press.

Learning in Higher Education (2013) *LiHE – Michigan – Learning spaces in higher education.* Online Resource: http://www.lihe.info/future-events/learning-spaces-in-higher-education/ [Accessed December 4, 2013].

Learning Spaces Development Group (2012) *A Learning Spaces Manifesto.* London: City University London.

Lee, A. (2008) How are doctoral students supervised? Concepts of doctoral research supervision. *Studies in Higher Education*, Vol. 33, No. 3, pp. 267-281.

Lee, N. (2006) Design as a learning cycle: A conversational experience. *Studies in Learning, Evaluation Innovation and Development*, Vol. 3, No. 2, pp. 12-22.

LeFebvre, H. (1974) *The production of space.* Malden, MA: Blackwell Publishing.

Lefebvre, H. (1991) *The production of space.* Oxford: Blackwell.

Leigh Star, S. (1999) The ethnography of infrastructure. *The American Behavioural Scientist.* Vol. 43, No. 3, pp. 377-391.

Lengel, T. & M. S. Kuczala (2010) *The kinesthetic classroom: Teaching and learning through movement.* California: Regional Training Center and Corwin, Sage Publication.

Levy, C.; A. Sissons & C. Holloway (2011) *A plan for growth in the knowledge economy.* London: The Work Foundation, Lancaster University.

Li, S. & Searle, C. (2007) Managing criticism in Ph.D. supervision: A qualitative case study. *Studies in Higher Education,* Vol. 32, No. 4, pp. 511–526.

Lin, W., Wang, L. & Chen, S. (2013) Abusive supervision and employee well-being: The moderating effect of power distance orientation. *Applied Psychology: An International Review,* Vol. 62, No. 2, pp. 308-329.

Lippincott, J. (2006) Linking the information commons to learning. In D. Oblinger (ed), *Learning spaces.* Washington, DC: Educause.

Lippincott, J. (2009) Learning spaces: involving faculty to improve pedagogy. *EDUCAUSE Review,* Vol. 44, No. 2, pp. 16–25.

Lippman, P. (2010) Can the physical environment have an impact on the learning environment? *CELE Exchange 2010/13.* Organization for Economic and Co-operation and Development (OECD).

Lizzio, A. & K. Wilson (2004) Action learning in higher education: An investigation of its potential to develop professional capability. *Studies in Higher Education,* Vol. 29, No. 4, pp. 469-488.

Locke, J. (1995) *An essay concerning human understanding.* New York: Prometheus Books. (Original work published in 1690.)

Lomas, C. & D. G. Oblinger (2006) Student practices and their impact on learning spaces. In D. G. Oblinger (ed) *Learning Spaces, 5.1-5.11.*

Lomas, C. P. & C. Johnson (2005) Design of the learning space: Learning and design principles. *EDUCAUSE Review,* Vol. 40, No. 4, pp. 16-28.

Long, P. D. & S. C. Ehrmann (2005) Future of the learning space: Breaking out of the box. *EDUCAUSE Review,* Vol. 40, No. 4, pp. 42-58.

Lovitts, B. E. (2005) Being a good course-taker is not enough: A theoretical perspective on the transition to independent research. *Studies in Higher Education,* Vol. 30, No. 2, pp. 137–154.

Lusted, D. (1986) Why pedagogy? *Screen,* Vol. 27, No. 5, pp. 2-14.

Mackinnon, J. (2004) Academic supervision: Seeking metaphors and models for quality. *Journal of Further and Higher Education,* Vol. 2, No. 4, pp. 395–396.

Malnarich, G. (2008) Increasing student engagement through faculty development: A practice brief based on BEAMS project outcomes. *Institute for Higher Education Policy,* pp. 1-4.

Manathunga, C. (2005) The development of research supervision: "Turning the light on a private space". *International Journal for Academic Development,* Vol. 10, No. 1, pp. 17-30.

Manathunga, C. (2007) Supervision as mentoring: The role of power and boundary crossing. *Studies in Continuing Education*, Vol. 29, No. 2, pp. 207–221.

Mann, K.; J. Gordon & A. MacLeod (2009) Reflection and reflective practice in health professions education: A systematic review. *Advances in Health Sciences Education*, Vol. 14, No. 4, pp. 595-621.

Marquardt, N. & S. Greenberg. (2012) Informing the design of proxemic interactions. *IEEE Pervasive Computing*, Vol. 11, No. 2, pp. 14-23.

Martin, J. P. & J. Goicoechea (2000) Sociocultural and constructivist theories of learning: Ontology, not just epistemology. *Educational Psychologist*, Vol. 35, No 4, pp. 227-241.

Martin, P.; R. Morris; A. Rogers; V. Martin & S. Kilgallon (2009) *Encouraging creativity in higher education: The experience of the Brighton creativity centre* In: Dialogues in Art & Design. Group for learning in Art and Design (GLAD) conference 21 October 2009.

Marton, F. & A. Tsui (2004) *Classroom discourse and the space of learning.* Mahwah, NJ: Lawrence Erlbaum Associates, Inc.

Mason, J. (2011) Developing tools to facilitate integrated reflection. In *ePortfolios Australian conference 2011: Making a difference, showing a difference.* E-learning Services, Queensland University of Technology, Curtin University, Perth, Western Australia, pp. 73-83.

Massey, D. (1994) *Space, place and fender.* Minneapolis, MN: University of Minnesota Press.

Maunder, R. E. & A. Harrop. (2003) Investigating students' perceptions of what contributes to productive seminars and lectures and staff predictions of students' perceptions: How well staff know their students? *Journal of Further and Higher Education*, Vol. 27, No. 4, pp. 443-456.

Maxwell, T. W. & Smyth, R. (2011) Higher degrees research supervision: From practice towards theory. *Higher Education Research and Development*, Vol. 30, No. 2, pp. 219–231.

McAlpine, L. & Norton, J. (2006) Reframing our approach to doctoral programs: An integrative framework for action and research. *Higher Education Research and Development*, Vol. 25, No. 1, pp. 3–17.

McCarthy, S. & C. Almeida (2002) Self-authored graphic design: A strategy for integrative studies. *Journal of Aesthetic Education*, Vol. 36, No. 3, pp. 103-116.

McCormack, C. & Pamphilon, B. (2004) More than a confessional: Postmodern groupwork to support postgraduate supervisors' professional development. *Innovations in Education and Teaching International*, Vol. 41, No. 1, pp. 23–37.

McGrew, J. & J. Northrup (2012) Reimagening space with rapid fabrication. In S. Doorley & S. Witthoft (eds) *Make space: How to set stage for creative collaboration.* Hoboken, NJ: John Wiley & Sons, Inc., pp. 79-104.

McNamara, D. (1991) Subject knowledge and its application: Problems and possibilities for teacher educators. *Journal of Education for Teaching: International Research and Pedagogy,* Vol. 17, No. 2, pp. 113-128.

McPhee, L. (2009) *Learning Spaces.* Online Resource: http://www2.nau.edu/lrm22/learning_spaces/ [Accessed December 12, 2013].

McWilliam, E. & Palmer, P. (1995) Teaching tech(no)bodies: Open learning and postgraduate pedagogy. *Australian Universities' Review,* Vol. 38, No. 2, pp. 32-34.

Melhuish, C. (2010) *Ethnographic case study: perceptions of three new learning spaces and their impact on the learning and teaching process at the universities of Sussex and Brighton.* Unpublished research report commissioned by CETLC, Universities of Sussex and Brighton, and CETLD, School of Arts and Architecture, University of Brighton.

Melhuish, C. (2011a) What matters about space for learning: Exploring perceptions and experiences. In Boddington, A. & J. Boys (eds) *Reshaping learning: A critical reader. The future of learning spaces in post-compulsory education.* Rotterdam: Sense Publishers.

Melhuish, C. (2011b) What do we know about the relationships between learning and space? In Boddington, A. & J. Boys, J. (eds) *Reshaping learning: A critical reader. The future of learning spaces in post-compulsory education.* Rotterdam: Sense Publishers.

Merleau-Ponty, M. (1962) *Phenomenology of perception. Translated from French by Colin Smith.* New Jersey: Routledge and Kegen Paul.

Meyer, J. H. F. & R. Land (2003) Threshold concepts and troublesome knowledge (1): linkages to ways to thinking and practicing. In C. Rust (Ed.= *Improving Student Learning: Equality and Diversity.* Oxford: OCSLD.

Meyers, N. M. & D. Nulty (2009) How to use (five) curriculum design principles to align authentic learning environments, assessment, students' approaches to thinking and learning outcomes. *Assessment & Evaluation in Higher Education,* Vol. 34, No. 5, pp. 565-577.

Mezirow, J. (1991) *Transformative dimensions of adult learning.* San Francisco: Jossey-Bass.

Millennial Branding (2012) *Millenial branding student employment gap study.* Online Resource: http://millennialbranding.com/2012/05/millenial-branding-student-employment-gap-study/ [Accessed October 31, 2013].

Milne, A. (2006) Designing blended learning space to the student experience. In D. G. Oblinger (ed) *Learning Spaces,*11.1-11.15.

Milne, A. (2007) Entering the interaction age: Implementing a future vision for campus learning spaces...Today. *Educause Review*, Vol. 42, No. 1, pp. 12-31.

Minor, A. J., Pimpletone, A., Stinchfield, T., Stevens, H. & Othman, N. A. (2013) Peer support in negotiating multiple relationships within supervision among counselor education doctoral students. *International Journal of Advanced Counselling*, Vol. 35, pp. 33-45.

Mitchell, G.; B. White; M. B. White; M. R. Pospisil; S. Killey; C. J. Liu & G. Matthews (2010) Retrofitting university learning spaces PP8-921. *Final report. Support for the original work was provided by the Australian Learning and Teaching Council Ltd., an initiative of the Australian Government.*

Moilanen, H. (2012) *Regional development zones in spatial development in Finland: Governing spatial development through new territorial frames.* Turku, Finland: University of Finland.

Monahan, T. (2002) Flexible space & built pedagogy: Emerging IT embodiments. *Inventio*, Vol. 4, No. 1, pp. 1-19.

Montgomery, T. (2008) Space matters: Experiences of managing static formal learning spaces. *Active Learning in Higher Education*, Vol. 9, No. 2, pp. 122-138.

Moore, A.; S. Fowler & E. Watson (2007) Active learning and technology: Designing change for faculty, students, and institutions. *EDUCAUSE Review*, Vol. 42, No. 5, pp. 42-61.

Murphy, E. (2004) Recognising and promoting collaboration in an online asynchronous discussion. *British Journal of Educational Technology*, Vol. 35, No. 4, pp. 421-431.

Murphy, M. & T. Brown (2012) Learning as relational: Intersubjectivity and pedagogy. *International Journal of Lifelong Education*, Vol. 31, No. 5, pp. 643-654.

Nair, P.; R. Fielding & J. Lackney (2009) *The language of school design: Design patterns for 21st century schools, revised edition.* Minneapolis, MN: Designshare.com.

Narum, J. (2004) Science spaces for students of the 21st century. *Change: The Magazine of Higher Learning, September/October*, pp. 8-21.

Newmann, F. M. & G. G. Wehlage (1993) Five standards of authentic instruction. *Educational Leadership*, Vol. 50, No. 7, p. 8.

Newton, T. (2011) Transactional analysis now: Gift or commodity? *Transactional Analysis Journal*, Vol. 41, No. 4, pp. 315-321.

Newton, T. (2012) The supervision triangle: An integrating model. *Transactional Analysis Journal*, Vol. 42, No. 2, pp. 103-109.

Nielsen, J. (1994) Heuristic evaluation. *Usability Inspection Methods*, Vol. 17, pp. 25-62.

Norman, D. A. (1986) Cognitive engineering. In D. A. Norman & S. W. Draper (eds) *User Centered System Design: New Perspectives on Human-Computer Interaction*, Hillsdale, NJ: Lawrence Erlbaum Associates, pp. 31-61.

NSSE (2013) NSSE updated for 2013. Promoting student learning and institutional improvement: Lessons from NSSE at 13. Annual Results 2012.

Nygaard, C.; C. Holtham & N. Courtney (eds) (2011) *Beyond Transmission: Innovations in university teaching*. Oxfordshire, UK: Libri Publishing Ltd.

Nygaard, C.; J. Branch & C. Holtham (eds) (2013) *Learning in Higher Education: Contemporary standpoints*. Oxfordshire, UK: Libri Publishing Ltd.

Nygaard, C.; J. Branch & P. Bartholomew (eds) (2014) *Improving University Students' Learning Outcomes through Case-based Learning*. Oxfordshire, UK: Libri Publishing Ltd.

O'Dea, J & J. Rowley (2009) A quantitative comparison of Change over 12 months in pre-service music and PE teachers experiences and perceptions of e-learning and a qualitative analysis of perceived benefits and enjoyment. *Proceedings of the 5th International Conference on e-Learning*. Universiti Sains Malaysia, Penang, Malaysia: Academic Publishing Limited, pp. 307-316.

Oandasan, I. & S. Reeves (2005) Key elements for interprofessional education. Part 1: The learner, the educator and the learning context. *Journal of Interprofessional Care*, Vol. 19, No. 1, pp. 21-38.

Oates, S. (2010) The indomitable spirit of Berne and Cohen: "If you can't do it one way, try another". *Transactional Analysis Journal*, Vol. 40, No. 3-4, pp. 300-304.

Oblinger, D. G. (ed) (2006) *Learning spaces*. Washington DC: EDUCAUSE.

OECD (2005) The OECD program definition and selection of key competencies. Executive summary. Online Resource: http://www.oecd.org/dataoecd/47/61/35070367.pdf [Accessed November 12, 2013].

OED (2013) Oxford English Dictionary. Oxford University Press.

Oliver, R. & J. Herrington (2001) *Teaching and learning online: A beginner's guide to e-learning and e-teaching in higher education*. Mt. Lawley WA, Australia: Edith Cowan University Centre for Research in Information Technology and Communications.

Osman, G.; T. M. Duffy; J.-Y. Chang & J. Lee (2011) Learning through collaboration: Student perspectives. *Asia Pacific Education Review*, Vol. 12, No. 4, pp. 547-558.

Overbaugh, R. C. & L. Schultz (2013) Bloom's taxonomy. Online Resource: http://ww2.odu.edu/educ/roverbau/Bloom/blooms_taxonomy.htm [Accessed November 23, 2013].

OWP/P Architects, VS Furniture & Bruce Mau Design. (2010) *The third teacher: 79 ways you can use design to transform teaching and learning*. NY: Abrams Publishing.

Öztürk, M. & E. Türkkan (2006) The design studio as teaching/learning medium – A process-based approach. *International Journal of Art & Design Education*, Vol. 25, No. 1, pp. 96-104.

Park, S. & P. Ertmer (2008) Examining barriers in technology-enhanced problem-based learning: Using a performance support systems approach. *British Journal of Educational Technology*, Vol. 39, No. 4, pp. 631-643.

Parker, J. (2003) Reconceptualising the curriculum: From commodification to transformation. *Teaching in Higher Education*, Vol. 8, No. 4, pp. 529-543.

Parlett, M. & D. Hamilton (1972) *Evaluation as illumination: A new approach to the study of innovative programmes*. Occasional paper, Edinburgh University Centre for Research in the Educational Sciences/Nuffield Foundation.

Pearson, M. & Kayrooz, C. (2004) Enabling critical reflection on research supervisory practice. *International Journal for Academic Development*, Vol. 9, No. 1, pp. 99–116.

Pennington, M. (1996) *The computer and the non-native writer: A natural partnership*. Creskill, NJ: Hampton Press Inc.

Peterson, J.; L. McWhinnie; J. Lawrence & J. Arnold (2012) The industry studio in the creative arts: Ten practitioner perspectives. In B. de la Harpe; T. Mason & D. L. Brien (eds) *TEXT Special*, No. 16.

Picard, M.; R. Warner & L. Velautham (2011) Enabling postgraduate students to become autonomous ethnographers of their disciplines. In C. Nygaard; N. Courtney & L. Frick (eds) *Postgraduate education - Form and function*. Oxfordshire: Libri Publishing Ltd., pp. 149-166.

Pilkington, R. M., & S. A. Walker (2003) Facilitating debate in networked learning: Reflecting on online synchronous discussion in higher education. *Instructional Science*, Vol. 31, pp. 41-63.

Poggenpohl, S. (2012) Envisioning a future design education: An introduction. *Visible Language*, Vol. 46, No. 1/2, pp. 8-19.

Postareff, L.; V. Virtanen; N. Katajavuori & S. Lindblom-Ylänne (2012) Academics' conceptions of assessment and their assessment practices. *Studies in Educational Evaluation*, Vol. 28, No. 3-4, pp. 84-92.

Preece, J.; B. Nonnecke & D. Andrews (2004) The top five reasons for lurking: Improving community experiences for everyone. *Computers in Human Behavior*, Vol. 20, No. 2, pp. 201-223.

Prensky, M. (2001) Digital natives, digital immigrants. *On the Horizon*, Vol. 9, No. 6, pp. 1-6.

Proctor, B. (2000) *Group supervision: A guide to creative practice*. London: Sage.

Prosser, M. & K. Trigwell (1997) Relations between perceptions of the teaching environment and approaches to teaching. *British Journal of Educational Psychology*, Vol. 67, No. 1, pp. 25-35.

Punch, K. (2009) *Introduction to research methods in education*. London: Sage.

Quality Assurance Agency for Higher Education (QAA) (2012) *UK Quality Code for Higher Education*. Gloucester.

Radcliffe, D. (2008) A pedagogy-space-technology (PST) framework for designing and evaluating learning places. In Radcliffe (*et al.*) (ed) *Learning spaces in higher education: Positive outcomes by design*. Brisbane, Qld: University of Queensland, pp. 11-16.

Radcliffe, D. (2009) A pedagogy-space-technology (PST) framework for designing and evaluating learning places. *Learning spaces in higher education: Positive outcomes by design*. Brisbane, Qld: University of Queensland and the Australian Learning and Teaching Council.

Ramsden, P. (1987) Improving teaching and learning in higher education: The case for a relational perspective. *Studies in Higher Education*, Vol. 12, No. 3, pp. 275-286.

Ray, B. B. & G. A. Coulter (2008) Reflective practices amongst language arts teachers: The use of weblogs. *Contemporary Issues in Technology and Teacher Education*, Vol. 8, No. 1, pp. 6-26.

Raymond, E. (2000) *Learners with mild disabilities: a characteristics approach*. Boston: Allyn & Bacon.

Reese, M. & R. Levy (2009) Assessing the future: E-portfolio trends, uses, and options in higher education. *Research Bulletin*, 4.

Reeves, S.; S. Lewin; S. Espin & M. Zwarenstein (2011) *Interprofessional teamwork for health and social care*, Vol. 8, Oxford: Wiley-Blackwell.

Reushle, S. (2011) Designing and evaluating learning spaces—PaSPorT and design-based research *Physical and virtual learning spaces in higher education: Concepts for the modern learning environment*, pp. 87-101.

Robertson, J. L. & R. P. Shrewsbury (2011) Video teleconferencing in the compounding laboratory component of a dual-campus doctor of pharmacy program. *American Journal of Pharmaceutical Education*, Vol. 75, No. 9. Article 181.

Rochester Institute of Technology (2008). Online Resource: http://www.rit.edu/cias/ritphoto/ifs-2008 [Accessed October 20, 2013].

Rodgers, J. (2002) Encouraging tutorial attendance at university did not increase performance. *Australian Economic Papers*, Vol. 41, No. 2, pp. 255-266.

Rogers, C. R. (1969) *Freedom to learn*. Columbus: Merrill.

Rogers, M. (2012) Palomar5: Exploring the space between work and life. In S. Doorley & S. Witthoft (eds) *Make space: How to set stage for creative collaboration*, Hoboken, NJ: John Wiley & Sons, Inc., pp. 125-144.

Rose, D.; L. Lui-Chiviizhe & A. Smith. (2003) Scaffolding academic reading and writing at the Koori Centre. *Australian Journal of Indigenous Education*, Vol. 32, pp. 41-49.

Rose, J. (2012) *How to break free of our 19th century factory-model education system. The Atlantic*. Online Resource: http://www.theatlantic.com/business/archive/2012/05/how-to-break-free-of-our-19th-century-factory-model-education-system/256881/ [Accessed December 4, 2013].

Rowan, J. (1983) *The reality game: A guide to humanistic counselling and psychotherapy*. Second Edition. London: Routledge.

Rowley, J. L. & J. O'Dea (2009) How do students perceive the enhancement of their own learning? A comparison of two education faculties' experiences in building an online learning community for bachelor of music education and bachelor of education students. Teacher education crossing borders: Cultures, contexts, communities and curriculum *- Proceedings of the Australian Teacher Education Association Annual Conference 2009*. Albury, NSW, Australia. pp.1-10.

Rubin, L. & C. Hebert (1998) Model for active learning: Collaborative peer teaching. *College Teaching*, Vol. 46, No. 1, pp. 26-30.

Rugg, G. & Petre, M. (2004) *The unwritten rules of PhD research*. Berkshire: Open University Press.

Saldana, J. (2009) *The coding manual for qualitative researchers*. London: Sage.

Sara, R. (2006) Sharing and developing studio practice: a cross-disciplinary study comparing teaching and learning approaches in the art and design disciplines. Paper presented at the *CLTAD conference*, London.

Savin-Baden, M. (2008) *Learning spaces; Creating opportunities for knowledge creation in academic life*. Berkshire: Open University Press.

Scheer, B., & F. E. Preiser (1994) *Design review: Challenging the urban aesthetic control.* London: Chapman & Hall.

Schein, E. H. (1992) *Organizational culture and leadership: A dynamic view.* San Francisco, CA: Jossey-Bass.

Schön, D. (1987) *Educating the reflective practitioner.* San Francisco: Jossey-Bass.

Schön, D. A. (1983) *The reflective practitioner: How professionals think in action.* New York: Basic Books.

Schön, D. A. (1995) The reflective practitioner: How professionals think in action. Aldershot, England: Arena.

Schulman, L. (2005) Signature pedagogies in the professions. *Daedalus,* Summer 2005, Vol. 134, No. 3, pp. 52-59.

Scott-Webber, L. (2004) *In Sync: Environmental behavior research and the design of learning spaces.* Ann Arbor, MI: The Society for College and University Planning.

Scott-Webber, L. (2011) *Design decoded: A journey of discovery in finding your authentic design self…your design voice.* Deer Park, N.Y.: Linus Publications.

Scott-Webber, L.; M. Marini & J. Abraham (2000) Higher education classrooms fail to meet needs of faculty and students. *Journal of Interior Design,* Vol. 26, No. 1, pp. 16-34.

Scott-Webber, L., Strickland, A. & Kapitula, L. (2013). Built Environments Impact Behaviors Results of an Active Learning Post-Occupancy Evaluation. *Planning for Higher Education Journal* | V42N1 October–December 2013, 1:12.

Scottish Funding Council (2006) *Spaces for learning: A review of learning spaces in further and higher education.* Edinburgh.

Sharma, D. S. (1997) Accounting students' learning conceptions, approaches to learning, and the influence of the learning–teaching context on approaches to learning. *Accounting Education,* Vol. 6, No. 2, pp. 125-146.

Sharpe, R.; G. Benfield; G. Roberts & R. Francis (2006) *The undergraduate experience of blended e-learning: A review of UK literature and practice.* Higher Education Academy, UK.

Shih, S.; T. Hu & C. Chen (2006) A game theory-based approach to the analysis of cooperative learning in design studios'. *Design Studies,* Vol. 27, pp. 711-722.

Shreeve, A. (2011) *The way we were? Signature pedagogies under threat.* Paper presented at the Researching Design Education: 1st International Symposium for Design Education Researchers; CUMULUS ASSOCIATION// DRS, Paris, France.

Shreeve, A., S. Wareing & L. Drew (2008) Key aspects of teaching and learning in the visual arts In H. Fry; S. Ketteridge & S. Marshall (eds) *A handbook for learning and teaching in higher education: Enhancing academic practice*. New York and London: Routlege, pp. 345-362.

Shulman, L. (2005) *The signature pedagogies of the professions*. American Academy of Arts and Sciences.

Sills, C. (2009) Training for supervisors of transactional analysis practitioners and others. In P. Henderson (ed) *Supervisor training: Issues and approaches*. London: Karnac.

Sills, C. (ed) (2006) *Contracts in counselling and psychotherapy*. London: Sage.

Sills, C. & Fowlie, H. (eds) (2011) *Relational transactional analysis: Principles in practice*. London: Karnac.

Sinha, K. (2005) The future of technology and its impact on our lives. *Businessworld*, April 11, 2005.

Sivan, A.; R. W. Leung; C.-C. Woon & D. Kember (2000) An implementation of active learning and its effect on the quality of student learning. *Innovations in Education & Training International*, Vol. 37, No. 4, pp. 381-389.

SKG (2013) *Spaces for Knowledge Generation*. Australian Learning and Teaching Council.

Skill, T. D. & B. A. Young (2002) Embracing the hybrid model: Working at the intersections of virtual and physical learning spaces. *New Directions for Teaching and Learning*, Vol. 92, pp. 23-32.

Smith, J. & R. Hu (2013) Rethinking teacher education: Synchronizing eastern and western views of teaching and learning to promote 21st century skills and global perspectives. *Educational Research and Perspectives: An International Journal*, No. 40, pp. 86-108.

Smythe, M. (2011) *Blended learning: A transformative process?* Online Resource: https://ako-web.ako-kvm1.catalyst.net.nz/mi/download/ng/file/group-3740/smythe---blended-learning-a-transformative-process.pdf [Accessed December 4, 2013].

Softpedia (2005) *Technology that changed our lives*. Softpedia Webservices.

Solomon, C. (2003) Transactional analysis theory: The basics. *Transactional Analysis Journal*, Vol. 33, No. 1, pp. 15-22.

Sommer, R. (1959) Studies in personal space. *Sociometry*, Vol. 22, pp. 247-60.

Sommer, R. (1969) *Personal space: The behavioral basis of design*. Englewood Cliffs, NJ: Prentice Hall.

Sommers, N. (1992) Between the drafts. *College Composition and Communication*, Vol. 43, pp. 23-31.

Sommese, L. (2007) Graphic design curricula: Another reconsideration. *Novum*, Vol. 10, No. 37, pp. 12-17.

Soroka, V. & S. Rafaeli (2006) *Invisible participants: How cultural capital relates to lurking behavior.* Proceedings of WWW 2006 Scotland, 15th International World Wide Web conference.

Souleles, N. (2011) *Elearning in art and design: Perceptions and practices of lecturers in undergraduate studio-based disciplines and the rhetoric of innovative practices.* Lancaster University.

State of Victoria (2011) Research into the connection between built learning spaces and student outcomes. Literature review Paper No. 22 June 2011. Education Policy and Research division. Department of Early Childhood and Early Childhood Development. Melbourne, Australia.

Steelcase Education Solutions (2011) *Applications & insights guide.* Michigan: Steelcase Inc.

Stevens, M. (2011) 21st Century Learner. *NEA Today Magazine*, National Education Association.

Stevens, R. (2012) Identifying 21st century capabilities. *International Journal of Learning and Change*, Vol. 6, No. 3/4, pp. 123-137.

Stewart, D. W.; S. D. Brown; C. W. Clavier & J. Wyatt (2011) Active-learning processes used in US pharmacy education. *American Journal of Pharmaceutical Education*, Vol. 74, No. 4, Article 68.

Stewart, H. & C. Kenyon (2000) *From androgy to heutagogy.* ultiBASE (Faculty of Education Language and Community Services, RMIT University).

Stonehouse, A. (2011) The 'third teacher' – Creating child friendly learning spaces. *Putting Children First*, No. 38, pp. 12-14.

STP (2009) Curriculum development in studio teaching: Volume one, STP Final Report. *Studio Teaching Project.*

Strong-Wilson, T. & J. Ellis (2007) Children and place: Reggio Emilia's environment as a third teacher. *Theory into Practice*, Vol. 46, No. 1, pp. 40-47.

Stupans, I. (2013) Online resource: http://pharmacylearning.edu.au/ [Accessed December 4, 2013].

Stupans, I., & L. Orwin (2012) *How do we connect and engage students, learning in a distance mode, to develop verbal communication skills?* Paper presented at the Research and Development in Higher Education: Connections in Higher Education, Hobart, Australia.

Sturpe, D. A. (2010) Objective structured clinical examinations in doctor of pharmacy programs in the United States. *American Journal of Pharmaceutical Education*, Vol. 74, No. 8.

Taylor, A. (2012) Here's what college education costs students around the world. *Business Insider International.*

Taylor, J.; P. Dunbar-Hall & J. Rowley (2012) Music education students and eportfolios: A case study in the 'digital natives' debate. *Australasian Journal of Educational Technology,* Vol. 28, No. 8, pp. 1362-1381.

Taylor, P. & D. Wilding (2009) *Rethinking the values of higher education - the student as collaborator and producer? Undergraduate research as a case study.* The Reinvention Centre for Undergraduate Research, University of Warwick/QAA.

Temple, P. (2007) *Learning spaces for the 21st century: A review of the literature.* London: Institute of Education, University of London.

Temple, S. (2004) Update on the functional fluency model in education. *Transactional Analysis Journal,* Vol. 34, No. 3, pp. 197-204.

Tepper, B. J., Moss, S. E. & Duffy, M. K. (2011) Predictors of abusive supervision. *Academy of Management Journal,* Vol. 2, No. 2, pp.279-294.

The Guardian (2012) *Guardian university tuition fees league table.* The Guardian, August 15, 2012.

The University of Sydney (2013) Office of the DVC [Education]; May 2013, pages 1-3.

Thody, A. (2008) *Learning landscapes for universities: mapping the field[or] Beyond a seat in the lecture hall: a prolegomenon of learning landscapes in universities.* University of Lincoln.

Thomas, L. (2012) *Building student engagement and belonging in higher education at a time of change: A summary of findings and recommendations from the what works? Student retention & success programme.* Higher Education Academy, UK.

Thrift, N. (2008) *Non-representational theory: Space, politics, affect.* London: Routledge.

Tolmie, A. & J. Boyle (2000) Factors influencing the success of computer mediated communication (CMC) environments in university teaching: a review and case study. *Computers & Education,* No. 34, pp. 119-140.

Trigwell, K. (2011) Scholarship of teaching and teachers' understanding of subject matter. *International Journal for the Scholarship of Teaching and Learning,* Vol. 5, No. 1, p. 1.

Trigwell, K.; M. Prosser & F. Waterhouse (1999) Relations between teachers' approaches to teaching and students' approaches to learning. *Higher Education,* Vol. 37, No. 1, pp. 57-70.

Tronto, J. C. (1993) *Moral boundaries. A political argument for an ethic of care.* Routledge: London.

Tuan, Y. (1977) *Space and place, the perspective of eExperience.* Minneapolis, MN: University of Minnesota Press.

Tudor, K. (2009) "In the manner of": Transactional analysis teaching of transactional analysts. *Transactional Analysis Journal,* Vol. 39, No. 4, pp. 276-292.

Tynjälä, P. (1999) Towards expert knowledge? A comparison between a constructivist and a traditional learning environment in the university. *International Journal of Educational Research,* Vol. 31, No. 5, pp. 357-442.

Van der Merwe, M. & R. M. Albertyn (2010) Transformation through training. *Community Development Journal,* Vol. 45 No. 2, pp. 149-168.

Van Dijk, L. A.; G. C. Van Den Berg & H. Van Keulen. (1999) Using active instructional methods in lectures: A matter of skills and preferences, *Innovations in Education and Training International,* Vol. 36, pp. 260-272.

Verplanken, B., & W. Wood. (2006) Intervention to break and create consumer habits. *Journal of Public Policy & Marketing.* Vol. 25, No. 1, pp. 90-103.

Vilkinas, T. (2002) The PhD process: the supervisor as manager. *Education and Training,* Vol. 44, No. 3, pp. 129-137.

Vygotsky, L. (1978) *Mind in society - Development of higher psychological processes.* Cambridge: Harvard University Press.

Waghid, Y. (2006) Reclaiming freedom and friendship through postgraduate student supervision. *Teaching in Higher Education,* Vol. 11, No. 4, pp. 427-439.

Walker, S. & L. Creanor (2012) Towards an ontology of networked learning. In V. Hodgson; C. Jones; M. de Laat; D. McConnell; T. Ryberg & P. Sloep (eds) *8th International Conference on Networked Learning 2012,* Maastricht, Netherlands.

Walliss, J. & J. Greig (2009) Graduate design education: The case for an accretive model. *International Journal of Art and Design Education,* Vol. 28, No. 3, pp. 287-295.

Wands, B. (2001) A philosophical approach and educational options for the e-designer. In S. Heller (ed) *The education of an e-designer.* New York: Allworth Press, pp. 20-23.

Warf, B. (2011) Anthony Giddens. In P. Hubbard & R. Kitchin (eds) *Key rhinkers on space and place.* London: SAGE Publications, Ltd., pp. 178-184.

Warschauer, M. (1996) Comparing face-to-face and electronic discussion in the second language classroom. *CALICO,* Vol. 13, No. 2, pp. 7-26.

Webb, C. A.; R. J. DeRubeis; J. D. Amsterdam; R. C. Shelton; S. D. Hollon & S. Dimidjian (2011) Two aspects of the therapeutic alliance: Differential relations with depressive symptom change. Journal of Consulting and Clinical Psychology, Vol. 79, No. 3, pp. 279-283.

Weller, S. (2012) Achieving curriculum coherence. In P. Blackmore & C. D. Kandiko (eds) *Strategic curriculum change: Global trends in universities*. London: Routledge.

Wenger E. (1998) *Communities of practice*, Cambridge: Cambridge University Press.

Wenger, E. (1998) *Communities of practice: Learning, meaning, and identity*, Cambridge University Press, Cambridge.

Wenger, E. (2006) *Community of practice: a brief introduction*. Online Ressource: http://www.ewenger.com/theory/ [Accessed December 4, 2013].

Werquin, P. (2010) *Recognition of non-formal and informal learning: Country practices*. Paris: OECD.

West, R. E., G. Wright, B. Gabbitas & C. R. Graham (2006) Reflections from the Introduction of blogs and RSS feeds into a pre-service instructional technology course. *TechTrends*, Vol. 50, No. 4, pp 232-247.

Whyte, J. & J. Bessant (2007) *Making the most of UK design excellence: Equipping UK designers to succeed in the global economy*, Innovation Studies Centre, Tanaka Business School, Imperial College, London.

Wild, L. (1998) That was then: Corrections and amplifications. In S. Heller (ed) *The education of a graphic designer*. New York: Allworth Press, pp. 39-52.

Wilson, G. & M. Randall (2012) The implementation and evaluation of a new learning space. *Research in Learning Technology*, Vol. 20, pp. 1-17.

Winnicott, D.W. (1953) Transitional objects and transitional phenomena—A study of the first not-me possession. *International Journal of Psycho-Analysis*. Vol. 34, No.2, pp. 89-97.

Winter, R. & C. Munn-Giddings (2001) *A handbook for action research in health and social care*. London: Routledge.

Wisker, G. (2005) *The good supervisor*. Baskingstoke: Palgrave Macmillan.

Wolfe, P. (2010) Brain matters: Translating research into classroom practice. Virginia: Association for Supervision and Curriculum Development (ASCD).

Wright, T. & Cochrane, R. (2000) Factors influencing successful submission of PhD theses. *Studies in Higher Education*, Vol. 25, No. 2, pp. 181-195.

Zamel, V. (1993) Questioning academic discourse. *College ESL*, Vol. 3, No. 1, pp. 28-39.

Zepke, N & L. Leach (2010) Beyond hard outcomes: 'soft' outcomes and engagement as student success. *Teaching in Higher Education*, Vol. 15, No. 6, pp. 661-673.

Zepke, N.; L. Leach & P. Butler (2011) *Student engagement: What is it and what influences it?* Wellington New Zealand: TLRI.